The Arun

Makalu

The Arun

A Natural History of the World's Deepest Valley

by Edward W. Cronin, Jr.

Illustrated with Photographs

Houghton Mifflin Company Boston 1979

Library of Congress Cataloging in Publication Data
Cronin, Edward W
The Arun: a natural history of the world's deepest valley.

Bibliography: p.
Includes index.
1. Natural history — Arun Valley, India-China.
2. Arun Valley Wildlife Expedition, 1972–1973.
I. Title.
QH193.N4C76   500.9549'6   79–12578
ISBN 0–395–26299–2

Printed in the United States of America

W 10 9 8 7 ·6 5 4 3 2 1

The epigraphs heading each of the chapters (with
the exception of chapters 7, 8, and 10) are transla-
tions from the Tibetan by Gordon Enders and were
excerpted from his book, co-authored with Edward
Anthony, called *Nowhere Else in the World*.

The map on page xii is by John V. Morris.

TO SUSAN

Acknowledgments

The success of the expedition and the development of this book depended on the assistance of people and organizations too numerous to thank individually. Many have been mentioned in the text, but I would like to extend special gratitude to Mr. Jeffrey A. McNeely and Dr. Howard B. Emery, steadfast companions throughout my journeys in Nepal. In addition, I would like to thank Mr. Pema Sherpa, who so helped me in my field research. And Mr. William Eddy, Jr., whose encouragement and support was largely responsible for the decision to write the book.

My editor, Ms. Ruth K. Hapgood, provided invaluable advice and counsel throughout this project.

Perhaps my wife, Susan, deserves the greatest share of my appreciation for her constant assistance and tolerance; she displayed incomparable endurance for putting up with me during this lengthy project.

Finally, a book of this nature is the product of numerous interactions with countless people and considerable literature research. If I have misrepresented the views or unwittingly borrowed the ideas of anyone, I would like to apologize here. The faults of the book are my faults, and I only hope that a measure of truth comes through about the serious situation of the fauna and flora in the eastern Himalayas.

Contents

The Arun

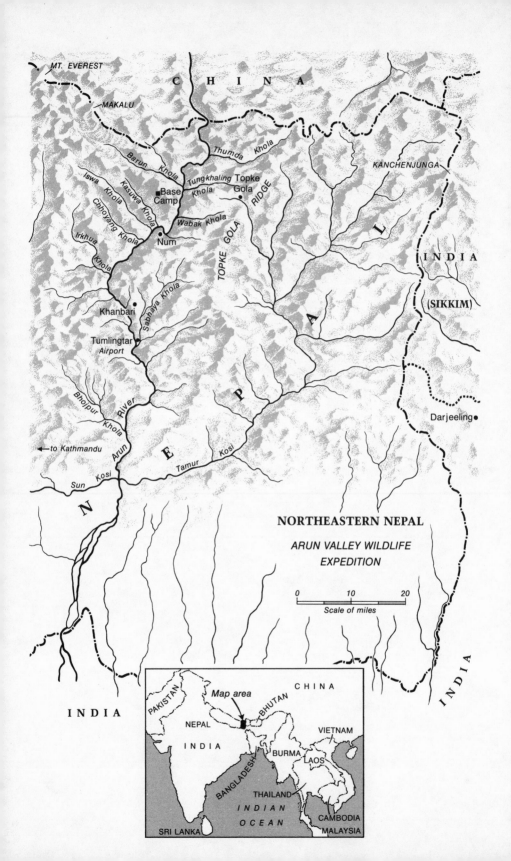

MT. EVEREST

MAKALU

C H I N A

KANCHENJUNGA

Thumda Khola

Barun Khola

Iswa Khola

Kasuwa Khola

Chhoyang Khola

Irkhua Khola

Tungkhaling Topke
Khola Gola

Base
Camp

Wabak Khola

Num

TOPKE GOLA RIDGE

S I K K I M)

I N D I A

Saphaya Khola

Khanbari

Tumlingtar
Airport

P

Bholpur Khola

River

Darjeeling

to Kathmandu

Arun

Kosi

Tamur Kosi

E

Sun Kosi

N

NORTHEASTERN NEPAL

*ARUN VALLEY WILDLIFE
EXPEDITION*

0   10   20

Scale of miles

I N D I A

I N D I A

CHINA

Map area

PAKISTAN

NEPAL

BHUTAN

VIETNAM

INDIA

BURMA

LAOS

BANGLADESH

THAILAND

SRI LANKA

CAMBODIA

MALAYSIA

*INDIAN
OCEAN*

Paper Birds, Feathered Kites

In the simplest words
That the guru writes,
Kites are paper birds
And birds are feathered kites.

Which do you prefer —
Shrieking living things,
Or the pleasant whirr
Of lifeless paper wings?
— *Tibetan Kite Song*

IN OCTOBER 1973, Pèma Sherpa captured the attention of everyone in camp by a curious comment that he made to Dr. Douglas Burns, expedition herpetologist.

"Yes, Sahib, I am exactly sure. It had a face like a frog but a body like a lizard."

"Pema, where did you see it?" Doug asked anxiously.

"Just downside from here, sir. Last year, when I was working with the Japanese Mountaineering Expedition we camped near here, and one time when I went down to the stream to wash dishes I saw it come up from the bottom of the stream and sleep for a few minutes on top of the water."

Dr. Howard Emery and I were at the front of the lab tent finishing up the last of the avian blood samples, but we put our work aside to listen in on their discussion. They were standing beside our field kitchen in the last light of a fading day. To the north, the rugged shapes of the Himalayas still showed their icy summits. To the south, the red plains of India vibrated in the final hot rays of the sun. A mature forest covered the steep slopes and ridges surrounding our temporary camp, slowly losing the details of its canopy to become a dark green blanket over the landscape.

"Do you think I could find one now, Pema?"

"I hope so, Dr. Burns. But the monsoon is over and I think the stream is dry at this season. You could look at the pond down in the valley," Pema answered.

"Can I go there tomorrow and be back in camp before dark?"

"Why not?" Pema said in his typical fashion, an indirect challenge to the Sahib's ability to walk. "But you should take a flashlight."

Doug was obviously excited, but Pema seemed to want to cut the conversation short, excusing himself by suddenly remembering some unfinished duties. He went over to the weather station to check his instruments, while Doug retreated to the warmth of the kitchen fire.

Like our other Sherpas, Pema became nervous whenever we showed such intense interest in something he took so much for granted — the animals and plants of the mountains. He considered it the proper business of a Sahib to be climbing mountains, or at the very least, to be pleasure trekking over the endless hills and valleys of Nepal. For foreigners to be interested in frogs and snakes, to appear content watching birds, to stay up all night capturing rodents, or to spend three weeks camped alone in the forests studying the red panda was to break all traditions.

It was not until later in the evening, while we sat comfortably around the campfire after a dinner of rice and chicken fried in mustard oil, that Doug offered an explanation. Apparently, Pema's description had been virtually unmistakable. A frog-lizard that swims in the streams must be a salamander. Salamanders have bodies like lizards in that they are quadruped and have slim bodies and long tails, but they reveal their brotherhood with frogs in their wet skins and broad flat heads. Although to the best of our knowledge salamanders had never been reported from Nepal, Doug felt certain that they should be found here because of the well-documented records from farther east in the Himalayas, in Assam and Burma.

As herpetologist, Doug's work with the frogs, lizards, and snakes had gone very well. He had made a large collection resulting in several new distributional records and maybe even a new species of lizard. There was one unusual specimen of lizard with a scale pattern distinct from any described in the literature, but Doug could not be certain until he reached a museum and conducted a comparative analysis. The previous week he had surprised everyone by bringing in a poisonous pit-viper that he had found within minutes of camp. Doug, his eyes sparkling with zoological joy, treated the discovery of the specimen as an important new altitudinal record; we treated it as an uneasy threat to our midnight runs to the latrine.

Despite his success, Doug still wanted very much to find a salamander because it would help prove his evolving theory about the zoogeography of the herpetofauna. Zoogeography is the study of the distribution of animals over the surface of the earth. Our camp was situated at 7200 feet above sea level on the top of a narrow ridge in the Arun Valley of far eastern Nepal. For a long time, biologists had wondered how eastern Nepal fitted in with the gradual transition of fauna and flora from the xeric forms of the dry western Himalayas to the mesic forms of the wet eastern Himalayas. Doug believed, as the rest of us were coming to realize, that the animals of eastern Nepal were most closely related to those of the eastern mountains of Sikkim, Bhutan, and Assam. The discovery of salamanders would be an important indicator of such eastern dominance.

In addition, the documentation of salamanders in Nepal would be a notable record in itself, representing not just a new species for Nepal, or just a new genus, but an entire new order (Urodela) of creatures that could be added to the list of wildlife known from this small country. Throughout the five months of his visit with the expedition, Doug had searched continuously for salamanders, dutifully turning over thousands of stream rocks, excavating damp rotten logs, and probing the mossy banks of every gully — but without any luck. Now, with Pema's tantalizing lead, he decided to make one final try. A veteran of expeditions from Alaska to Tasmania, Doug knew he would never find a salamander by sitting in camp.

Doug wanted to take Laadee Bal with him. This old Chetri porter knew the trails in the area well and spoke of two other ponds that they could visit along the way. Most porters were local villagers whom we hired to help carry our equipment from one camp to the next and, as such, were on the payroll for only a few days at a time. But Laadee Bal was a permanent member

of our staff, because he was the best woodsman we had encountered in Nepal. More than once he had been responsible for
finding a rare plant or animal that we had overlooked. An expert
tracker, he could translate an innocent-looking forest clearing
into what it actually was — a complex intersection of animal
trails. The delicate imprints on a crushed leaf would enable him
to tell us the story of how a female ghoral, a goatlike creature of
the deep forests, had passed during the early morning. Mud on a
low branch would indicate her size and maybe even something
about her behavior. A small, thin, gentle man, his light feet
would dance across the forest floor like one of the spirits he
would speak of late at night.

They left at dawn the next day, just as the bright flames of
the sun illuminated the tops of the mountains but long before
the damp shadows had left our clearing. After many months
in the hills, Doug was sprouting a dark beard and had that lean
appearance everyone acquires from hiking daily over the narrow
mountain trails. The chilly winds of October prompted him to
wear a sweater over his normal trail clothes: a woolen shirt,
baggy shorts, sneakers, and his constant companion — an old
canvas bag worn at the hip and containing his camera, collecting
equipment, water bottle, and other necessities.

By contrast, Laadee Bal wore the typical Nepali dress of white
jodhpurs, short tunic, a dark vest, and a long length of cloth
wrapped several times around his waist and hiding among its
folds his tobacco pouch, dry kindling, and medicinal herbs. Like
other hill people, he seldom wore shoes, except perhaps on special
days at large bazaars of the full moon or when visiting the government offices down in the valley. He tucked between his belly
and waist cloth a two-foot-long kukri knife that had been carefully warmed near the fire that morning to serve as a source of
heat during the early hours. His constant companion was a red
turban, made by twisting a long scarf around his balding head.

Heading down the slope, Doug and Laadee Bal took a short
cut through the forests, winding their way among the tall oaks.
At this altitude, the forests receive the full brunt of the monsoon, and the seasonal rains support rich growths of arboreal
plants. Orchids, ferns, mosses, and epiphytic herbage of all kinds
flourished on every branch and tree trunk. An understory of
laurels fit beneath the oaks and was also decorated with strands
of moss. The dim variegated light permitted a carpeting of ter-

restrial ferns to grow across the forest floor, but, along the edges of the clearings and streams, dense clumps of bamboo took advantage of the direct sun. Pushing their way through the bamboo, Doug and Laadee Bal found the stream that Pema had talked about. It was typical of many of the smaller streams in the Himalayas — a swirling torrent during the monsoon but barren soon after the winds shift in September and cold air flows dry across the hills.

They reached the pond in the valley around nine o'clock and immediately waded in, searching the shallows for any sign of life. The water was slimy green with algae along the edges, but in the middle it was clear and placid, revealing a bottom of rotting leaves and colored rocks. Several times their groping fingers touched something that moved, and Laadee Bal's quick hands would retrieve a sleeping frog or an angry water beetle. Spending almost an hour, they found many of the common inhabitants of a Himalayan pond, but nothing unusual.

Laadee Bal then showed Doug the way to the second pond near Machay Village. As they approached the village, the forest gave way to scrub and secondary growth where the trees had been cut to provide grazing areas for domestic animals. A few trees remained, scattered across the slope like lonely animals lost from their herd; they showed the scars of frequent cutting for firewood and fodder and stood as mutilated skeletons over a contagion of brush.

Machay was a small village of thatched roofs and terraced rice fields that depended on a small reservoir near the village temple for its water supply. It was a mixed village of both Rai and Chetri people — an out-of-the-way place that saw few visitors and really didn't care whether outsiders came or not. The mud-and-stone houses were spread out, each placed close to its own fields. The larger houses were surrounded by a vegetable garden, a few tobacco plants, and often a fenced enclosure for pigs and sheep. There were usually one or two outbuildings, such as an elevated shed for storing grain or a crude structure of sloping boards for chickens. The shrill cry of a rooster and the plaintive bleat of a goat could be heard over the laughter of playing children.

On approaching the pond, Doug realized that its artificial construction would limit the normal aquatic life one could expect in more remote ponds. He did not bother to search it closely.

Doug Burns examining the "frog-lizards"

Instead he went over to the little stone temple, at first out of curiosity, and then to pay homage. Of his 38 years, Doug had spent the last ten in Asia and had become deeply involved in the Buddhist religion. He had spent nine months in a Buddhist monastery in Thailand and had been formally accepted as a monk; he had studied the Buddhist way with a sincere heart. He slowly rang the temple bell three times and stopped for several minutes to meditate.

Trekking back up the hill toward camp in the late afternoon, they took another forest trail to visit the final pond along the top of the ridge. A small depression collected water from a spring in the middle of the forest. All but the center of the pond was in deep shade caused by the broad leafy arms of oaks. Still thinking about the temple at Machay, Doug quietly waded out into the water to see a small figure rise from the bottom. Doug gently cupped his hands beneath the creature and slowly lifted the object of his search — the first salamander ever found in Nepal.

It is a truism of field zoology that no animal is rare once you discover its specific range and habitat; Doug was able to capture three specimens in a matter of minutes and saw several others in the pond. Later, back at camp, he carefully examined his specimens by placing them in a shallow dish. He photographed them, then weighed and measured their wiggling forms, noting the condition of their skins. They had a distinctive character of larval salamanders, external gills that extended out from the side of the head like backward-pointing antlers. Depending on the temperature of the water and the abundance of the food, these antlers would soon disappear as the immatures metamorphosed into adults. Doug was going back to his home in Thailand shortly and so decided to take some live specimens with him in the hope that he could study them in captivity. He was especially interested in their process of maturation, their feeding habits, and their social behavior. As with all field research, the completion of one project invariably leads to another project and a new set of questions to be answered.

The documentation of salamanders in Nepal might seem at first an uninteresting example of scientific minutiae, an esoteric detail of little importance. And yet, we have recently entered an age of widespread concern about the natural environment. While pollutants contaminate our drinking water and chemicals corrupt our food, we are beginning to learn something of the interrela-

tionships on our tiny planet. While the diversity of wild species
in the world continues to decline, threatening the basic life systems of the earth, we are becoming increasingly aware of our
absolute dependence on nature. While our eyes stretch toward
the stars, following man's first ventures into outer space, we are
discovering our own position in the black emptiness that sur-
rounds us. We have finally realized that both knowledge and
understanding of the world's wildlife is imperative to our own
global survival. The discovery of this innocuous little creature
in a remote valley of the Himalayas is perhaps an apt example
of the many small steps that are required to gather that knowledge and develop that understanding.

A cursory search of the literature on the natural history of the
Himalayas reveals that remarkably little is recorded about the
animals and forests. Most species are hardly known beyond their
museum specimens, and the ecosystem is at best a vague impression left by the books of mountaineers and the occasional
trekker. The proper distribution and habitat of many species,
such as the salamander, are still an enigma. Basic life histories
of countless creatures remain a complete mystery: There are
species of birds, for example, whose eggs and nests are as yet un-
documented; even large mammals, such as the ghoral, are known
only from the superficial accounts of hunters. Botanists are still
struggling with a valid classification of forest types, while they
have not yet even begun to catalogue the full variety of plants.
There are probably new species to be discovered.

Certainly the hidden valleys of the Himalayas should offer an
irresistible lure tempting a multitude of biologists. The varied
altitudes of the world's highest mountains contain a wealth of
species in habitats that range from the tropics to the equator.
Strategically situated in the center of a vast continent, the Himalayas are the crossroads of Asia and offer a study site with an
incomparable diversity of material. Here is the stuff that all field
biologists dream of — and more. Yet since the work of Brian
Hodgson and Sir Dalton Hooker in the nineteenth century, surprisingly few men have dared even to enter the inner hills, and
our knowledge of the wildlife has increased pathetically little.
In today's shrinking world this oversight seems all the more dis-
graceful: The Himalayas are less than two days' travel, by airplane, from any point on the globe.

Why then this appalling ignorance? The Himalayas do pose

severe hardships to the enterprising biologist. Most roads stop at the foothills, and travel is confined to narrow footpaths that wind their way endlessly up and down the countless ridges. All equipment and supplies must be carried into the hills on the backs of porters or their domestic animals. Communication is equally difficult, and one finds oneself cut off from the outside world for months at a time. The seasonal monsoon unleashes its torrential rains in May, and for three or four months many streams and rivers are impossible to cross as the daily downpours flood waterways and swamp bridges, isolating one side of a valley from the other or the safety of the plains from a visitor trapped on the wrong side of a swollen, debris-clogged stream. Cholera, dengue fever, hepatitis, tuberculosis, dysentery, and other diseases are still common enough to present real threats. Blood-sucking leeches, abundant during the rainy season, are a painful and ghastly ordeal.

Such working conditions are enough to keep many biologists within their air-conditioned offices at home, but possibly a greater obstacle has been the sheer foreignness of the Himalayas. Modern biologists never study an animal in isolation from its environment and constantly strive to learn as much as possible about the ecosystem of their study subject. But a satisfactory knowledge of an ecosystem is acquired only after years of familiarity and personal experience — time to learn the birds and mammals, the major plants, and perhaps something of the geology and soil. It is not surprising that most field biologists tend to continue studying in their home environment or in the area where they have already developed some expertise.

Ordinarily, the daring individual who ventures into foreign lands to conduct his study is still accustomed to being able to carry out his research within a framework of previously acquired knowledge. In studying the habits of nectar-feeding birds of Hawaii, for example, an English ornithologist can rely on a small library of reference material on the plants, their flowering times, growth patterns, nectar production, and so on. For a similar study done in the Himalayas, the ornithologist would have trouble even identifying the plants.

There is also a growing trend among field biologists toward specialization. Today, our schools, institutions, and museums tend to promote specific studies on individual animals, such as single species, or a particular biological problem, such as the ecological influences on clutch size in birds. But the Himalayas still require the kind of biological research performed during the nineteenth century, a basic exploration and documentation. Many modern biologists are ill-prepared for such research and often consider it lacking in the challenges they seek with their new sophistication. While our general knowledge of the natural world, as measured by the increasing number of articles and books published each year, is expanding tremendously, our knowledge of many of the more remote and isolated areas is falling far behind. There is reason to wonder whether it will ever catch up.

The Arun Valley Wildlife Expedition made an attempt to learn something about one remote place. The original sponsor of the expedition was the Association for the Conservation of Wildlife, a small organization headed by one of the foremost naturalists of Asia, Dr. Boonsong Lekagul. Dr. Boonsong is an energetic man whose love for wildlife is shown in the warmth of his bird paintings, the thoroughness of his research, and the fervor of his outrage at mindless destruction of wild things and wild places. Under his guidance, the association has become a major force in the conservation and research on the wildlife of Southeast Asia and has long been the representative for the primary international agencies that deal with wildlife, such as the World Wildlife Fund and the International Union for the Conservation of Nature and Natural Resources.

In 1970, I was working at the association as staff ornithologist and spent much of my time at the central offices of the association in Bangkok, Thailand. The association's museum is located there, an enormous building that houses the private collection of Dr. Boonsong; the tall walls are covered with mounted specimens of bison and deer, and as in all museums, the acrid-sweet smell of naphthalene permeates the air. My close friend, Jeffrey McNeely, was the staff mammalogist at the association, and we often worked together on special research or conservation projects. Naturally, much of the wildlife we handled also lived in the Himalayas, and this bred a desire to see and visit the high mountains.

With Dr. Boonsong's support, we evolved a program to visit the Himalayas, but the limited financial resources of the association dictated that our research be confined in both time and scope. Other organizations and institutions around the world took an interest in our plans, however, and offered assistance in carrying out a more thorough study. The expedition grew into an interdisciplinary venture, incorporating the varied talents of ornithologists, mammalogists, botanists, herpetologists, parisitologists, and so forth; the goal of the expedition was expanded to undertake a basic ecological survey of the Arun Valley, the principal watershed of eastern Nepal.

The expedition began work in October 1972 and continued for fifteen months, through December 1973. Fourteen primary scientists and over 40 different workers were involved in the expedition at one time or another. The hardships and difficulties already mentioned took their toll, and, despite many successes, the expedition members suffered greatly from sickness and deprivation.

Obviously, no one person could hope to tell the story of such a varied expedition adequately, much less provide a full explanation of the natural history of the Arun Valley. Rather, I would like to provide an overview of the mountains, touching here and there on the more important aspects of the natural environment and explaining something about an environmental problem in the Himalayas that has become my major concern. I stayed on in Nepal after the expedition, spending another year in the field and eventually making two additional trips to the Himalayas. I returned from my third trip to Nepal in February 1977, this time to discuss with government officials and concerned citizens the growing problem of environmental abuse.

Nepal, like other countries of Asia, is threatened with a plight that has spread around the world, now a familiar story to those who watch the painful development of Third World countries. A rapidly expanding human population is causing an unprecedented demand for food, energy, and space, straining the natural ecosystem upon which it depends for its survival and jeopardizing the very existence of wildlife and forests. It is a situation radically different from that experienced in the richer countries of the world, where environmental problems are the result of industrial pollutants or the excessive use of the natural environment for the luxury of recreation or the greed of commercial enterprise. In Nepal, there is a much simpler and more basic relationship: Too many people, using primitive agricultural techniques, are forced to depend on the land itself for their survival.

In our shrinking world, the dilemma of a distant mountain valley has more than mere passing interest. Today, the fate and well-being of any citizen on the planet can intrude on our own quiet existence. No longer is there anywhere to hide. Isolationism is an archaic philosophy for anyone who drinks South American coffee, uses African minerals, drives a European car, eats American grain, or desires Asian oil. Poverty and hunger were once deplorable conditions seeking our generosity but have now become political forces demanding our attention. Nepal was once a sleepy hermit in the mountains but has now become a restless land squeezed between two nuclear powers with a history of animosity, China to the north and India to the south. Land — and its forests and wildlife with their ability to feed, shelter, and provide for people — is the most precious commodity on the planet, an irreplaceable substance that is easily destroyed, a limited resource that is in increasingly short supply.

Like most foreigners, I first imagined the Himalayas as snow-clad peaks dominating the horizon and deep pristine valleys providing in their remoteness a rugged terrain of rich forests teeming with wildlife. This vision can still be found in the Himalayas. It is impossible for me to forget my first sight of such a panorama. On the expedition reconnaissance, for two days we had climbed up a dry and dusty trail through a confining land of terraced fields and yellow mud houses. Finally, at the top of a ridge, we rounded a corner of the trail to enter the cool green twilight of my first Himalayan oak forest. As a connoisseur of forests I had explored jungles from the Americas to Asia, but there was a qualitative emotional difference here. The place was alive in a Shangrila sense: A red-billed leiothrix uttered a lilting melody, a wistful song that carried through the damp moss and ferns, and there was the clean smell of freshly washed vegetation. The dense canopy was broken open in several places, for the giant oaks had to abide their irregular footing on the sloping land. Here and there large holes in the canopy framed, as if from some romantic painting, the distant icy peaks of Makalu and Chamlang. The view combined both the privacy one associates with a forest interior and the vast, almost stunning, dimension of the Himalayan giants.

Surely here was a land so wide and tall in its immensity that one could measure himself against the scale and find an answer to the meaning and worth of the individual in nature's often impersonal world. It was, at the time, inconceivable to me that such a boundless landscape could ever be subdued by man's heavy hand. But I have since learned that, even in the Himalayas, man in his numbers and constant hunger can overwhelm the tallest mountains of the world.

Makalu

CHAPTER TWO

The Arun

Let your soul move to and fro,
Else it will not bloom;
Buddha let his stomach grow,
To give his soul more room.
— *Invocation to the*
Laughing Buddha

The Land

THE HIMALAYAS are young mountains, jagged forms not yet ground smooth by wind and rain. From the torpid plains of India they appear as white ghosts vibrating in the sun, a vague presence along the northern horizon that blends with the clouds, visible for a moment, then lost again in a confusion of ice and vapor. From the foothills, they appear slanted back by perspective into tolerable peaks, and one can daydream, boldly examining the distant snows for the best route to the summit. But up close, beside the main massifs, they are giant towering shapes, brilliant patterns of ice and rock, fluted gullies leading up cliffs, past spurs and crests, up corniced airy ridges, higher and higher, to a frozen summit wasteland.

Cold and gray, the Arun River is older than the Himalayas. Her advanced age is indicated by her drainage, for she defies the normal laws of watershed and cuts right through the axis of the mountains. Her waters first collect north of the wall of peaks, flowing slowly across the barren expanses of Tibet, a sparse land dwelling in the rain shadow of the Himalayas. Then, gathering power in descent, the Arun turns south to excavate a wide breach between the mountains. Waves, whirlpools, and churning foam mark a precipitous fall. Rock crushed by her power and silt eroded from the slopes color her waters dark as weathered slate. Finally, she emerges quietly on the plains of India, a subdued wanderer that flows through rice paddies and muddy canals to meet the Ganges and later empty into the Bay of Bengal.

The river and mountains were born in a mesozoic collision that began less than seventy million years ago, perhaps as recently as forty million years ago, an astonishingly short time in geological reckoning. At that time, India and Eurasia were separate land masses sliding across the surface of the planet, driven by an engine of heat from the earth's core. India drifted north to collide with Eurasia, and the ancient sea bed which had divided them cracked, faulted, and pushed upward. As the two land masses merged to form one, a series of low hills was formed: the Tibetan Marginal Mountains. These new hills trapped moist winds from tropical seas and a system of rivers developed, one of them the Arun, which flowed south and out of the hills.

But the land masses continued to crush into each other in a catastrophic event beyond human memory or comprehension. A second great flow of earth was squeezed up in front of the Tibetan Marginals. This material came from the northern edge of India and formed a nappe of overthrust rock stretching from east to west along the entire junction of the land masses. This nappe was the foundation of the Himalayas, and its folds momentarily trapped the Arun, blocking her passage. She had to retrace her channel, but carving waters won the race with rising earth and the Arun River gouged through to maintain a southerly drainage. Constant pressure between the land masses caused a complex series of tectonic thrusts, creating taller and taller summits in the growing Himalayas. Again the Arun cut through. Some two million years ago, the rate of rising over the nappe increased; within the last six hundred centuries, and before the eyes of primitive man, the Himalayas have risen their final four thousand feet, to become the highest mountains in the world.

Resting directly over the nappe, today the Himalayas continue to rise, while the Arun continues to erode through. The vagaries of mountain building make it difficult to estimate, but the Himalayas appear to be climbing several inches each year. The tremendous force required for this upward motion still comes from India, maintaining a northward movement into Eurasia of about

two inches per year and causing tectonic activity to recur throughout Asia. The Tibetan plateau has been compressed and thick-
ened so that it now has an average elevation of more than 15,000
feet and forms a vast high-altitude land that out-tops all but the
three highest peaks in the United States and all but the six highest in Europe. The crush of the Indian land mass is also causing
a lateral displacement of earth across eastern Asia and resulting
in earthquakes and strike-slip faulting as far away as Lake Baikal,
along the Chinese coast at Macao, and Tangshan, off the Yellow
Sea. The meeting of these two great land masses was, and continues to be, one of the great geological events in the history of
the earth.

The Arun River now forms one of the deepest valleys on any
continent. Less than eighty miles separate the summits of Mount
Everest, on the Arun's western flank, and Mount Kanchenjunga,
on the eastern flank. Everest, at 29,028 feet above sea level, is
the highest mountain on the planet, while Kanchenjunga, at
28,159 feet, is the third highest; and yet where the Arun crosses
between them the water flows at a meager 7600 feet. Thus the
valley is over 20,000 feet deep and the landscape is on a scale that
dwarfs such geological spectacles as the Grand Canyon in North
America or the Great Rift Valley in Africa.

Between the summits and the river are the repeated patterns
of canyons and slopes, ridges that echo each other down a winding valley. Each tributary creates its own small valley, and the
main Arun Valley is a series of parallel canyons, one after another, like furrows in a freshly plowed field.

There is something in the human eye that enjoys geometric
figures, and the valley provides sculptured forms of earth and
rock to capture the attention of the most insensitive visitor. I
have spent hours upon hours enjoying this geological entertain-
ment. Walking up a steep trail one gains new vantage points; a
distant slope that at first appeared to be a blank wall because of
foreshortening gradually changes into a giant stage of cliffs with
swirling patterns of rock or huge slabs of earth standing on end
like balanced dominoes. Even the single view from a campsite is
an animated play; the changing light of day, with its slanted rays
in the morning and flat light at noon, transforms the crisp profiles of a ridge hovering over a void into a dizzy scene of descending lines that plunge to a shimmering river bed. Unlike flat
plains with their tedious monotony, here one finds spirited views
that seem to breathe and grow under examination.

Two-dimensional maps of the valley tend to disguise its actual size. The compressed details of contour lines condense on a flat piece of paper the enormous surface area of this vertical world. One learns of the real magnitude of this land only by walking across its face. An exhausting day's hike can be less than three linear miles on the map when, as is common, it involves a climb or descent of several thousand feet. The peaks which stand out sharp and hard in the clear skies of the post-monsoon months can appear to be within a few hours' walk and yet actually take many days to reach. Distances are seldom calculated in miles or kilometers, but rather are figured by the hours of walking time or the number of campsites. Thus, a distance between two points can expand or contract according to the local weather or the time of year. A sudden rain can mire the trail in mud, increasing the time for a journey by a factor of two or three. The amount of water in a monsoon stream can determine whether it may be waded easily or require several hours to build a temporary bridge. A quick route along a high ridge may be impossible in the winter season when water holes dry up and there is nowhere to camp. For the visitor accustomed to standardized space and regulated measurements, the valley imposes a new concept of space.

The land is in perpetual change. While the mountains are rising, the slopes are being cut away at their base by the river or stripped bare of their soil by the rain. The landscape is littered with gray scars where erosion marks soil lost to the river. Occasionally, a landslide will dump its debris into the river or one of its tributaries and form a natural dam across the waters. The massive quantities of silt carried by the currents settle out to build a flat bed of sediment in the still water behind the dam. When the current finally cuts a channel through the debris, a small plateau is left standing beside the river; in time, the river channel is cut deeper and deeper until the plateau stands high above the waters. Hiking along the river's edge, following the bends and curves of the Arun from north to south, you will see many such plateaus. Most are quite small, but a few are several miles long, and all seem completely out of place in this land of angles. By their contrast they bear witness to the restless forces that continue to create the most rugged topography in the world. The mountains are a sign of life — evidence of the unconsumed fires and pressures within the earth.

Uniting the land and the water, the clouds drift back and forth in a communion of mist and mountain. They are a constant companion and create the many moods of the mountains, emphasizing the profiles of the ridges, accenting the thrust of the summits, blanketing flat the bottom of the valley. I have no favorites for I enjoy most the process of change, but certain of my images of the mountains are forever linked to specific cloud conditions. Once, when I was on an early morning walk along a narrow ridge, clouds like gray velvet enveloped me so that I could not see beyond a few feet; I thought I knew the trail well and could remember in my mind's eye the spacious views on all sides, but suddenly it was a new trail, a private one that existed for the fleeting moments of a single morning. I have gone back and walked that same path again, but the trail of that morning no longer exists.

On certain windy days in the late fall there are white billowy clouds which surge across the ridges like waves along an ocean front, and, if one is standing high enough to be in their face, the clouds become vital forces that affect the emotions and one can never again look upon them as inanimate vapors. I have known clouds in the Arun which are as real and lasting as any creature of flesh and blood. There is one that dwells behind a notch on a ridge where prevailing winds form a constant eddy. By day, this cloud wanders beneath the notch, swimming here and there over the canopy or stopping to feed over a particular gully. At night, it sleeps in the notch itself, resting quietly in the canopy like a giant white whale.

There is also a rhythm to the seasons. Typically, the winter dawn sees few clouds, perhaps only some extremely high cirri that glisten in the upper air or maybe thin streamers that cling to the summits like loose prayer flags. But small clouds form quickly, and by late morning delicate white cumuli float against a still blue. The afternoon is usually chilly as the clouds build in size to dominate the sky and to block out the sun, sometimes releasing a light winter rain over the countryside. But, at dusk, the clouds disappear again, their energy dissipating with the setting sun; and the heavens are open to reveal Taurus and Orion battling.

The summer sky is more turbulent. Between May and September, a monsoon deluge from the Indian Ocean strikes the valley and as much as a foot of rain can fall in a day. In certain parts of the valley, almost sixteen feet of water fall during this

Chital Deer

short four-month summer monsoon, comprising over 80 percent
of the year's annual precipitation. Thick gray quilts hang low
through the mountains. Below the clouds, a constant drizzle in
dull light is common. Water thoroughly saturates the soil, increasing its weight many times and occasionally causing it to
overcome the frictional forces that bind it to the rock beneath;
on a rainy monsoon night, with thick drops drumming down on
the tent fly, one can feel a sudden deep tremor from the ground,
a solid groaning shudder, as somewhere the soil breaks loose and
comes rumbling down a slope. But the mountains are often taller
than the clouds, and on a high ridge one can still find warm
summer sun while looking down on a restless sea of vapor that
fills the valley.

The Wildlife

Nature abhors a vacuum and when the Himalayas first rose they
offered a naked empty land. Their newly created space was
quickly invaded, however, by the surrounding plants and animals
of India and Eurasia. Indeed, the Himalayas became a great mix-
ing area as the two land masses collided. Species which had
evolved for millions of years independently on the separate con-
tinents suddenly came face to face, causing a revolution in ecosystems, and resulting in new competition as species flowed back
and forth to explore the new lands available to them. The most
startling example occurred in India, where mammals were unknown prior to the collision; the oldest fossils of mammals in
India date back only to the Eocene, or about 45 million years ago.

Today it is almost impossible to make out the details of these
original invasions. The changing climate, shifting topography,
competition between forms, and new speciation have greatly altered the modern distribution of plants and animals. Any statements about the origins of present distributions must be subject
to numerous qualifications and exceptions. Yet clearly there are
two basic trends of geographic distribution based on the two principal climatic gradients that the Himalayas experience.

One trend is along the north-south axis of the mountains and
reflects the differences of average temperature between modern
India and Eurasia. Indian life forms adapted to the heat of the
tropics, such forms as the exotic pangolin and langur monkeys,

colorful leafbirds, trogons, and malcohas, and graceful palms and bamboos, spread north into the lowlands of the mountains where high temperatures prevail. Conversely, durable and hardy species that were adapted to the cold temperate life of Eurasia, such as the wolf and brown bear, or rosefinches and grosbeaks, extended south into the harsher higher elevations of the Himalayas.

The second trend is along the east-west axis of the mountains. The Himalayas stretch in a narrow belt for over 1500 miles, from the borders of Afghanistan to those of Burma and Thailand; there is considerable difference in rainfall between the two ends, creating an east-west gradient of moisture. Species from the arid Middle East and Mediterranean lands, such as mouflon sheep, larks, and cedar trees, extend east following the drier climate of the western Himalayas. Species from humid southern China and Southeast Asia, such as the red panda, laughing thrushes, and rhododendrons, stretch their range west, occupying suitable damp habitats of the eastern Himalayas.

The Arun Valley is situated near the intersection of both of these trends. The north-south trend is found throughout the mountains but is particularly prominent in the Arun, where the unusually deep valley, with its broad shoulders open to the warm Indian air currents, acts as a topographic funnel channeling species up and down between the north and south. The proximity of the Bay of Bengal causes the valley to receive a relatively heavy and lengthy monsoon, fostering damp habitats, and allowing an eastward extension of many species.

There is a third pattern of distribution of animals and plants in the Himalayas that is based not on geography but on altitude; it is a helpful pattern to learn for it serves to sort out the confusing diversity of species. Briefly, the different altitudes, with their varying conditions of temperature and humidity, have caused the plants and animals to segregate themselves according to remarkably narrow elevation belts. Botanists still dispute the specific boundaries and composition of these belts, but in the Arun Valley there appear to be six zones of plants and animals stacked one on top of the other in rapid succession up the slopes. These zones or belts correspond broadly to basic climatic divisions, and thus reflect the geographic trends of distribution. In essence, the mountains are a microcosm of the gradual changes that occur across the latitudes, and the valley embraces within its comparatively small area habitats ranging all the way from the equatorial tropics to the frigid lands of the arctic.

From 600 feet above sea level, the lowest elevation in the valley found at the edge of the plains of India, to an altitude of about 3000 feet, there is a tropical belt where heat-resistant sal forests bake dry under a merciless sun. Jackals, civets, and jungle cats roam the forests at night. At dawn, a flowering silk cotton tree will be alive with flocks of racquet-tailed drongos, spot-winged stares, and mynas feeding on the new blossoms. During the heat of midday, the relentless call of the crimson-breasted barbet will ring out, an endlessly repeated note on the same pitch, the same even spacing, on and on, producing unbearable irritability in its hearer.

A subtropical zone occupies the elevations between 3000 and 6000 feet, and contains *Castanopsis* and *Schima* trees, curious splayed tree ferns, and the unusual palm *Pandanus furcatus*. Golden-fronted leafbirds, rufous-bellied bulbuls, and white-crested laughing thrushes are common in the forests; but many of the trees have been cut and commensal or secondary-growth species are prominent. This is the area of greatest human inhabitation, and terraced fields occupy most slopes. The only remaining forests are isolated patches confined to ravines and ridge tops where infertile soil limits cultivation. It is hard to make out the original fauna and flora of this belt, and one is forced to extrapolate data from the forest remnants.

The upper limit of cultivation stops at around 6000 feet in the Arun; local villagers say that above this point there is often insufficient sunlight for domestic crops because of the constant cloud cover during the monsoon. The continuous forests begin again and there is a lower temperate zone stretching up to around 8500 feet. Oak and laurel forests, supporting rich growths of mosses, ferns, and orchids, flourish in this humid cloud belt. Giant flying squirrels sail on silent membranes through the canopy, while the chestnut-headed tit babbler and the yellow-naped yuhina scurry through the undergrowth.

From 8500 feet up to 12,000 feet, an upper temperate zone harbors a variety of forests depending on the exposure of the slope and local climate. Maples are often abundant, at times mixed in with other trees, and occasionally dominate the forest canopy. One also finds the flower forest within these elevations; during the pre-monsoon rains, a canopy of magnolia trees gives forth giant white blossoms, and an understory of rhododendrons is painted in delicate shades of crimson, yellow, and white by the abundant flower clusters. The shy ghoral and the tame serow travel along hidden paths through the jungle; the red panda favors the dense growths of bamboo.

From 12,000 feet to the upper limit of plant life, usually at 16,000 feet but in some places as high as 20,000 feet, an alpine zone exists with the characteristic low shrubs, open meadows, and moraine-covered slopes typical of alpine areas throughout the world. Fir and birch form part of the transition forests between the upper temperate and alpine zones; rhododendrons are prominent everywhere, from an understory plant of the transition forests to pure stands that cover some slopes in tall shrubs, fifteen to thirty feet high, and cloaked in color during the pre-monsoon blooming period. During the winter, the open meadows are blanketed in snow, but when the spring melt comes the meadows are alive with dense growths of alpine flowers. This is the home of the snow leopard, considered by most who have seen one to be the most beautiful of all the large cats.

The high-altitude zone of perennial snows has seldom been recognized as a separate entity, for in the past biologists have not believed that much life can exist under such harsh conditions. Starting in some places at about 16,000 feet, it continues up another 12,000 feet to the top of the peaks — almost half the total height of the mountains — to include an incredibly large area. Many animals found there are merely visitors enjoying brief periods of mild weather during the summer, but there is also a substantial number of endemic life forms. Invertebrate creatures are the rule, including many spiders and springtails. Some feed on plant debris, especially pollen, that is blown by the mountain winds to these high elevations; there is often an elaborate hierarchy among the insects of predator and prey, carnivore and herbivore.

These six different zones of plants and animals are not isolated worlds that abut each other like bricks in a mason's wall. There is always a gradual transition of forest types between any two zones, and some plant species live in two or even three different zones. Among the animals, there are birds which regularly migrate between zones, spending their summer months breeding in the upper temperate or alpine zones and descending to winter in the subtropical or tropical zones. Even individual animals of a species, particularly large mammals, will travel each day between any two zones. The zones, then, are merely broad outlines that conform to a basic progression of changing temperature and rainfall, and each contains a preponderance of particular species that give it a characteristic identity.

And the patterns of life in the valley are truly endless. Forests growing at the same elevation can be different depending on whether they occupy a north- or south-facing slope. South-facing slopes receive more direct solar radiation, favoring the growth of certain species. North-facing slopes suffer less from rapid evaporation so that they are often damper and more humid and thus favor other species. The farther north one travels in the valley, the more dissipated are the effects of the monsoon; the land becomes drier, resembling more and more the western Himalayas. Similarly, certain side valleys are protected by their steep walls and convoluted topography from the monsoon and are comparatively dry and sparse. One is never sure of the specific animals and plants that dwell on any particular slope until it has actually been visited.

One aspect of distribution that intrigues biologists is the ability of mountain terrain to promote speciation. The deep canyons and high ridges tend to separate populations of a species that on the plains would be continuous and freely interbreeding. The populations of a species, for example, that inhabit the upper elevations of two adjacent mountain peaks might be only a few linear miles apart but would be separated by a possibly insurmountable obstacle: the lowland habitat in the valley between them. Many alpine animals find subtropical and tropical vegetation as effective a barrier to their travel as a broad ocean. In effect, the mountains break the population of any species down into small units. Whenever a population is broken up, there is always the possibility that these isolated units will change independently in time as mutations, genetic drift, and new adaptations occur.

A case in point is the kalij pheasant, a large black-and-white bird with metallic hues; this pheasant of the subtropical zone shows five distinct color phases across the Himalayas. Ornithologists have recognized each color phase as a separate subspecies and believe that each phase represents delicate adaptations to slightly different climatic and vegetational conditions. The drier environments of the western Himalayas are producing paler forms while the damp conditions of the eastern Himalayas are producing those with darker pigmentation. Thus we could be watching the evolution of several new species of kalij. These minor adaptions might develop into major ones that in the future would prevent interbreeding even if there was a chance encounter between two individuals of different phases. During breeding and mating displays, a light-colored male from the western Himalayas might not accept a dark-colored female from the eastern Himalayas.

Sometimes a separated part of a population will continue to exist after the other parts of the population become extinct. These remnants are spoken of as relict populations. The insect fauna of certain Himalayan areas shows this phenomenon, and many species still protected in alpine regions most closely resemble insects common in central Asia millions of years ago. As the oceans protected the coelacanth until some unsuspecting fisherman caught this living fossil, the heights of the mountains could well protect similar living fossils. There is always the possibility that ancient creatures, long extinct elsewhere, can be re-discovered still dwelling in the inaccessible Himalayas.

Some authorities explain the mysterious stories of the Yeti or Abominable Snowman with such a hypothesis. During the past several decades, reports have filtered out from the Himalayas about the existence of a creature as yet unknown to science: half-man, half-ape, it is said to be a large creature that walks on two legs and wanders the high snow fields, feeding on small animals and alpine vegetation. Numerous local villagers have seen the creature and a few foreigners, mostly mountaineers, have reported catching brief glimpses of it, or of finding its footprints that match those of no known animal, but the world's scientific community remains skeptical. Those authorities who have studied the problem, however, suggest that it is not such an impossible idea, for at one time many species of ape roamed the forests of India; although all of them except the gibbon are believed to be extinct, it is conceivable that another species, a large one in the fashion of the African gorilla, managed to find refuge in the remote and isolated valleys of the Himalayas.

To the person who has actually traveled in the Himalayas, such an idea does not seem far-fetched at all. The land is big enough to hold all the mysteries, and more, that are attributed to it. Places like the Arun Valley, with their countless canyons and side valleys, inaccessible slopes that have rarely, if ever, been visited, could easily contain new or old species unknown to man. The abundance and diversity of wildlife alone suggests it. There are over 600 species of bird found in the valley, more than are commonly found in all of the continental United States. Indeed, the Arun contains an interwoven mixture of plants and animals of unsurpassed complexity, providing the valley with a beauty and fascination rarely found elsewhere.

The People

There is no record of when man first invaded the Himalayas. Neolithic hunters appear to have visited the mountains as early as 3000 years ago, for their weapons have been found in the foothills. Perhaps the first men actually to cross the high mountains were Indian merchants searching for a route to link the growing markets of two major civilizations, India in the south and the Tibetan extension of China in the north. Or the first men could have been Tibetan, for after living on the high desolate plateau of Tibet, life in the sheltered valleys of the Himalayas must have seemed very appealing.

Some agriculturalists were apparently already settled in the Himalayas when, in the sixth century B.C., an auspicious event occurred in the foothills just west of the Arun Valley. A prince of the Sakya clan walked out of his father's palace to spend a lifetime wandering and searching for religious insight. He founded one of the world's principal religions, Buddhism, and later came to be known as the Enlightened One.

At that time, the rulers of this area were the Kirantis, and they helped spread Buddhism through the mountains. Later the hills were controlled by Indian rulers, such as the Licchavis and Thakuris, who established a series of small kingdoms in different valleys along the Himalayas. The activities and history of these small kingdoms have been lost in the passing of time, and only a few reports have filtered down about them, oddly enough from foreign visitors.

In the seventh century A.D., a Chinese emissary reported back to China about one of these kingdoms which he had visited. He described a small kingdom ruled by King Narendradeva. For dress, the people used a single long cloth wrapped around the body. The customs dictated that they pierce their ears and place pieces of bamboo or horn in them, thereby extending the earlobes, which was considered a sign of beauty. They did not eat

with spoons or utensils, but used their hands to scoop rice. Large dishes were made of copper for the rich and wood and bamboo for the poor. The houses were made of wood and rock, and the walls were covered with colorful designs and carvings. A highly artistic people, they were passionately fond of music and dancing. They worshiped five gods and made stone images that were washed every day with holy water.

The king's crown had jewels of pearl, rock crystal, nacre, garnet, and coral. In his ears he wore golden rings and jade pendants. At receptions he would sit on a throne of richly carved wood in a hall scented with incense and carpeted with flowers. Noblemen, officials, and courtiers would squat in front of him and hundreds of armed soldiers lined the side of the chamber.

After the Thakuris, the Mallas came to power, and during their reign a cultural isolation began that still continues today. This isolationism was a reaction to the Islamic conquests of northern India during the thirteenth century when Muslims destroyed the spiritual centers of Buddhism, repressed Hinduism, and threatened the independence of all people living in India. Following the Mallas, members of the Rajput family, who had originally fled to the Himalayas because of the Muslims, conquered the various kingdoms and in 1768 united the area into the single kingdom that is today the modern country of Nepal. The leader of these conquests was Prithvi Narayan Shah and his family continues to rule Nepal today.

It is a country stretching some 500 miles along the central portion of the Himalayas. The Himalayas are narrow mountains, at places less than 80 miles across, and Nepal is similarly a narrow country. At its widest, it is less than 145 miles, and in one place is only 56 miles across; the extra width beyond the mountains includes portions of the Indian plains, a lowland area called the Terai, and averages only some 600 feet above sea level. Nepal is in the lower latitudes and averages about 28° north of the equator, a latitude roughly equivalent to that of the Hawaiian Islands, Miami, Florida, and Cairo, Egypt. The total area of the country is only about 56,000 square miles, an area comparable to that of the combined areas of the states of Indiana and Illinois. Physically and emotionally, it is a small country wedged between the giants of India and China.

Events in the recent history of Nepal have reinforced its feelings of xenophobia, greatly inhibiting foreign ideas from penetrat-

Lhomis Village

ing what remains one of the most primitive countries of the world. In 1846, the Shah dynasty lost control of the government to the Rana family and although Shahs continued as the figureheads of a monarchy, real power was vested in the Ranas, who ruled through the hereditary position of Prime Minister. The Ranas refused outside intervention in the country, and the borders were largely closed to foreigners while the Ranas conducted a selfish and bizarre reign over Nepal. Finally, after over 100 years of supremacy, the Ranas were overthrown by King Tribhuwan, who opened his country's borders to the world for the first time in history in 1951.

Kathmandu, the capital, located in central Nepal, is situated in an old lakebed that has drained to leave a unique flat valley in the center of the hills. The town, for it really is more of a town than a city, is refreshing. Some concessions to the tastes of the outside world have been made along a few wide boulevards, where new hotels advertise separate baths and European cuisine. But most of the town is taken up by small two-story houses that crowd over narrow cobblestone streets, winding back and forth in odd sequences, obviously designed more by the genius of a thousand footsteps than by a conscientious city planner.

One's first day in Kathmandu is a sensuous experience. You are drawn to walk back and forth, investigating every alley and path until exhausted. Here and there, tucked back from the roads in large courtyards, are the colorful, almost garish, temples where images of Buddhism and Hinduism are freely mixed. Ancient fetishes are still venerated and blood sacrifices persist. Near the center of town is the bazaar, a loose designation that applies to the shops, stalls, and open-air venders which line some of the narrowest and most crooked streets. Villagers from the hills roam through in search of vegetables, rice, wool blankets, tobacco, brass cooking pots, brightly colored beads and jewelry, or baskets of woven bamboo in all shapes and sizes. An occasional cow, sacred in the eyes of the Hindu religion, wanders freely about with a look of bovine condescension.

Each tribe of people wears its own traditional dress: Sikhs in carefully folded turbans sell cloth and blankets; Newaris in their crested topis, or hats, sell brass ware; a Chetri woman with a quilted shawl barters her vegetables. Government officials wear western jackets over their Nepali jodhpurs. The smell from the open sewers mixes freely with that of the flowers sold at every

corner. The intensity of sights and sounds collides to give everything a richly textured quality.

The town really has not changed much over the centuries, and
that seventh century emissary from China would probably make
an identical report if he were reborn to visit again. In Kathmandu
on February 24, 1975, Birendra Bir Bikram Shah Dev was formally
crowned King of Nepal in a courtyard of the ancient palace of
Hanuman Dhoka. While ancient Vedic hymns were chanted,
King Birendra was washed and anointed by Brahman priests, and
then enthroned on a dais facing east. Nepal's superb helmetlike
crown, encrusted with pearls, diamonds, rubies, and emeralds,
and crested with billowing bird of paradise feathers, was placed
on his head. Soldiers and trusted priests once again crowded
around, and the young king left the palace to be borne on a towering elephant through streets packed with subjects and carpeted
with flower petals.

But Kathmandu, with its kings and merchants, cows and crooked streets, constitutes only 10 percent of modern Nepal. The
vast majority of the populace lives out in the hills. As with the
wildlife, the people of the hills represent many different groups
from originally distant lands that have come to live together.
They, too, have segregated themselves according to the altitudes.
In the Arun, the lowest elevations are inhabited by Satars, Bauns,
and Chetris, who build mud-and-wood houses, sometimes elevated on platforms, with sloping grass roofs. They grow rice and
corn and own many chickens, goats, and cows. Many of these
people first came from India, and their customs closely resemble
those of their southern neighbors.

The middle elevations are inhabited by Rais, Thamangs, Newaris, and Gurungs, among others. Their houses are usually two
stories high and are built of rock plastered over with mud in dark
earthen shades of red and brownish gray. Crude designs in
brighter colors often ornament the front walls. They also own
many domestic animals and grow rice as their staple crop. They
continue to spurn the use of eating utensils, preferring to scoop
rice with their hands. They rely on wild tubers, mushrooms, and
a variety of forest plants to cure illness. Shamans, preaching an
elaborate religious mythology, are still popular. Hinduism mixed
with Buddhism mixed with Animism makes even major religious
distinctions hard to draw. Some of these groups are the oldest
inhabitants of the mountains and their origins are obscure.

Bhotias, Lhomis, and other people originally from Tibet occupy the highest settlements. They are often the poorest of the hill tribes. They build squat houses of wood and use large rocks to hold the roofs down against the strong mountain winds. They wear coarse dark clothes, and the women often have heavy necklaces of silver coins or colorful beads of red and yellow stones. A few, the rich, have shoes, but most go barefoot. Barley, wheat, and potatoes are the most successful crops. They rely on the forest not only for medicinal plants, but also for basic foodstuffs; wild animals provide a major source of protein. The mountain streams are too cold for bathing and many people never wash more than their hands and face.

Altogether in the Arun Valley there are six to seven major ethnic strains and over twenty different human groups that follow individual linguistic or social customs. Since all roads stop at the foothills, communication is limited and the people live in isolated communities sometimes a ten- to twelve-days' walk from the major bazaar towns. Except for salt, metal for their knives, and luxury items such as brass ware or jewelry, each village is self-sufficient, capable of providing its own food, clothing, and shelter. Intermarriage between tribes is uncommon, and some people spend their entire lives within one small village or side valley. In the past, they have had little desire and almost no need to care about events in the outside world. They have maintained their ancient customs and habits that have served them well for generations.

CHAPTER THREE

Cloth Walls

They tell of Chumbo who aspired
One day as mail-man to be hired.
To prove that he could make the run
He vowed that walking he would shun
And do his eight miles in a dash
So rapid would he surely smash
All records for the distance. Well,
He sprinted for a mile and fell
Exhausted by the roadside, where
He lay and panted hard for air.
Next day he learned there was no need
For mail-men who make too much speed.

— *Gartok Fable*

I MUST CONFESS at the outset that our start in the field gave
little indication of our later success. Indeed, it was a sputter-
ing, erratic, agonizing kind of affair, and I really wondered during
those first few days whether we were going to survive at all.
None of us was in admirable physical condition after spending
the previous two years at our respective desks in Bangkok. And
although we had done considerable work in the wilds of Southeast Asia and the more remote forests of America, we knew little
about the practical matter of traversing the roughest topography
on the face of the earth. Still, these were but minor problems.
With hindsight, I realize that we fell prey to a series of basic misconceptions about the simple art of walking.

Our first false assumption was a reliance on the Boy Scout ethic

— the spirit of preparedness. With faithful twentieth-century minds we had searched among the technological wonders of our age for all possible devices that would help us meet any threat the trail might provide. For example, I carried with me to the airport on the day of our first trip to the Arun Valley a special aluminum-framed knapsack containing such necessities as water bottle, poncho, sweater, fresh socks, extra shoelaces, plastic tube tent, and so on. Fittingly, I was dressed in my custom-designed field jacket, complete with dashing epaulets, and eleven pockets offered precise space for other necessities, from compass to moleskin to waterproof container of matches.

After all, a Sahib, as we were now called in Nepal, should cut a jaunty, handsome figure, and I had watched the NASA landings on the moon and had duly noted proper procedures for explorers. For the purpose of recording our experience, I wore around my neck two camera bodies, a host of lenses and light meters, a pair of binoculars, and a tripod. It made little difference that I had a large duffel bag for my personal gear or that we were going to hire a team of porters to carry all of our equipment. I felt the need to maintain independent life-support systems.

The small charter airplane carrying Jeff, Howard, Nima Chottar, our head Sherpa, and me, and all of our tents and field gear, took off late in the morning for a spectacular fifty-minute flight over hills and ridges, gorges and canyons, of impressive scale. We landed at the dirt airstrip at Tumlingtar, elevation 1500 feet, in the center of the valley. This large plateau was once the bottom of a lake, but the Arun had since eroded a deep channel on the western side and the plateau now stands some 500 feet above the river. Nima had arranged by letter to have several porters meet us at the airstrip so that we could begin trekking on the first day.

I descended laboriously from the plane, conscious that all eyes were on me. I thought at the time this was because I was new and lacked a sunburn, but later realized it was because I carried more wealth on my person than the average porter, making the equivalent of $1.20 per day for his efforts, could accumulate in a lifetime. Adjusting straps, buckles, and epaulets, I started off across the flat plateau with determined strides, even if a bit noisy from the clang and rattle of my assorted paraphernalia. My companions followed and we soon launched far ahead of the porters, keeping to the trail as it wound its way past thatched houses and rice paddies toward the Khanbari ridge.

By now, it was well past noon and we were in the full heat of the day. At this tropical elevation the sun beat down like molten gold over the landscape, and everything blistered under its touch. The red lateritic hills surrounding us on all sides seemed to glow with a fire of their own. Heat, in all its oppression, and sweat turned the camera cases into wet, slippery surfaces, and my shoulder straps cut cruelly into my flesh. Our strides became shorter, less determined; walking grew to be a chore, then a burden, and slowly, as the parched trail turned from side to side, on and on, a torture.

In vaguely worded hints on the subjects of weather and terrain, my companions and I discussed the wisdom of waiting for the porters to catch up. We should make sure that all of our gear had arrived safely. And maybe we were going too fast for them. When they arrived, only minutes later, we took advantage of the meeting to give them some of our less important equipment as a kind of test of their willingness to be helpful. In truth, the fashion show was over. I had come so prepared for everything that I was barely prepared to stand up.

The first rise of the Khanbari ridge exploded my second misconception about walking — that it could be learned from a book. There is, in the mountaineering and outdoor circles, a collection of treatises on the proper and efficent methods of walking. I had read each with due thoroughness back in Bangkok and so felt ready to race across the mountains. As I felt the slope slowly steepening under me, I began a semi-religious chant of advice from the books: "Step around not over, Tra-la, Tra-la. Shorten the steps not the pace, Tra-la, Tra-la."

Gradually, the Tumlingtar plateau dropped below us, and the Arun River, surging its way south through the canyon, came into view, Tra-la, Tra-la. Sweat stung my eyes and the heat seemed to swarm round my head like an amorphous cloud of insects, buzzing incessantly, and hungry for the dehydrated body of a bleached Sahib. The lifeless rocks and increasingly steep trail didn't seem to give a damn whether I knew how to walk or not. I started stopping every few feet, bracing myself on one leg or the other and readjusting my pack in every conceivable way, searching for some comfort from the expensive design of nylon and metal alloys. My legs seemed possessed by a spirit of their own, a demonic one that cared little about my memorized axioms on walking, Tra-la, Tra-la.

The refrain was more difficult: "The mountaineering step is

performed by locking the knee on each stride, swinging forward, and thereby allowing the muscles of the weight-supporting leg to rest while the other repositions itself, Tra-la, Tra-la." The agony of climbing was enough, but the constant and unrelenting heat grew and grew. A hideous fascination with watching my own boots took over: Each step created a small cloud of dust that reminded me, of all things, of powdered snow. Numb, I thankfully slid into a semi-conscious state of walking and forgot all the rubbish from the books.

My third explosion of myths about walking — that walking was a matter of muscle — occurred slowly as the afternoon wore on. Every half mile or so it was the custom of the villagers to plant banyan or pipal trees; these giant fig trees take decades to grow, but once mature they have great horizontal branches that provide a luxurious shade. A wooden bench is constructed beneath the shade and these rest stops offer a tempting place to linger and enjoy the views while catching one's breath. Needless to say we recuperated as best we could at every rest stop. But we were careful to keep ahead of the porters, for somehow we had unanimously arrived at the unspoken idea that Sahibs belonged in front of porters. Sahibs were the leaders, the first to explore the trail.

Still, there came a point in our growing exhaustion when the porters reached a rest stop at the same time that we did but instead of resting they kept walking on. Since we had already shown our hands by taking off our packs, we quickly brought out our cameras and made showy motions with lenses and tripods as if we were taking vital photographs. Photography is a magical process that has given Sahibs all over the world the chance to rest under the guise of business.

With the pressure of their presence behind us gone, we adopted a new, more deceitful strategy. We completely abandoned the idea of photography, observation, everything but survival, and put all of our loose gear inside our backpacks so that it would be easier to carry. With grim expressions we marched on at the fastest possible pace, calculating that the pain would be easier to bear the shorter its duration, and made increasingly lengthy stops between our efforts. A sick kind of game developed: a race between rest stops, then, winded and sore, a long break while the embarrassment of showing up late in camp slowly re-entered our collective consciousness and sparked a new race to the next stop.

Khanbari, the main bazaar town of the upper Arun

It seemed to go on forever. The innate drive for survival common to all creatures has strange ways of expressing itself in man.

We arrived at Khanbari at four in the afternoon, just as the sun dipped down behind a high ridge to the west. A marvelous view for beginners, Khanbari stands at 4000 feet on a long ridge and looks south across a panorama of the lower hills. Terraced fields, like a thousand staircases, climb up all the surrounding slopes. Mud-and-rock houses of the villagers are scattered here and there on the larger terraces and are painted in ocher shades of the soil so that they blend with the land as if they were natural formations. A procession of ridges marches south toward the plains of India, and Tumlingtar can be seen below, as if again from an airplane.

Khanbari is the major bazaar town for the upper Arun, and there is a single street of loose cobblestones and dirt that is lined with whitewashed houses. The larger houses are two stories high and belong to merchants, who sell their goods, mostly foodstuffs, cloth, and such odd items as cheap Indian tennis shoes or Chinese flashlights, in low, poorly lit rooms on the ground floor. Several tall banyan trees stand at the entrance to the town like sleeping watchdogs. Sparrows and swallows fly back and forth between the houses and nest in specially built holes in the walls. It is a quiet, soothing place that has never seen a motorized vehicle or even a gasoline engine.

After catching our breath, we discovered that no one else had arrived from Tumlingtar. We could not find our porters, Sherpa, field gear, or anything. A few villagers kindly invited us into a tea shop where we hid from a growing crowd of children and waited to find out what had happened. We were not in the mood to go looking. Around six o'clock, Nima Chottar arrived with a disheartening appearance of relaxation and good humor. He explained that the porters had stopped shortly after they passed us. They had hurried along the trail at first so that they could reach a house where chang, the locally made beer, was sold. "It was much too hot to walk, Sahib. We waited until the sun went down."

The porters arrived later, in the cool hours of the evening, joking, intolerably pleasant after their chang. There was, it appeared, more mind than muscle in walking. Strategy was as important as steps, and one had to bring a certain understanding to the process, a knowledge that the trail was indeed finite. A steady

Porters must carry both the expedition load and their own belongings

pace was more important than any technological toy. Self-control was more valuable than glib advice from a mountaineering book. And Sahibs were not measured by their strength, a currency that is devaluated in the hills, where the villagers have such abundance of it.

Thus, I made it my business to learn the way the porters walk. The standard expedition load is 75 pounds, but each porter actually carries significantly more, for added to the expedition weight is the weight of their own blankets, food, and cooking pots. To some experienced backpackers of America and Europe, this might not seem unduly heavy, and it isn't; the able bodied men of the hill tribes carry it with ease. This is the weight, arrived at after years of expedition experience, that all porters are expected to be able to carry — not only men, but also women, and children in their teens. The stronger men will often carry two loads at once in order to double their daily salary, and I have seen village men carrying three times this weight when hauling their own supplies.

The porters prefer to carry the loads in a woven bamboo basket secured to their backs and supported by a tumpline that runs across the forehead. Almost 80 percent of the weight is thereby supported by the head and the muscles of the neck. They tire from such a weight, to be sure, but they can still hike impressive distances each day over impossible terrain and can easily keep up with most beginning Sahibs. Even at the end of a long day in which we have climbed several thousand feet, the porters have an elastic gait that seems to vibrate with the very pulse of the mountains. They have, it appears, the resilience of the earth itself.

I have spent many days following porters step by step as they walk. I would place my feet in their footsteps, imitating if not the spirit then at least the mechanics of the way in which they walked. Especially when climbing uphill, they break the mountains down into thousands upon thousands of small increments. The smaller the stride, the less the muscles of the leg must work and the more one can take advantage of the natural fulcrums and balancing movements of walking. After a while, I found I could usually keep pace with a loaded porter going uphill. But going downhill, such as on one June day when afternoon rains spurred us on to camp, they could still quickly leave me behind. Despite their loads, they ran down the trail, hopping from rock to rock, jumping steep sections until it seemed that they must crash at the bottom, only to catch themselves at the last moment with a deft movement and hurtle down another declivity. Their skill reveals a conscious knowledge of gravity.

I have also learned that each man has his own pace. There is a rhythm to walking that is determined not by the distance to be covered nor by the condition of the trail, but by the individual size and proportion of legs to body, weight to muscle. I have short legs in relation to my body and find I can go up and down hills faster than others; Jeff, who is my height, has proportionately longer legs and quickly outwalks me on flat sections but lags behind wherever the trail steepens. Each person has his or her own equation, and it is needlessly exhausting to walk with a companion whose size dictates a different pace. The delights of companionship never make up for the strain of going too fast or too slowly.

Indeed, the development of our skills and attitudes toward walking seems to me now to parallel the development of the expedition itself. Looking back, I realize that the expedition as a group entered the mountains with all the same naïveté that we showed individually toward that first climb to Khanbari. Our elaborate preparations in Bangkok were of little help, and we had to learn how to succeed in the mountains by actually working and living there. The hardships which at first seemed to be overwhelming soon came to be welcome friends and a natural part of the job.

Altogether there were seven members who spent from five to fifteen months in the field. Douglas Burns was expedition herpetologist. Howard B. Emery served double duty as expedition parasitologist and medical officer. James and Karen Foster, a husband-and-wife team, were in charge of the botanical research. Jeffrey A. McNeely was our expedition mammalogist and served with me as expedition co-leader. His younger brother, David McNeely, was our logistical officer. And I was responsible for supervising the ornithological research in addition to my administrative duties. But many others, such as a team of mammalogists from the Field Museum of Natural History in Chicago or several groups from Educational Expeditions International, joined us in the field for one- to three-month periods. In all, some forty-three people participated in the expedition at one time or another, making it the largest wildlife expedition ever to visit these mountains.

At first, we organized the expedition according to the familiar model of previous mountaineering expeditions. The logistical problems presented by the Himalayas are similar whether you are supporting a team of climbers or a team of scientists. In mid-October 1972, seven charter airplanes flew us and the bulk of our equipment to Tumlingtar. We then spent a week at Khanbari organizing our supplies into loads and purchasing additional foodstuffs before starting north for the higher elevations and the forests. There was the typical long train of porters, more than 300 men and women, who carried our gear slowly along the narrow rocky trails. It was a laborious process, and we had considerable difficulty in maintaining contact between the front and rear of our supply chain, which stretched for more than a mile. We had hoped to keep this initial phase of the expedition as simple as possible, but when you have to carry 15 months' worth of food and equipment all at one time there are unavoidable complications and an unbelievable amount of gear — more than twelve tons in all.

Among our first tasks, we recognized the need for a base camp to serve as a central storehouse and offer protection from the harshness of the Himalayan weather. After a careful search, we chose a clearing at about 9000 feet inside a healthy upper-temperate forest of the Kasuwa Khola. It was a perfect site, close to a variety of habitats, centrally located in the upper Arun Valley, and less than a seven-days' walk from the airstrip at Tumlingtar. The local name for our adopted forest clearing was Labar, and, since it was to be our home for more than a year, we tried to make the camp as comfortable as possible, within the limits of local materials.

We hired forty of the more industrious porters to stay on for three weeks to help us construct two crude buildings. Their only tools were macheté-like kukris to roughhew beams, and large sledgehammers and wedges to carve rock, and yet within a surprisingly short time they had erected solid walls, complete with windows, and fashioned waterproof roofs out of woven bamboo. The main building had sleeping quarters for all members, a large central room with fireplace, and a permanent kitchen that could provide meals well above trail standards. The second building was given over to the Sherpa staff, who outfitted it with a large dormitory for themselves and two secure storerooms. In the end, we calculated that the total cost of the buildings was less than $1000, or about the cost of a single large frame tent!

Temporary base camp at Labar

Expedition Sherpas tending the campfire; note the plant presses drying on the pole above the fire

At the beginning we worked closely together as a group, all the members coordinating their research efforts to study the plants, mammals, birds, snakes, and amphibians of a single selected plot of forest. We surveyed the forests surrounding base camp first and then gradually, as the months passed, began taking longer and longer trips out to explore neighboring side valleys or new country farther north. Typically this would involve camping for several days in the same locality while we worked the surrounding forests and then trekking onward for a day to another study site where we would begin again. Sometimes, we would make a transect of a particular hill or slope, slowly ascending in altitude as we worked each 1000-foot elevation. Or, we might make a south-north transect, working our way across the country in gradual stages. These were especially productive times both for the group as a whole and for us as individuals.

Our trail camps consisted of a variety of sleeping tents all clustered around a central field kitchen. We had little trouble finding good campsites for there were numerous clearings within the forests, wide meadows in the alpine highlands, and open fields or pastures in the inhabited lower hills. The field kitchen was a practical design used by Sherpas throughout the mountains: A large tarp, suspended by a simple pole frame, was stretched high over a main cooking fire so that the fire was protected from rain and snow. The sides were open, of course, and it was a primitive, drafty shelter, but the combination of warmth from a roaring fire and the semblance of a roof overhead made it an inviting retreat.

Our diet was as varied as we could make it, considering that all canned and imported food had to be carried into the hills on porter back and thus was too expensive to use regularly. Coffee, tea, jam, sugar, and dried fruit were brought from Kathmandu in limited quantities. Some supplies — spices and tobacco, for example — could be purchased in the large bazaar towns, such as Khanbari. But we lived as much as possible off the local produce from the villages. Rice and potatoes were the constant staples. Occasionally we could get corn or wheat milled by hand into a coarse flour for making breads and pancakes. A local domestic plant that resembled spinach (and tasted much as its local Nepali name, "Saag," might suggest) was our principal green vegetable. During the wet season, though, we could gather many wild vegetables from the forest, including nettles, fiddleheads, and mushrooms. Fruits and squashes were grown in most villages but were highly seasonal. We would gorge for several weeks on oranges or apples before facing many months without them. The local supply of meat, mostly arthritic billy goats, decrepit roosters long past their prime, or water buffalo that had suddenly died from some unknown disease, turned us into unwilling vegetarians much of the time.

Eight or nine Sherpas worked with us full time: Two or three would be kept busy in the kitchen under the guidance of Dave McNeely. One Sherpa would always be on the trail making the long run down to the airstrip to carry mail. And one was assigned to each of the primary researchers to assist in their particular work. Pema Thamchen from Thami Village of Khumbu was my assistant, and he quickly learned enough about avian field techniques to be a tremendous help. He became proficient in preparing museum specimens, operating the mist nets, and even the more difficult procedures like taking blood and albumin specimens. He came to know most of the bird species and could identify with remarkable reliability even the small confusing species of warbler. Other Sherpas were equally helpful to Jeff, Howard, and the Fosters so that we soon had difficulty working without their constant assistance; Sherpas show a singular talent in learning the wide variety of tasks that Sahibs, from mountaineers to field biologists, ask of them.

There is often some confusion about the difference between porters and Sherpas. In fact there is almost none except time and experience. The term *Sherpa* refers to a specific group of hill people, originally from Tibet, who live in the Khumbu Valley at the foot of Everest. When Nepal first opened her doors to foreigners around 1950, the mountaineering expeditions used the Khumbu Valley as a route to reach Everest and hired Sherpas as porters. The Sherpas quickly graduated from the menial labor of carrying loads to the better paying jobs of cooking food and setting up camp. Today, the Sherpas are very sophisticated. Some are extraordinary cooks and can produce everything from Japanese to American cuisine over the capricious flames of a campfire. A few are now quite knowledgeable about the technical aspects of mountain climbing and are much in demand. All know how to care for Sahibs while trekking, including the packing of loads, choosing routes, hiring porters, and protecting a precious bottle of liquor. The term *Sherpa* has become synonymous

Permanent Base Camp

Pema Sherpa of Thami Village

in the Himalayas for guide or cook, while the term *porter* still refers to someone whose sole responsibility is carrying loads.

The Arun Valley was seldom used as a route for early mountaineering expeditions and even today is considered too remote for most pleasure trekking. As a result, the hill people of the Arun have not had the opportunity to learn how to cook and guide foreigners; but they are most eager to learn, for they recognize the economically favorable position that Sherpas have achieved.

Porters are paid only on a daily basis — usually the equivalent of $1.20 to $1.80 per day depending on the size of the load and the area to be visited. They receive no extra benefits and must find their own sleeping arrangements at night. They receive food from the expedition kitchen only if they help fetch firewood and water, a minor task requiring at the most one or two men. Sherpas, on the other hand, command twice to three times the daily salary. They are entitled to food from the kitchen and expect free clothes, boots, backpacks, and substantial tips if the expedition is large and spends a long time in the mountains.

The inability to speak the foreigner's language is the main obstacle keeping the hill people of the Arun as porters. During my second year in the valley I had mastered enough Nepali to converse freely with the villagers and found that many of them would make excellent guides. They are hungry to learn and quick in picking up the Sahib's ways.

At present, however, the artificial hierarchy continues. Our working camps reflected this economic gradation in many ways, even including the sleeping arrangements. The Sahibs would sleep in small nylon alpine tents, one or two people to a tent, and often separated off at corners of the camp to provide some privacy. The Sherpas would use the large six-man tents which they would pack full with eight or nine men at once. They enjoyed staying up late at night talking and laughing, so that at a distance the tent seemed like an animate creature with its sides heaving and making strange squealing and giggling sounds. The porters would sleep out in the open under fair skies or beneath the kitchen tarp during inclement weather. They preferred to sleep close together, each tribe forming its own cluster, their bodies touching like logs in a wood pile, and their assorted blankets shifting around like waves on a sea of bodies.

The center of our working camps was the single large frame

tent that acted as the central laboratory. Inside, it was more than
10 feet across, with ample room for the aluminum folding tables
and three chairs which we brought to save our backs from the
constant bending over required in some of our work. This crude
field tent was truly the heart of our roving expedition and the
nucleus of our daily activities. On any given day each of us
would be involved in a variety of tasks, but the lab was always
the central meeting ground.

Howard was unofficially in charge of our impromptu laboratory since almost all of his work took place there. A precise and
methodical man in his late thirties, Howard was well suited to
the demanding research on ectoparasites that was one of the more
difficult activities of the expedition. Ectoparasites are those small
insects, such as ticks, chiggers, mites, and lice, that live on the
exterior surfaces of animals. These microfaunae have considerable zoological interest in themselves, but the pressing need for
such research is because of their ability to transmit diseases dangerous to man. Ticks, for example, pass through a series of molts
on their way to becoming adults, and at each stage they must
feed by sucking blood; if an immature tick feeds on a wild animal that is infected with a disease it can pass the disease on to
a second animal, sometimes a different species, during a later
feeding. Encephalitic viruses, rickettsial fevers such as typhus,
and bacterial diseases such as plague are all known to be harbored by wild animals and are transferred to man by ectoparasites.

The mechanisms by which such diseases operate are often mysterious and complicated. Not long ago an epidemic broke out
in the northern region of rural India. Suddenly, without any
warning, people in a few remote villages began suffering from
intense fevers accompanied by vomiting and severe headaches.
The symptoms grew worse, afflicting both young and old, but
the local health officials were helpless in the face of this disease
that was unlike anything they had seen before. By the time the
epidemic had run its course thousands of people had been affected, some permanently disabled. Many had died. A special
team of epidemiologists was brought in, and only after months
of work were they able to piece together what had happened.

The disease was indeed new to the area. It seemed to have
originated farther north in central Asia, where a similar disease
was maintained by wild animals and periodically spread to local
villagers there. But how had it traveled some 1000 miles and

Howard Emery working inside the field laboratory

over the Himalayas to India? The researchers hypothesized that it had been carried by a migrating bird that itself was infected or was carrying an infected ectoparasite. Once in India, a parasite spread the disease to the local population of monkeys, which the researchers discovered were suffering from milder, but almost identical, symptoms. The monkeys had maintained the disease in sufficient fluency so that it could later be spread to man. Perhaps a woodcutter visiting the forests for the day had been innocently bitten by a tick that had previously fed on one of the monkeys; once inside the village the disease spread quickly. This instance demonstrated the interconnected way in which wild animals and ectoparasites can act to spread dangerous disease around the world.

It is obvious that in order to control these diseases we must first document the kinds of ectoparasites and the ecology of their hosts. Such work requires an elaborate array of scientific equipment, including microscopes, centrifuges, syringes, assorted vials, and chemical preserving solutions. Howard would set these out on the table inside the lab tent and spend most of his day there slowly processing the bird and mammal specimens that Jeff and I brought to him. Each specimen would be carefully examined for ectoparasites, a task often requiring up to an hour per specimen, so that Howard was invariably up late into the night working. It always seemed odd — Howard cloistered in the tent amid the accessories of modern science, while just outside Himalayan winds blew across a tribal landscape of primeval mountains.

The rest of us followed more traditional pursuits at our working camps. Jeff, thin and lanky as a spring bear in search of his first meal, spent most of his time in the forests looking for animal trails, spoor, and other signs that would reveal the kinds and activities of the local mammals. When most people think of a mammalogist they imagine a stalwart individual concentrating his attention on a particular species of large mammal, perhaps a leopard or a wild goat. But the fact is that out of the 2600 species of mammal in the world only a few hundred are the typical large mammals, and the great majority consist of rats and mice, squirrels, moles, voles, bats, and so forth. Since the first priority of our wildlife research was a basic species census, Jeff had to pay attention to the entire gamut of wild animals and somehow keep in mind the confusing diversity of identifying characters separating *Rattus eha* from *Rattus fulvescens*, and so on.

Jeff McNeely was co-leader and expedition mammalogist

Such small mammals are difficult to study, to say the least, and Jeff had to complement his visual observations with an extensive trapping program. At each study site, he would set out a long line of traps, often several hundred at a time; he used aluminum box traps whenever possible so that he could release unharmed those specimens not needed for later museum analysis. Many small mammals are arboreal, spending their entire lives above the ground. These include not only such obvious examples as squirrels, but also many others, such as certain rodents and shrews. Thus, Jeff constantly had to invent new trapping techniques, setting up special snares high among the branches of the forest canopy. Bearded, dressed in his khaki field jacket, and with a camera slung over his shoulder, Jeff would disappear each day into the woods loaded with traps and notebooks in the most businesslike fashion.

Part of Jeff's job was to concentrate on the intriguing study of microhabitats. The basic habitat type of any area is usually indicated by the principal components of the vegetation, for example, an oak-laurel forest; but within any given habitat, there are also a thousand small areas that offer distinct temperature, humidity, and vegetational characteristics that directly affect the kinds of small mammals able to exist there. Even on a single tree, for instance, there might be different species of small mammal that inhabit the upper branches where there are abundant light and access to arboreal insects, the middle branches where epiphytes and climbers provide a darker, damper existence, or the base of the tree trunk where there is access to the forest floor and a third kind of food resources. Jeff wanted to take his studies beyond simple collecting and to gather as much information as possible on the interactions between individual species and their particular environment, their behavior, and their niche.

Indeed, Jeff's studies encompassed both ends of the spectrum of modern mammalogy. When there was time and opportunity, he would conduct visual studies of the behavior of large mammals; he was particularly interested in studying the daily and seasonal activities of serow. On the same day, he might find himself processing a series of karyotypes. After a careful chemical treatment, sections of bone material are placed on a microscope slide so that later, in a laboratory, their chromosome structure can be compared and their phylogenetic relationship determined. Many small mammals are so similar in form and color that it is difficult to distinguish between species; a study of their chromosomes often provides a more definitive insight into how species are related to each other.

Fortunately for me, the birds were somewhat easier to study in that most species are conspicuous and I could rely largely on visual sightings to record the local avifauna. Still, there are always some species whose secretive habits or rarity makes them difficult to observe and I would also set out at least a few mist nets at each study site. These large nets are constructed much like fish nets and are aptly named in that they are woven of such fine nylon thread that when set up they are almost invisible and appear like a vague mist that lingers between bushes. Unknowingly, birds will fly directly into the nets, which are so elastic that the birds can be captured without harm. Like Jeff, I could release most of the specimens I trapped, but occasionally there were individuals that I was forced to sacrifice and make into museum skins.

The taking of museum specimens is certainly the most unpleasant task required of any field biologist. You argue to yourself that such specimens are absolutely mandatory to document the presence of a new species in an unexplored area. In fact, the most experienced biologist can return from the field with the firm belief that he observed a certain species, and yet his testimony can never have the conclusive authority that a single specimen of that species has. Further, certain specimens are desperately needed for basic biological studies that can be conducted only back at the museum. And the fact is that the death of a few individuals out of a total breeding population makes little or no difference. Care should of course be exercised when dealing with species whose population is small or endangered. But the real threats to the survival of a species come from such factors as habitat destruction or abusive commercial hunting.

I guess the part of taking specimens that saddens me so is not the actual killing of an individual bird. My views on the sanctity of life do not distinguish between a dinner-table chicken and an exotic forest-dwelling babbler. What saddens me is that we live in a world where the worth and prospects of a species depend on its relationship to man.

I found the business of conducting a thorough species census of the birds of the valley to be an overwhelming task. Some idea of the magnitude of the problem can be understood when you multiply the basic climatic divisions (at least five) times the basic habitat types within each division (at least three per division) times the number of seasonal occupants. For any given study site, there would be birds that live in the locality year round, birds that live at a higher altitude and visit the locality only during the winter, birds that live at the locality but descend to lower altitudes during the winter, and birds that merely visit the locality en route from distant wintering or summering grounds. In addition, there were the problems of visiting the various side valleys and ridge tops, the distinctness of climate provided by geographical variations, and the unavoidable problems of searching out species whose population was so small that they were extremely rare and only sporadically present throughout the range.

Consequently, I had to recognize the limits of my time and opportunity to carry out the kind of thorough census I wished to conduct. I tried to vary my research accordingly, branching out into other activities when it would prove more productive. Much of my spare time was devoted to tape recording the vocalizations of birds, one of the most pleasant field activities I have ever undertaken. The sounds of many Himalayan bird species are virtually unknown and yet are extremely important to any understanding of their behavior and habits. During the summers, I gathered as varied data as I could on the breeding biology of species whose nests we would discover, including information on the number of eggs, the time of incubation, and the parental roles in bringing up the young. I also became involved in an in-depth study of the ecology and behavior of one particular species, the orange-rumped honeyguide.

Because of obligations in Bangkok, Doug Burns could not stay with the expedition full time; instead, he made three separate visits, each of two months or more, according to the seasons. He concentrated all his efforts on compiling the most comprehensive list of amphibians and reptiles he could. His visits had a frantic quality about them as he rushed across the hills searching out species, and toward the end of each trip he would become almost desperate to explore one more forest or look over just the next hill. His enthusiasm was a tremendous lift for the entire expedition and his warm friendship around the campfire a source of special joy. He is, I suspect, the most unassuming man I have ever met, and his scientific research reflected his honest and forthright manner, totally devoid of the trappings of jargon and masquerade.

The complex botanical situation in the Himalayas made Jim and Karen's work particularly confusing. The incredible diversity of soil types, altitudes, exposures, and weather patterns causes a corresponding diversity of plant life. Antiquated texts made field identification of all but the most common species impossible, and the Fosters were forced to gather an extensive collection of specimens. Typically, they would delineate small plots of ground, usually a meter square, within each study site and examine each plant found within the square, hopeful that it contained plants representative of the entire study site. As their collection grew, they tried to identify and collate specimens into what appeared to be individual species, a terribly time-consuming task.

Individual specimens would consist of small sections of a branch or a few leaves. They laid them carefully out on a flat piece of newspaper and attached a small label to them on which they wrote a number that identified the specimen in their collecting notebook, where they kept careful notes on the specific locality, the surrounding plant life, conditions of the soil, descriptions of the adult plant, and so on. Then, another piece of newspaper was placed on the top of the plant, and plant and papers were sandwiched between two pieces of cardboard. When a sufficient number of these sets was made up all were stacked together, one on top of another, and squashed tightly inside a wooden frame. The papers served to wick moisture away from the specimens so that they were soon dry and effectively preserved for posterity.

Karen was thin, with long auburn hair; Jim was heavier, and after he grew a beard, reminded one of a friendly mad scientist. I'm still not sure how Karen was able to put up with us. As the only woman on the expedition she was hypothetically at a disadvantage. It was her first visit outside the United States and, for all intents and purposes, the Midwest, where she and Jim had grown up. Jim, sophisticated in his science and completely immersed in the intellectual activities of botany, was a serious prodigy of academia. The expedition offered him the opportunity to pursue his science to the utmost, and coupled with the ethic of conservation, there was a religious fervor to his concentration. But he was like a ship without its rudder at times. Karen was his rudder.

Jim Foster crossing the main bridge at Paksinda

Dave, as logistical officer, managed supplies and equipment for the expedition. He also directed the daily operation of the base camp and was generally responsible for supervising the kitchen, although his southern California background prompted him to produce the most exotic foods in the middle of the Himalayas. Somehow, he was able to teach the Sherpas how to produce a rude imitation of tacos and spicy Mexican beans, a queer meal to have while sitting in an Asian forest. In addition, we set up a meteorological station at base camp; the weather records for the Arun Valley were hopelessly incomplete and consisted of scattered, unreliable data from a few poorly outfitted government stations. Dave kindly volunteered to add this to his duties — volunteered, that is, in his own way, for Dave had a sense of independence, an unfettered self-reliance resembling that of a wild mountain lion.

Still under twenty, Dave was the youngest member of the expedition, and although he conducted himself and his responsibilities in an efficient and competent manner beyond his years, he seemed bent on playing the youthful role of camp agnostic. Any suggestion or advice we might give about the kitchen, logistics, or meteorological project would be duly questioned and examined before he would agree. And even then he would have to change things just a little, as if to demonstrate that he was his own man. A heated argument would always ensue, and Dave would respond by rubbing the toe of his moccasin in the dirt and hiding beneath the wide brim of his western hat, with a certain quiet smile of determination that drove everyone else slightly furious. When things calmed down we would realize that Dave was perhaps the truest scientist on the expedition in that he questioned everything. And the fact was that Dave was a terribly likable and personable young man, intelligent and eager. Just stubborn.

Evenings in camp were a learning process as we exchanged notes and ideas from our respective disciplines. The Fosters might explain about the local forests and teach each of us something about the methodology of botany, while Jeff might inform the group about his recent mammal discoveries, or I might describe the avifauna of the present study site. Traveling and working with such large groups was exciting and stimulating in the beginning of the expedition. There was always something to do, and even if your own research was experiencing a lull, other members would appreciate your assistance. The interaction of disciplines and people was as rewarding as it was spirited. We seldom stayed up late, though, preferring to adjust our schedules to the natural cycles of light and dark that the sun and stars provide.

As I think back upon the general business of living and working in the Himalayas I find that although the hardships will always be remembered — the leeches and rain, the constant moving from place to place — I dwell more on the good parts. There were comforts to our life in the field, comforts that go beyond friendships and beautiful views, that I now miss sorely.

Walking, for one. The rhythm and feel of one foot after another was a comfort like no other. If I was sick or depressed, there was no surer cure. If I needed to think and was not able to muster the discipline to sit and contemplate, I found that walking would free my mind as no other exercise could. As the months passed my muscles became conditioned to the steepest hills, and I discovered the healthy exhaustion which followed a long climb to be the perfect sleeping potion. Later, I hiked that same section of the trail mentioned earlier, from Tumlingtar to Khanbari, and found that it took less than two hours and was hardly a strain at all.

But walking was much more than just a physical exercise. Although at first a burdensome labor, it grew to be second nature and as much a part of my consciousness of the Himalayas as any rocky peak or spring blush of rhododendrons. Walking became an act of rejoicing to travel along a high ridge where the views of mountains and valleys, space itself, walked with us. It became an act of real achievement to climb 18,000 feet to the top of a mountain, for when we finally reached the summit we knew in our minds and bodies the true height of the mountain. It became an act of pilgrimage to toil for days over a curving trail to a distant mountain, and the use of a plane or helicopter to reduce those days to minutes would detract not only from the trip, but also from the mountain.

Cloth walls were another comfort. For most of my two-year stay in the Himalayas, there was nothing more substantial between me and the forests than the thin fabric of my tent or the synthetic shell of my clothes. The transition to such an existence went completely unnoticed — only a slow awakening of sensors that had long lain dormant. But upon my return to Kathmandu

Mountain trail

and then America, I found the wood and concrete walls that we have adopted as our civilized skin to be walls around emptiness. I no longer knew the temperature of the air, the direction of the wind, the more subtle sounds of the animals that always tell, by their kind and abundance, the locality, season, and even the time of the day. A whole range of sensitivities has been abandoned in exchange for more potent and jarring stimulations.

CHAPTER FOUR

The Lower Hills

Trees are safih infidels,
In them no devotion dwells.
But when God among them strides
There's a surge of holy tides,
And the irreligious trees
All go down upon their knees,
Saying prayers and singing hymns
As they bend their leafy limbs.

— *Ballad of Koko Nor*

I CAN REMEMBER with great clarity my various flights from
Kathmandu to Tumlingtar. The charter plane was always
loaded heavily with supplies and people so that we were invariably crammed together like boxes on a supermarket shelf; and
the fierce, irregular winds of the mountains tossed the tiny plane
back and forth like a flimsy straw on a great wave. It seemed a
most uncomfortable, if not terrifying, experience, but I found I
still enjoyed the flight, for the plane offered a special vantage
point. I could look out through the curved windows and observe
the landscape as it flowed by beneath us. Fascinated, I would
study the pattern of villages and forests and try to come to know
the land as soaring eagles must know it.

At first the flight swings south from Kathmandu and then
heads east toward the Arun Valley. You fly at only 12,000 feet,
cruising slowly over the convoluted land of the lower hills. These
hills seldom climb above 8000 feet, and the white massifs are
far enough to the north so as not to cause alarm. On a clear

day, especially in the rain-washed sunshine of the post-monsoon
months, you can make out the basic features of the geology. Far
to the south is the flat ground of the Terai, a smooth plain that
stretches in an unbroken line to the southern horizon. Polit-
ically, the northern portion of the Terai is part of Nepal, but
geologically the area is merely a northward extension of the
Gangetic plains.

A narrow belt of land slopes gently uphill from the Terai to
meet the first foothills; this belt, called the Bhabar by the natives, consists of alluvial soils and debris washed down out of
the hills. Crisscrossed by broad rivers that glisten in the sun,
the Bhabar appears wrinkled and folded like a cloth ribbon in
need of ironing. The first foothills erupt out of the Bhabar like
a low wall. Known as the Siwaliks or Churia Hills, they form a
regular band of low ridges that stretch across the southern front
of the Himalayas. Immediately inside their slopes is a series of
low-altitude valleys called the Duns, which separate the outer
foothills from the inner range of main hills, the Mahabharat
Range, a wide band of increasingly taller ridges climbing north
to where the giant peaks rise from the Great Himalayan Range.

The Mahabharat Range was the original home of the Nepalese
hill tribes and was the first area to be cleared and settled. Here
one finds the oldest and most established villages, many of which
are at least 200 years old. Some of the hills reach up over 8000
and 9000 feet, and as we flew over them I could usually see a
distinct line across their faces at about 6500 feet where the terraced fields of the villagers gave way abruptly to forests.

Although the general panorama of the Himalayas was always
spectacular, I found that it was the land below the line of cultivation that most consumed my attention, the land of human
inhabitancy, the land comprising the Bhabar, the Siwaliks, the
Duns, and the lower portion of the Mahabharat Range that is
commonly referred to as the lower hills. I don't know what I
expected, but looking down all I saw was a depressing barren-
ness — mile after mile of parched terrain that had already felt
the abuse of weather and man. It was obvious that most of this
area had been worked for centuries and that the villagers had
cut and pruned, plowed and burned, until most of the natural
vegetation had been removed.

I would crane my neck back and forth to find some forests in
this settled land. Scattered stands of sal trees occupied the lowest

elevations, and on the slopes of the subtropical belt I could occasionally spot an isolated patch of castanopsis forest. In some places, a small stand would be situated just above a village, obviously a woodlot that had been selectively preserved by the villagers to serve as a source of firewood and fodder. But generally the forests were confined to the very steepest slopes, the crests of ridges, or the rugged shoulders along the rivers where the villagers found the terrain too difficult to cultivate. The forests were surrounded by fields and pastures like city parks in a concrete wasteland.

I was always struck with the transition that occurred as the plane descended to land at Tumlingtar. From the air, the predominant color of the landscape was red, a burning rust tone from the exposed lateritic soils. The naked fields and slopes seemed to blaze with reflected sunlight, and the impression was one of a ravaged, desperate land. But once on the ground, although the views were still harsh and the heat intense, the homes of the villagers offered an agreeable, comforting quality. Thatched houses dotted the ridges and slopes and were nestled among clumps of giant bamboo or in the leafy arms of the banyan trees swaying gently in the slightest breeze. Native women threshed grain in the shade of nearby houses, talking cheerfully and keeping a watchful eye on playing children. In the distance, I could see darkly tanned men toiling behind teams of oxen as they slowly plowed the fields. Their relaxed, almost leisurely movements seemed to keep pace with the languid quality of the climate.

This conflict of images, an abused land versus friendly villagers, was part of our thoughts whenever we worked in the lowlands. Like most westerners, we were drawn naturally to the villagers, and felt a strong attraction to their simple lifestyle and vital energy. But we felt a parallel concern for the missing wildlife as represented by the endless terraced fields and worn pastures that covered the landscape.

The world's tropics possess some three quarters of the total species of plants and animals found on the planet. In the minds of biologists, the tropics are always equated with an inordinate complexity of life forms, and yet the tropical elevations of the Arun had been reduced to the most meager ecosystem. Above all, we were biased by our responsibility to view the land in terms of the natural fauna and flora. It was our job to discover how much wildlife was left, to examine the specific effects of the villagers' activities on the forests, and to understand something about the future prospects of the remaining wildlife.

Our first investigation was in a small sal forest growing in a narrow belt along the nearby tributary of the Sabhaya Khola. From the literature, we had some idea of what to expect. Sal is one of the more common forest types of the subcontinent and has been extensively studied because of its importance as a source of timber. On the plains, it grows into a magnificent tree, over 120 feet in height, but the steep slopes and shallow soils of the hills limit its height to less than 80 feet. Its large rounded leaves, six to ten inches long and shiny yellowish green, make it an easy species to identify. Although never quite leafless, sal sheds much of its foliage during the dry season. And it is a highly gregarious species, only infrequently found with other canopy species. It never lives up to the popular conception of Asian forests as tangled growths which hinder travel and create fear with their dank obscurity, but in many places sal does foster a rich and diverse forest.

Armed with such knowledge, our first visit to the sal forest along the Sabhaya was a rude surprise. Inside, the forest was open and spacious. The canopy was seldom continuous and in many places the crowns of the trees were widely separated, so that light flowed through to brightly illuminate the forest interior. We could not detect any real understory layer beneath the canopy. Arboreal plants, with the exception of a few ferns and perhaps some moss, were almost absent. And the forest floor was practically naked; there might be scattered seedlings of young sal or occasionally a clump of other small shrubs, but in most places the ground was covered only with dry brown leaves. The list of plant species Jim and Karen compiled was discouragingly short. Indeed, this sal forest seemed almost a monoculture.

A cursory examination revealed many of the causes of these conditions. Scarring on the trees demonstrated that the villagers regularly cut the foliage for fodder and firewood. Wandering domestic goats and sheep showed that the villagers normally allow the forest interior to be used as pasture. But the full extent of forest disruption was the result of a more powerful influence: the annual practice of burning the forest floor. The villagers believe that burning helps promote new growths of grass and seasonal plants which they desperately need to feed the insatiable

Sal forests growing along the shores of the lower Arun

appetites of their domestic animals. To some extent, it probably does. But it also reduces the forest to only those species which are resistant to fire — a new factor in the process of evolution for which few plants are prepared.

The impact of burning can only be appreciated by actually witnessing it. One April night I watched the villagers burn the floor of the sal forest around our camp on the Sabhaya. A thin line of red, yellow, and smoldering greenish flames moved across the slopes, as if a searing iron were being drawn over the land. A bright torch could be seen chasing back and forth behind the line as a villager set and reset the flames in orderly fashion. The flames moved quickly with the wind, but wherever the debris was sparse the flames would die out and the villagers would have to run over to relight the fire. The ash-laden vapor became so thick that it could be tasted and almost handled like a palpable substance. Even the stars and moon were obscured by the pasty smoke. Fortunately, the fire moved fast so that the trees seldom burned, although when I examined the forest the next morning I found scorched trunks and twisted branches and limbs. I also found the burned bodies of squirrels and birds, countless small mammals, reptiles, amphibians, and insects.

What I had seen was not a new sight for the Himalayas, nor for that matter a new experience for any part of South Asia. Buried in the literature of early explorers to the subcontinent are repeated references to this common theme of a dry season land in flames. I have personally observed this primitive technique of controlling the natural vegetation in the Chieng Mai Province of northern Thailand and along the rolling hills of the Isthmus of Kra. But nowhere have I seen the villagers burn the land so completely as in the Arun Valley. The sal forests were only the beginning, and later that same April I saw villagers burn scrub and forests throughout the lower hills. Toward the end of the dry season the atmosphere became so saturated with the accumulated smoke from the fires and dust from the exposed soil that the air was turned dark. Visibility was reduced to the point where I had trouble seeing nearby ridges, and the charter flights to Tumlingtar were canceled because the pilots could no longer make out the landing field. The sky did not clear again until the first monsoon rains of late May.

As a result, there is no way now to ascertain what might have been the original condition of the sal forests in the Arun. There is even some evidence to suggest that sal, at present the most common forest type, was once much less prevalent. In addition to sal we found a second major forest type in the tropical lowlands; this was the tropical evergreen forest and in the past it was believed that this latter forest was replaced by sal only along the deep, shady gullies where the ground occasionally becomes waterlogged. But as John Stainton points out in his excellent book, *Forests of Nepal*, "... it may be that in Nepal, or at any rate in its eastern parts, tropical evergreen forest is confined to damp and shady sites not so much by reduced rainfall as by the fires which sweep the country periodically."

Our research faced a real dilemma. It was impossible to make any concrete statements about the present status of the wildlife when the past status was unknown. And it was impossible to say anything about the past status when we were even in doubt about the basic forest type which once occupied any given tract of land. Was sal the dominant forest type of the inner lowlands because of its ability to excel in the tropical heat, or merely because of its resistance to fire? Man's intervention in the lowlands had been so pervasive that all judgments about the natural fauna and flora were subject to serious qualifications.

Our investigation of a tropical evergreen forest revealed that this forest type indeed favors special conditions. Not far from Tumlingtar a gorge narrowed to form steep walls that allowed more shade in the morning and evening hours than occurred on neighboring slopes. The soil was comparatively moist and rich in humus. It appeared from the topography of the site that the ground suffered regular flooding during the monsoon overflow of the stream. The villagers, although they still cut the foliage for fodder, obviously had difficulty in burning the damp debris on the forest floor. The success of the tropical evergreen forest type at this site could well have been an artifact of man's use of fire.

The forest was immediately distinguishable from sal by virtue of its darker green vegetation. The canopy was composed of many species, such as *Eugenia, Michelia*, and various *Lauracea*; it was generally continuous and provided deep shade and a controlled climate for the forest interior. There was a thick understory and many arboreal plants, including growths of mosses, ferns, orchids, and climbers. The forest floor was alternately covered with shrubs, bamboos, palms, and ferns. Even in sparse sections, it was apparent that this forest was dramatically more diverse and lush than any sal forest we had visited.

The animal life of the tropical evergreen forest was also much richer. Both forest types harbored primarily Indian species of birds, but whereas the sal forest birds would include only a handful of species, perhaps a haircrested drongo, a common iora, or a gray-headed flycatcher singing its plaintive song among the dry branches, the tropical evergreen forest contained such variegated species as the green-billed malkoha, the golden-backed woodpecker, the red-capped babbler, the large necklaced laughing thrush, the silver-eared mesia, the verditer flycatcher, the pale blue flycatcher, and many others. The increased number of understory, terrestrial, arboreal, and canopy plants of the tropical evergreen forest provided numerous microhabitats and thus a greater variety of bird life.

In surveying the avifauna of the tropical elevations I discovered two other distinct groups in addition to the forest birds: those common around houses and cultivated fields, and those characteristically associated with the streams and rivers. Among the commensal species, house sparrows built their nests in the thatched roofs of the villagers' homes. Mynas and barbets fed on the fruit of the fig trees that stand along the trails. Black drongos complacently rode the backs of domestic sheep and water buffalo, occasionally descending to the ground to feed on insects kicked up by their larger companions. On almost any day I could find along the hedgerows and scrub that lined the fields a flock of spotted doves, several species of shrike, tailor birds, bee-eaters, and numerous bulbuls.

The streams and rivers provide a very specialized habitat for typical water-loving birds. Although they are generally confined to the tropical elevations, the Himalayas possess many species of kingfisher: I frequently encountered the large pied kingfisher, both the tiny Eurasian kingfisher and its similar-looking blue-eared kingfisher, the white-breasted kingfisher, and the stork-billed kingfisher. Other water birds included the large cormorant, the merganser, several species of duck, both the gray-headed and the red-wattled lapwings, and during the winter a confusing number of sandpipers, stints, and plovers.

Forever etched in my mind are the mixed images of sal trees and the midnight screams of jackals — a weird, laughing, chortling sound that seems to come from nowhere and yet is everywhere around you at once. Jackals, together with wolves, foxes, and dogs, both domestic and wild, comprise the family Canidae; the jackal's closest relative is the wolf, but the jackal is much smaller, almost the size of a fox, and it has a malign, sinister quality about it that has created its distasteful reputation. Jackals can succeed in almost any environment, from the humid forests to the dry, open plains, and they are found as high as 12,000 feet in the Himalayas; but in the Arun I have always thought of them as a species of the lowland forests where they persist in surprising numbers.

During the day, they are seemingly invisible, hiding in the scrub and forests or among rock shelters. But at dusk they secretly come forth in ones and twos, sometimes in small packs, and hunt together or, like their spiritual compatriots the vultures, scavenge on animal carcasses, refuse, and offal near villages. It is at this time that they begin their calling and like most members of the dog tribe, their vocalizations must play an important role in communicating information about food, mating, and the presence of other predators. Little is known of their behavior and biology, however, and they remain mysterious creatures whose ghostlike voices cry out across the dry hills.

The pangolin is also found around Tumlingtar. It is a strange animal that resembles the armadillo of the New World in that it is covered, from its head all the way down its back and along its tail, with hard overlapping scales. Pangolins are frightening things to look at, although they are actually quite harmless as they lack teeth. Their principal form of defense is to roll up in a tight ball and rely on their armored body to protect them from predators. They live in burrows and their food consists almost exclusively of the eggs, larva, and adults of termites or ants. Like the jackal, they are nocturnal creatures, active after the sun sets, and as a result are seldom seen by people.

Indeed, most of the mammals of Asia are very difficult to observe. Asia has few scenes comparable to the wide savannas of Africa with their grassy expanses teeming with vast herds of wildebeest, zebra, antelope, elephant, and others. Asia is far more typically a land of forests, with secretive animals that hide from the visitor. Himalayan mammals are seldom concentrated as in Africa, and many are exclusively nocturnal or favor dense vegetation so that wildlife enthusiasts are often frustrated, especially those who expect nature to resemble a zoo, with each animal carefully presented for easy viewing. But for the serious enthusiast, one willing to undergo the rigors of the field in exchange for a singular adventure, the fleeting sight of one of Asia's unusual creatures invariably provides a marvelous and enduring experience.

Around Tumlingtar, habitats that during the day would seem empty and barren of wildlife at night would be alive with the shining globes of animal eyes reflecting from our flashlights. One evening in some scrub beside the river, we discovered a small fishing cat; its spotted coat made it look like a small leopard, only paler and grayer. We were not sure what it was doing but suspected that it was searching for roosting birds among the bushes that lined the water. Shortly afterward we noted another pair of eyes that belonged to a Himalayan palm civet, a long-tailed creature that seems a cross between a cat and a dog. It prefers a more vegetarian diet and we guessed that we might have interrupted it en route to nearby houses where there was half-eaten fruit and old food lying on a compost pile. We were careful not to approach it too closely for the Himalayan palm civet, like a skunk, has a reputation of secreting a horrid-smelling liquid when irritated. On the way back to camp we sat for a moment beside a large mango tree and counted the number of large fruit bats scurrying among the branches after ripening fruit. There were at least several dozen.

Most mammals of the lowlands survive simply because they are nocturnal and thereby avoid direct contact with man. Large diurnal mammals, like the chital deer, are all but gone from the Arun. When there is a report or sighting of them, word spreads quickly through the villages, and men flock to the place armed with their crude muzzle-loading rifles. Firearms are strictly controlled in Nepal and supposedly illegal without special permits, but many villagers possess handmade weapons or old arms smuggled into the country from India and Tibet. Local government officials, often the most avid hunters, own modern cartridge rifles and shotguns. And most villagers are adept trappers, with extraordinary expertise in the use of all kinds of snares, deadfalls, pits, nets, and so forth. With their limited diet and often severe shortages of protein, the villagers consider any wild animal as fair game and a valuable addition to the pot.

Typical of the waning numbers of mammals is the wild water buffalo. A small population can still be found at Koshi Tappu on the riverine flood plains of the Terai, just south of the Arun

Valley. They resemble the domestic water buffalo common throughout the subcontinent, but the wild species is much heavier and of greater stature, with long corrugated horns that give it a nobler appearance. Unlike their docile domestic counterparts, wild buffaloes are aggressive and unpredictable and truly deserve the respect that their size and strength warrant. These animals once ranged widely over the subcontinent but now are confined to a very few areas in Assam and at Koshi Tappu. They have been protected at Koshi by the maze of interwoven channels and islands created as the river flows out onto the plains and acting as a natural barrier against man's intrusion. They are still threatened, though, by natural hazards such as the disastrous flood in 1968 which reduced their already meager population to fewer than fifty animals. Since then the buffalo population has recovered somewhat although it is still dangerously small.

The Koshi Tappu area is a natural sanctuary for many animals that have long since disappeared from the accessible regions of the Arun's lower elevations. The dominant forest type is a mixed assemblage of khair and sissoo trees, a very common growth along the Bhabar and Terai. It is sometimes considered a successional forest since it helps reclaim soil along river banks and is often replaced after several years by deciduous riverine forest. At Koshi Tappu, however, it appears a stable forest type, perhaps because the frequent flooding removes whatever soil the khair and sissoo can consolidate. The combination of diverse vegetation and mixed water/land habitats provides for a wide range of large mammals, including wild boar, the gaur, hog deer, chital deer, and, according to recent reports, the tiger.

The Koshi Tappu has an equally rich avifauna. The mudflats and shallow waters are attractive resting areas for numerous species of migrating birds. Ducks, geese, cranes, herons, terns, and many others visit the Koshi each year. Drs. Robert Fleming, Sr. and Jr., two of the most knowledgeable and respected naturalists in Asia, reported that during the course of a single week's observation in 1971 they were able to count over 32,000 ducks representing 19 species! This abundance of visiting birds is matched by a host of residents, including peafowl, jungle fowl, ibis, egrets, quail, and numerous smaller species. Unfortunately, the poaching and hunting pressure has increased during the years, and it appears now that the numbers of both birds and mammals are declining proportionately. But this limited area still gives some indication of the numbers and diversity of wildlife once common throughout the tropical elevations.

The tropical habitats ascend only to about 2500 feet in the Arun, and above this is a band of subtropical fauna and flora that continues up to 6500 feet. This subtropical band is usually included in the lowland area, however, because it suffers from the same disruption by man and generally lies below the upper limit of cultivation. In the same way that sal forest is the most common forest type of the tropical elevations and serves to characterize that zone, the subtropical zone is characterized by *Castanopsis*, a beautiful tree not familiar to the westerner but quite common in South Asia.

There are 28 species of *Castanopsis* in the world and most are confined to East Asia. They do well in the damp conditions of the eastern Himalayas and are much less common in drier climates; in west Nepal, for example, there is substantially less rainfall and the subtropical belt there is usually occupied by forests of pine or oak. *Castanopsis*, closely related to oaks, are usually classified in the same order, Fagaceae, because they produce a woody nut much like the oak's acorn. The nuts of *Castanopsis* are hard, coriaceous, and covered with spines, which makes them very useful in the field as a means of quickly identifying the genus; indeed, they are often distinctive enough to enable positive identification of individual species.

The three chief species of *Castanopsis* found in the Arun Valley provide a dramatic example of the powerful effect altitude can have on the distribution of any particular species. *Castanopsis indica* favors the lower elevations, from 2000 to 4500 feet; typically it is mixed with other trees, especially *Schima*, but also *Mallotus*, *Bombax*, *Terminalia*, and *Eugenia*. Starting around 3500 feet, *indica* is slowly replaced by *Castanopsis tribuloides* in mixed forests with *Schima*. And around 5000 feet, *tribuloides* is slowly replaced by *Castanopsis hystrix*. This latter species is the one that sometimes forms an almost pure forest by itself.

In our investigation of the subtropical zone we visited many forest stands throughout the Arun. Most of them could hardly be called forests, though, and resembled the sal growths we had surveyed along the Sabhaya, where the disruption by man had been so extensive as to totally change the natural composition of the fauna and flora. Typically, the stands consisted of only a few scattered *Castanopsis* trees, perhaps interspersed with one or two

Much of the lowlands is inhabited, and terraced fields cover the slopes

Many of the lowland forests, such as this Castanopsis stand, have been severely damaged by the grazing of domestic animals

other species, but with no real understory or undergrowth. Almost all of the trees showed signs of having been pruned, with their lower branches, and sometimes even their upper branches, lopped off close to the trunk. Dry scrub grew between the trees like a malignancy. The ground, wherever it was exposed, was hard as concrete.

Not unexpectedly, we found that the animal life of such stands was also limited. In the worst woodlots, for example, the birds were as much secondary growth species or commensal species as they were forest species; these included such birds as the spiny babblers that hide in the cutover brush, the white-crested laughing thrushes that travel everywhere in raucous flocks, or the Himalayan tree pies that constantly declare their presence in the loudest possible voices. Healthier woodlots contained a greater variety of birds, for example, the Eurasian cuckoo, the yellow-bellied fantail flycatcher, the chestnut-bellied nuthatch, the white-bellied yuhina, and the beautiful yellow-throated minivet. Among the mammals, we found the Indian porcupine, the Indian hare, and the rhesus macaque monkey to be common in the subtropical zone. But in general we discovered that many of the birds and mammals of this zone were the same as those of the tropical zone. Although at times we thought we could detect larger concentrations of a species in one particular zone versus the other, the great mobility of animals allows them to travel freely between zones.

To our surprise, we did find one or two forests in the subtropical zone that appeared to be substantially intact. One such forest was at Dahbalay in a remote area that was some distance from any village. From the outside, the Dahbalay forest seemed remarkably verdant, with notable growths of arboreal plants and a continuous canopy. The forest floor was rich in ferns and seedlings. To all intents and purposes, it looked like a healthy, mature *Castanopsis* forest, and we decided it would be an excellent study site for an extended survey.

We were intrigued with the possibility that an undisturbed forest remnant might be able to preserve wild species in an area long after the bulk of the countryside had been turned into cultivated fields. Like a zoo, a forest remnant might act as a sanctuary and maintain small breeding populations of native species that could later re-inhabit the region when suitable vegetation had regrown. Dahbalay seemed a perfect candidate for such a sanctuary.

We set up a comfortable camp and field laboratory just outside the forest. At the time a team of ten Americans from Educational Expeditions International was visiting us, and we took advantage of the extra manpower to conduct as thorough a survey as possible. Jim and Karen marked off a series of transects through Dahbalay and began collecting and cataloguing the variety of plants. Howard took charge of the mammal research and put out three trap lines, which he moved through each quadrant of the forest on a rotating basis. I began a program of daily visual censusing of the birds and set up numerous mist nets to sample each of the basic components of the forest — the canopy, understory, forest floor, interior clearings, and exterior edge.

Almost at once, data from the various disciplines demonstrated that something was wrong. Dahbalay was situated at just over 6500 feet, right on the border with the lower temperate zone, and Jim was half convinced that the exclusive dominance of *Castanopsis* was artificial. Both Howard and I reported curious data about the animals; many species appeared to be missing. I found that among the birds, for example, an entire microfauna — those birds which frequent the forest understory and floor — was absent. I had expected to find the slaty-headed ground warbler, the yellow-billed scimitar babbler, the black-faced flycatcher, and a host of other species which favor the forest interior. The normal birds of canopy and forest edge were present, indeed plentiful; but somehow the Dahbalay forest had been altered so that inner forest species were just not there.

Suspicious about our findings, we decided to investigate the history of the forest by talking with the nearest villagers. We invited several village men to dinner one evening, and, sitting around the campfire, we had a lengthy discussion about Dahbalay and the village use of surrounding forests.

The men explained that the Dahbalay forest was a purposefully preserved remnant that served as a minor source of firewood and timber for the village. The soil at Dahbalay was too poor to be used for agriculture. By mutual agreement, everyone in the village shared the right to use the forest as they needed, but no one was allowed to clear the land. The village, through its elders and elected headmen, attempted to regulate the amount of cutting and in essence was practicing a primitive form of forest conservation.

The men said that many villages had such a system because the need for forest products was so crucial. The prosperity of a village was directly dependant on a healthy woodlot. To promote a sustained yield, the headmen of the village assign rights to gather firewood in certain areas of each woodlot, and households jealously guard their territories; many territories represent traditional claims that date back several generations. Trivial uses of wood are discouraged, and when a household needs a particularly large tree for a construction project they must pay a sizable sum to the village headmen. The fundamental concept of a renewable resource is also recognized, and the headmen will sometimes declare a moratorium on cutting if a certain plot shows signs of really excessive use that will soon lead to complete exhaustion.

Most villages tried to designate a small plot of land as their forest preserve somewhere nearby their village. The men said that their village had done so and that there were several good woodlots in their immediate vicinity that served as a source of daily firewood. But during the past generation these woodlots had not been large enough to supply all their needs for fodder and timber for construction. They had been forced to come farther afield to places like Dahbalay to find sufficient wood. The men also explained that they could remember that when they were young Dahbalay was considerably different. At that time the trees were mostly oaks, not *Castanopsis,* and the forest was lush, with more moisture and a greater variety of plants.

It did not take Jim and Karen long to realize what was happening. The villagers had, in effect, been altering the entire composition of the Dahbalay forest through the years in a significant yet almost undetectable way. They had been selectively cutting the oaks in favor of the *Castanopsis* trees, and the latter species had become dominant only because of this human influence.

After questioning, the men said that they did prefer oaks. The wood was better for lumber than *Castanopsis,* and their domestic animals much preferred eating the foliage of oaks over that of other species of tree common to these altitudes. The gradual cutting and pruning of the oaks over the years was not enough to destroy the appearance of a mature forest stand, but it was enough to change the vegetation and markedly affect the microhabitats required for the survival of certain species of animals and plants.

Many species of birds, for example, are specifically adapted through natural selection to an extremely specialized microhabitat. Their feeding habits and breeding biology are dependant on a complex arrangement of physical, climatic, and vegetational factors. Certain species of scimitar babbler are specialized, with their long scimitar-shaped bill, to feeding on insects among the dense mat of mosses and arboreal plants that grow along the moist branches and trunks of the shaded forest interior; if the canopy of the forest is pruned and excessive sunlight dries the arboreal plants to the point where they die off, the scimitar babbler loses its prime feeding area and the advantage of its specialization. It can no longer compete and can quickly disappear.

Cases in point are several species of bird that were reported as quite common by ornithologists visiting the eastern Himalayas during the nineteenth and early twentieth centuries. The blue-fronted long-tailed robin which affects the floor of lowland forests, the dusky-green tit babbler which affects the forest understory, and the green cochoa which affects the lower canopy were all found in sufficient numbers at that time. Despite special efforts, I was unable to locate them anywhere in either the subtropical or tropical zones of the Arun. It is not unlikely that these inner forest species are now extinct in the valley.

Dahbalay was really a turning point in my understanding of what was happening to the wildlife of the Arun Valley. Before Dahbalay, I had been basically surveying and studying, a wide-eyed spectator of the animals and plants. The obvious forest destruction of the lower altitudes depressed me, but I held out hope for remnants such as Dahbalay and was elated by the dense forests of the middle and upper elevations and the sanctuary that they might provide. But our study at Dahbalay demonstrated that even a seemingly healthy forest could be suffering from serious environmental problems. It was such an insidious form of environmental disruption that I became quite apprehensive about the future of all Himalayan wildlife.

Looking back I realize that a broad pattern emerges of the changes in the status of the wildlife occurring throughout the lowlands. A lack of data precludes detailed statements, but it is possible to outline a series of stages in the gradual progression from a natural environment to a man-dominated one.

Stage one would be the virgin forests, without any significant human influence. These are limited to a very few areas, certainly less than one or two percent of the total land area and possibly as little as a fraction of one percent. In our entire survey of the two zones the only place where we thought such conditions

Black drongo riding the back of a domestic sheep

Macaque monkey searching for fruit in a pipal tree

might prevail was at Koshi Tappu, and there the status was a function of natural barriers that prevented man's interference. As the need for land and natural resources increases, however, these natural barriers will doubtless be overcome and the virgin forests will disappear. It is also apparent that the number of such forests is already so low that they no longer hold a representative sample of the plants and animals once found in the lowlands.

Stage two is a place like Dahbalay, where minimum human use of the forest is taking place. Squirrels still run through a full canopy and birds sing from a rich undergrowth; the changes are not conspicuous but they are nonetheless significant. The general fauna and flora of the forest are preserved, especially those of the forest edge and canopy, since these microhabitats are less affected. But the plants and animals of the inner forest begin to disappear as the special conditions of shade, humidity, and temperature are altered.

Stage three is the disrupted forest remnant, such as the sal growths around the Sabhaya or the *Castanopsis* woodlots. Here the natural vegetation is completely altered. Some of the major trees continue because of their size, but the constant cutting and burning modify the physical structure of the forest to the point where a host of minor plants, the arboreal and terrestrial species, disappear.

A curious phenomenon of species replacement begins. This stage is very much like secondary growth, with a corresponding increase in the number of secondary-growth fauna and flora. At first, those forest species which occupied microhabitats resembling secondary growth, like the forest edge and canopy, persist; these include birds like the black-headed yellow bulbul, the rufous-necked scimitar babbler, and Brook's flycatcher, which do well in both forests and cutover scrub. Later, as the forest is broken up more and more, these forest species are displaced by true secondary-growth creatures, those specifically adapted to scrub and brush, such as mynas and white-cheeked bulbuls.

Stage four is the cultivated field, the open pasture, or the continuous scrub. Trees are incidental. The fauna and flora have been reduced to the most meager level. Such gross destruction of the forest habitat has a simple and straightforward meaning for biologists. Studies in Malaysia, for instance, have shown that over 80 percent of the original bird species disappear when a forest is clear cut. Some birds attempt to migrate to remaining forests, but those forests already have a full contingent of animal life; most of the migrating birds merely die. Where the forest with its diverse vegetation provided many microhabitats for numerous birds, the clear-cut areas with their limited plant life allow for only a few; one exchanges myriad species, each with moderate population sizes, for a scant number of species, most with a rather large population size.

This simplified ecosystem is vulnerable to disease, weather changes, and invasion by foreign species. In 1973 and 1974 surveys we found that one of the most common plants of the sub-tropical zone was *Eupatorium adenophorum*, a conspicuous low shrub with deltoid leaves, reddish stems, and small white flowers. It grew over vast areas of abandoned fields, along trails, and paddy dikes, and seemed to dominate the secondary growth of the Arun lowlands. Villagers explained to us that it was causing a great hardship since few domestic animals would eat it and, being resistant to fire, it was almost impossible to destroy. They called it "ban mara," which in Nepali means dead forest, and said that only twenty years ago it was unknown in the Arun. Apparently, this plant is native to eastern China, and it has only recently been able to invade the Arun as man creates a suitable habitat for it. There are similar examples of invading species in both the birds and mammals, but this one suffices to demonstrate the tremendous changes that are occurring in the ecosystem of the lowlands.

These four stages are gross generalizations, and I am sure that the knowledgeable reader will discover a number of exceptions. But the stages do point out the basic trends in the natural environment. Indeed, it is not hard for me to use these trends to further generalize and hypothesize a fifth stage. Given the continued human interference, *stage five* would see the disappearance of all forests in the Arun lowlands. The vegetation would be cut until nothing but scrub and bare slopes remain. What few forest animals now find refuge in the present remnants would also disappear. New species from other parts of Asia would continue to invade. The ecosystem would be reduced to only those plants and animals that can co-exist with man.

But the principal difference between stages four and five would be a new factor. Habitat destruction would not be confined merely to scattered slopes here and there but would encompass every square inch of the lowlands. The power of forest vegetation to modify the climate would no longer occur. With no forests to absorb rainfall, control run-off, and maintain a moist soil, there would exist the possibility for a basic change in the climate of the lowlands, a change that I believe is already beginning to take place. Stage five would be a vast desert, certainly not a desert of sand dunes, but an arid, treeless wasteland stretching across the lower hills. If it seems far fetched, remember the history of places like the sub-Sahara or the Fertile Crescent. If this seems a terrible prospect for the wildlife, imagine the prospect for man.

CHAPTER FIVE

Middle Altitudes

There's only one escape from crowds:
Live in the sky among the clouds.
— *Lama Proverb*

THE LAST CALLS from a familiar owl echo out of the forest around our camp. Soft guttural notes of contentment speak triumphantly of a successful night of hunting, patient and mindful. It is a shy and unobtrusive tawny wood owl that has called from the same part of the forest each dawn. As I lie in my sleeping bag, I imagine his earless, brown-eyed form sitting hunched in the black retreat of the forest canopy. I feel a special delight in learning the pattern of his calls, an emotional appreciation that comes when one spends enough time in the wilderness to recognize the flow of the day and the rhythm of the animals.

"Coffee ready, Sahib," Pema Sherpa announces through the front flap of the tent. I sit up as he passes a steaming cup of Nescafé in, its heartening aroma challenging the cold dark interior of my tent. An awakening sip, and then I wedge the cup between frozen water bottle and sleeping mat to free my hands. I slip on my pants inside the warmth of my sleeping bag, and finally, with a crinkling swish of nylon fabric, put on my down parka.

I emerge from the tent to meet the penetrating chill of a December dawn in the Himalayas. Venus is still bright against a paling blue-black sky. My breath freezes in transient clouds and a lacy frost clings to the trampled grass of our forest clearing. I walk up a small hill at the end of the clearing, tucking cold fingers beneath my armpits to warm them and listening to a growing chorus of song. Trills from a blue-fronted redstart and chattering expectant sounds from a nutcracker punctuate the silence left by the owl. A tiny black-crested coal tit, uttering peeps and buzzes, starts an acrobatic dance among the sparse branches of a nearby bush. They are in a hurry to begin the day. Their calls make a vigorous statement of life that breaks the chill and beckons the sun.

The first rays, golden white and dazzling, strike the summit of Kongmaa La across from us, illuminating its jagged dome of rock and snow that crowns the line of five peaks rimming the northern ridge. At this season, they are white brooding shapes that seem unapproachable. Although Kongmaa is fourteen thousand feet above sea level and would rightfully be considered a tall mountain anywhere else, here it is a trivial peak that is not even mentioned on the map. Indeed, Pema considers it at best a nuisance, an obstacle that blocks from view the many giant massifs located just beyond. From the top of the ridge one can see beyond Kongmaa to Makalu, the fourth highest mountain in the world, a huge hump-backed monster of ice that rears its head among the spires of Umpha Lapsa, Chamlang, Tuche, and countless others.

Steep slopes fall from the peak of Kongmaa. In stark contrast to the lowlands, they are carpeted with luxuriant forests that slowly emerge from the shadows of dawn. Maples, magnolias, and rhododendrons crowd the slopes around us, and I can look down into the basin to see the lower temperate forests of oak and laurel. The slopes, like angular planes on a gabled roof, descend to a turbulent streambed far below. The stream, known as the Kasuwa, flows south for five miles to join the main Arun River at less than three thousand feet, almost two vertical miles beneath the summit of Kongmaa. The scale is imposing and no matter how long one spends in the Himalayas it is impossible ever to overcome a simple wonder at the size of everything.

I walk back to the tents. Pema is busy with breakfast under the kitchen tarp, shuffling pots and stirring rice porridge amidst the smoke. The porters are huddled beside the fire and Pema must dance among them as he adjusts the pans and checks the progress of the porridge minute by minute. Waiting there for breakfast, Jeff and Howard, Jim and Karen, talk quietly about our plans for this morning. It promises to be another blue-sky–green-forest day like those of the past. The early hours will find me searching for finches in the undergrowth. The afternoon I have reserved for a nearby stream where babblers bathe.

For the past two months we have concentrated our studies in these middle elevations, those altitudes of the Arun that lie above the disrupted lowlands but below the spacious alpine zone. It has been one of the most exciting times we have known. Everything is new to us, and the days rush by filled with countless discoveries. Unlike the lowlands, with their Indian influence, the fauna and flora of these elevations are truly Himalayan and hold their affinity to that portion of the earth that biologists call the Sino-Himalayan. This broad area, a wedge out of the center of Asia, stretches from the eastern Himalayas through southern China toward the island of Taiwan. It is an exotic land typified by such plants as the rhododendrons or animals like the pandas and babblers. Inaccessible by even Asian standards, it contains what is probably the least known wildlife in the world.

The forests are lush and wild, rank with an organic energy. Oak forests occupy the lower zone starting at around 6500 feet (the upper limit of cultivation) and continuing up to almost 8500 feet. These are stately forests with tall trees that vault upward from huge buttresses. The canopy hangs overhead like the broad ceiling of a giant auditorium, creating silent chambers where even sunlight is green. In some places, the canopy is almost pure oak, usually *Quercus lamellosa*, but it is often mixed with other species, including maples. Laurels are also prevalent, both in the understory and blending into the canopy. An evergreen forest, it keeps its leaves even during the winter.

The upper zone extends from 8500 feet up to 11,500 feet and is dominated by an upper temperate mixed broad-leaved forest. This name is derived from the fact that the most prominent trees have broad leaves, the canopy consists of a mixed association of maples, magnolias, rhododendrons, *Osmanthus*, and others, and the climate there is typically upper temperate, with winters and summers not unlike those of the northern United States and portions of Canada. The trees are seldom very tall, usually under 60 feet, and by comparison it is a congested forest, with numerous overhanging branches and a dense understory. In the winter, snow lingers on the forest floor and branches are bare. In the spring, the magnolias blossom forth in giant white flowers, which set off the varied shades of reds and pinks of the rhododendron flowers.

Oak-laurel forest of the middle altitudes

Both forests show the evidence of a heavy annual rainfall. Thick blankets of arboreal plants infest every tree. Mosses drape thickly from the canopy like spiderwebs in an abandoned house. Endless rows of ferns and orchids march up the trunks. And here and there a cluster of epiphytes sits in the crook of a sweeping branch. The summer monsoon hits these middle elevations with particular intensity, drenching the landscape until streams overflow and the slopes themselves flood with sheets of water flowing downhill.

In addition, the dampness here is a function of the ability of the forests actually to comb moisture from the sky. During much of the dry season these slopes are inundated with fog and clouds. The small droplets of moisture that make up the fog are too light to fall to the ground by themselves but are carried along in the air currents from which they are blown against the foliage. There they collect on the edges of leaves and tiny stems, for the narrow sharp surfaces serve to precipitate the moisture. The tiny particles of water coalesce and grow and, when they are heavy enough, fall to the ground as drops of rain. This phenomenon is typical of montane cloud forests throughout the world and helps account for the consistently damp conditions. Arboreal plants flourish for they no longer have need of a root system penetrating the earth. They merely pluck their water directly from the sky.

There are other forests in these middle elevations. In many places rhododendrons come to dominate the slopes and form an almost pure forest, to the exclusion of the mixed broad-leaved assemblage. Birch forests of *Betula utilis* are common in the higher elevations at the edge of the tree line. Farther north, where the monsoon is effectively blocked by the high ridges, forests of the fir *Abies spectabilis* occupy the broad slopes of the inner valleys. And there is even an occasional pine forest in the driest, most northern sections. But these forests are generally in the minority and are usually confined to the zone transitional with the alpine belt.

One forest, however, forms a quite distinct type and is found throughout these middle altitudes. Indeed, it is also plentiful in the subtropical belt, although it is in such a mutilated condition there that we seldom bothered to study it. It is a strange forest, simple and sparse, and consists almost entirely of an east Himalayan species of alder called *Alnus nepalensis*. This singular tree has deciduous branches that during the dry season break off at the slightest touch. Walking through such alders, we have merely to extend our arms to rake off multitudes of branches, and it takes but seconds to collect a night's firewood. As a result, these alders have straight, slender trunks with few if any lower branches and gaunt, lean crowns.

Jim and Karen became intrigued with these alder forests because they appear to act as successional forests that help reclaim slopes recently cleared of soil by landslides or erosion. Landslides are a common occurrence in the Himalayas because of the steep, fragile slopes. They exert a powerful influence on the fauna and flora, in one dramatic moment changing the composition of plants and animals across an entire hillside. Jim thought that he could detect a regular progression from the naked gravel and sand left after a landslide to the reappearance of a normal climax forest such as a mature oak stand.

At first, the bare sand is invaded by moss that grows out across the impoverished ground with the same vitality moss often shows growing out over rocks. The strong valley winds and constantly shifting soils soon bury the moss under new sand and gravel. Just below the surface, however, the moss absorbs moisture as a sponge, enabling the sand above to support the invasion of the first grasses and low shrubs. These, in turn, as they grow and die contribute humus and nutrients to build the soil for the first alders. The alders appear specifically adapted to the dry soil conditions at this point and are remarkable in their ability to grow quickly into a forest. Conceivably, their deciduous branches help speed the process of soil development. Finally, as the alder forest matures to provide shade over the ground and further develop the soil, the first oaks and maples invade. They grow slowly but eventually will replace the alders with a complete forest.

As one might expect, we found few animals in the alder forests. Jeff and I visited them frequently, but the birds and mammals there appeared to be chance visitors rather than regular residents. The alders are unadorned and elemental in comparison with the verdant oak and magnolia forests surrounding them. Arboreal plants are absent, the forest floor is a mat of grasses and low shrubs growing up among the rocks and fallen branches, and the naked trees seem sadly undernourished, like neglected house plants.

The other forests of these middle elevations, however, hold an incredible diversity of some of the most remarkable creatures in the world. The serows are typical of the many unusual herbivores of the Himalayas. Perhaps resembling large goats more than any other creatures, they are related both to wild goats and to that heterogeneous group, the antelopes. Old male serows stand about three and a half feet at the shoulder and can weigh over 200 pounds. At first glance they seem awkward and clumsy because of their short limbs and thick bodies. Once in motion, however, they are sure-footed creatures with an easy gait that takes them safely over the precipitous rocks and cliffs.

Serows are found from the Himalayas through Southeast Asia to Malaysia and Sumatra. In the Arun Valley, they inhabit the middle altitudes from 6500 up to 11,000 feet. Once they may have ranged lower, but widespread disturbance by man throughout the lowlands has probably pushed them above the upper line of cultivation.

Serows are shy and when we did see them it would only be a fleeting glimpse, always of a solitary animal and usually at the edge of a forest clearing on some distant slope. During the day they hide away inside the forest, frequenting rock shelters and overhangs that provide protection from weather and predators. Some rock shelters are traditional sites and bear well-worn signs of where serows have rested regularly. In the late evening they come out and we found indications that they seem to travel in a circuit, for on their regular paths the tracks led in a single direction, as if the serow were following a one-way street. Apparently they traveled uphill at night along the gullies and canyon bottoms, stopping to feed, drink in the streams, or visit natural salt licks. At first light, they would disappear back into the forests, returning downhill along different and more sheltered paths.

Closely related to the serow are two other herbivores of the middle altitudes, the ghoral and the takin. A small, stocky animal, the ghoral has short coarse gray hair, a white throat patch, and stubby horns. It is more gregarious than the serow, and commonly travels in groups of four to eight. Though scarce in the Arun, they are well known in other parts of the subcontinent, where they frequent hill villages.

There is almost no way to explain a takin. Part this, part that, it looks as if it humbly adopted all the attributes that other goats and antelopes refused. Ponderous and unwieldy, its heavy body sits on fat, stubby legs, and is covered with a dingy, drab coat. Its horns look like a cross between those of the gnu and musk ox, and its face seems to have suffered a terrible accident, while the expression of its droopy lips makes one think it has been sucking a mixture of lemon and garlic. It too occupies the same forest zones as the serow, but it shows some preference for the higher elevations.

Perhaps the handsomest of the Himalayan herbivores is the tahr. More of a true goat than the serow, it is roughly the same size, but its neck and shoulders are covered with long, flowing reddish-brown hair, forming a mane much like that of a lion and giving him a similar dignified bearing. Of all the herbivores, the tahr favors the highest elevations and the most difficult terrain. Twice I have seen them above the tree line, climbing among the rocky ridges and desolate moraines of the glaciers. (The hill villagers often use the name *tahr* in referring to the serow, and call the tahr instead by the name *jharal*, thereby creating much confusion, although the serow's dark coat, ranging from almost black to a paler reddish white on the limbs, and its white patch on muzzle and throat make it easy to distinguish from its lion-maned relative.)

Although the macaque monkeys found around the lowland villages also frequent the lower reaches of the oak forests, the more common primate of the middle elevations is the langur. It is an exquisite creature with an impressive ability to bound through the tree tops, often taking prodigious leaps from tree to tree, or gliding among the branches with effortless movements. By contrast, the macaques are clumsy animals and generally stay close to the ground; langurs probably displace the macaques in the forest zones because of the former's superiority in climbing.

Found throughout India, the langur inhabits regions of the Himalayas as high as 12,000 feet, where it is known to occasionally visit the snows. The Himalayan race is perhaps the most spectacular, noted for its dark face and hands contrasting with a bright gray coat, and its long agile tail that sometimes exceeds three feet in length and serves to distinguish it immediately from the macaques. Langurs live in large and relatively stable family groups. Like many primates, there is a well-defined social order within each troop: Males are dominant, older ones having authority over younger ones. Within their own group they are generally peaceful and rarely display the furious aggressive gestures that mark some primate behavior, but they can become quite antagonistic and territorial when two different groups meet. We saw langurs frequently in the Arun and thought them tame creatures. Once, a large troop of ten or more individuals lounged complacently in the high branches of a tree while we marched with a noisy, grunting team of porters through the brush below.

Other mammals of this region include an occasional leopard, several species of smaller cat, giant flying squirrels, a large bamboo rat, many smaller rodents, and at least two species of bear. But certainly, the most beguiling mammal of the Arun is the red panda, a close relative of the famous giant panda — the teddy bear come to life. There has always been controversy about whether these two species are more closely related to bears or raccoons, and their strange assortment of characteristics suggests affinity to a wide variety of animals. The latest findings, however, favor the raccoons.

While the giant pandas are known only from China and northern Burma, red pandas are common throughout the eastern Himalayas and southern China and are quite abundant in the Arun. During the monsoon, one sees them often in the rhododendron undergrowth. The red panda is considerably smaller than its black-and-white brother. Chestnut-colored, it is only about two feet long, and the large bushy ringed tail adds perhaps another sixteen inches. The rounded head, large erect pointed ears, and short muzzle resemble the raccoon, but it is far more appealing. The red-and-white markings on its face give it a comical, cheerful expression that never fails to elicit a smile, regardless of one's mood. Watching it climb through the crisp lines of the bamboo or meander through the green luxuriance of the rhododendrons is one of the finest sights of the Himalayas.

The red panda lives above 5000 feet in the Arun, traveling as high as 12,000 feet during the summer, but generally keeping below 9000 feet in the winter. During the day, it seeks the shelter of the tallest trees, preferring to sleep among the high branches with its tail wrapped over its head, like a child hiding beneath the sheets on early mornings. Occasionally, it adopts a most curious posture: lying prone along a branch with its head tucked under its chest between its forelegs, and its tail hanging down like an abandoned feather duster. In the evenings, it descends to the ground to hunt for food — fruits, leaves, and flowers. It also eats some insects and grubs. Captive pandas have shown a more cosmopolitan diet, including an unaccountable preference for Mars Bars.

Little is known about the social life of red pandas. I have seen only solitary animals, with one exception, and that appeared to be a mother with young. Local villagers have told me that mothers are very protective of their young and will care for them long after they appear able to forage on their own. A few villagers are quite knowledgeable about pandas and trap them occasionally to keep as pets or to trade to the animal dealers. According to villagers, pandas have regular habits and follow a definite schedule in their daily routine, making them easy to capture at their favorite drinking places.

One more mammal needs to be mentioned, as it created quite an uproar in the expedition. This is the unique Tibetan water shrew, an animal so rare that hardly a handful of mammalogists even know it exists. Jeff had been interested in it before we came to the Arun, and his greatest wish was that he would at least see one and document its presence in Nepal, even if he could not find the opportunity actually to study it in the wild. In the beginning of the expedition, he spent weeks wading up streambeds, shining flashlights at night over ridge tops, and belly-flopping his way through the mire of swamps and bogs, only to have a villager fortuitously appear in camp one day holding a perfect specimen. When Jeff asked the villager about it he said, "Oh yes, the pani musa (water mouse) are very common here. During the monsoon, we have so many in the streams and rice-fields that they become a pest!"

The Tibetan water shrew is a highly specialized creature remarkably well adapted for life in the fast-moving mountain streams. Larger than a mouse, it has a wide otterlike snout with long sensitive whiskers and a dark brownish-gray coat giving it the general appearance of a large rodent. The resemblance stops there, however, for close examination reveals a longitudinal row of white hairs along its tail, other stiff hairs forming a fringe around each foot, and even a series of suction discs on the bottom of the feet. This arrangement of hairs and suction discs obviously helps the Tibetan water shrew maneuver through Himalayan torrents and cling to slippery, wet rocks. It can actually climb straight up a smooth vertical surface, a feat more in keeping with a lizard than a warm, furry mammal.

Many creatures of the Himalayas are adapted with similar precision to specialized conditions. Doug Burns found a tree frog of the genus *Rhacophorus* that is able to live an almost exclusively arboreal life among the tree tops. Such a lifestyle presents

Arboreal moss

Poisonous pit viper

serious problems for an amphibian, which normally must lay its
eggs in water. Doug found that these frogs overcome the difficulty by laying their eggs in an aerial mass high above a body
of water. As she lays the eggs, the female kicks them into a
frothy mass whose outer surface soon dries into a crust that pre-
vents the loss of moisture from the eggs. When the eggs hatch,
the tadpoles stay in the egg mass for a while, but when they
become too heavy to be supported by the crust they drop down
into the water. Such a breeding system might seem a precarious
way of producing tadpoles. It does, however, offer the advantage
that when the tadpoles finally reach the water they are older
and stronger and far better prepared to face the hazards of pond
life than when they were first hatched.

The oak and magnolia forests of the Arun harbor many bird
families common to temperate forests throughout the world,
along with others that would be completely strange to an American visitor. I remember that once, early in the expedition, I was
surveying an area in the transition zone between the oak and
magnolia forests. I had had little luck in seeing birds that morning, and, discouraged, sat down beneath a large tree to rest before
returning to camp. To my delight, a pair of barwings very quietly
appeared; they sat for a while before moving on. Immediately,
other species started coming in: first some green-backed tits, then
nuthatches, followed by goldcrests, yuhinas, tit babblers, least
warblers, laughing-thrushes, tree creepers, and so on. Within a
matter of minutes over twenty different species paraded before
me. They all seemed to come from and depart in the same general direction. When they had gone, the forest was quiet again,
almost as birdless as it had been at first.

It was originally believed that such diverse species stay together
for protection from predators, there being safety in numbers. But
there are probably other advantages equally, if not more, important. Possibly the different species band together in order to hunt
for food as a group, each species specializing in its own particular
niche. The large laughing-thrushes search the low bushes and
ground for insects, while the barwings hunt the epiphytic mosses
and arboreal plants. The nuthatches and tree creepers comb the
larger branches and bare bark as the tits and warblers are busy
looking among the outer foliage and leaves. The sudden com-
motion caused by the flock surely scares everything in its path,
and probably helps expose insects that would successfully hide

from individual hunters. The greater number of individuals in any one flock proportionally increases the likelihood of the entire flock's finding any given food resource. And there are probably still other benefits that result from such affable flocking behavior.

Some of the most beautifully plumaged birds in the world are the pheasants of the eastern Himalayas and the mountains of southern China, where the family is believed to originate. Our North American pheasants are not native species, and the ring-necked pheasant is a recent immigrant from Asia. We found pheasants in amazing abundance in the Arun, where there are four species in addition to the closely related red jungle fowl, a bird of the lowest elevations that resembles the common chicken and indeed is probably the ancestor of most domestic poultry.

The kalij pheasant is a striking silky black bird with a red facial patch; the eastern subspecies found in the Arun is quite dark and shows little of the white coloration on the crest and back that is seen in birds from western Nepal. The kalij inhabits a wide altitudinal range stretching from the tropical lowlands through the temperate zones and is found wherever there is sufficient forest to offer it shelter at night. Like most pheasants, it feeds on the ground during the day but prefers sleeping on an elevated perch in the trees. Omnivorous, it eats almost anything it can find, from insects and grubs, to nuts, berries, and grain. There are occasional reports of kalij taking lizards and amphibians.

The crimson horned pheasant, also known as the satyr tragopan, is confined to a narrower range within the temperate zones. It is strictly a forest dweller and as a result is particularly vulnerable to habitat destruction of any kind. Males are brilliantly red with white spots, black speckling, and curious blue fleshy horns that extend back from the head. It feeds on buds, leaves, and fern tips. Normally shy and wary, during the breeding season the crimson horned pheasant is easily decoyed by villagers who imitate the calls of the soberly dressed female and are able to bring the male in within a few feet. It is perhaps the most arboreal of all pheasants and sometimes makes its nest high in the trees.

The impeyan pheasant is the national bird of Nepal and was named after Lady Impey, the wife of the first British Governor of Bengal. It goes by at least two other names: the Himalayan monal pheasant and the daphne pheasant. The males are noted for their dark plumage with extensive metallic hues; in different lights they alternately give off bronze, green, or blue sheens of sparkling iridescence. They are easily identified in the field for they typically flush when approached and sail downhill displaying their diagnostic chestnut tail and wing patches contrasting with a white rump. During the winter they seek shelter in the oak forests of the lower temperate zone, but in summer they visit both the magnolia and fir forests of the upper temperate zones and often can be found searching for berries and seeds among the scrub of the alpine zone. More gregarious than the solitary crimson horned pheasant, the impeyan normally nests on the ground.

The blood pheasant is hardly a pheasant at all, and appears to be a link connecting the partridge-quail group to the true pheasants. It closely resembles a partridge in size, shape, movements, and in the way it holds its relatively short tail. Its name comes from the red streaks on its greenish breast that from a distance appear to be blood stains. It is the highest altitude pheasant of the Arun and keeps to the upper margins of the magnolia, rhododendron, and birch forests. The blood pheasant feeds on a variety of vegetable and animal matter and seems particularly fond of mushrooms in the spring. With a tameness bordering on stupidity, it is easily killed or captured by village hunters, who can approach it within yards before it flees. One dawn while I was camping in a rhododendron clearing, a blood pheasant walked right into my tent as if it wanted to share my morning coffee.

We found many familiar bird families in the inviting habitats of the middle altitudes: There are many kinds of woodpeckers, including a sapsucker. Members of both swift and swallow families are present in large concentrations, finding the cliffs and strong valley winds well suited to their lifestyle. Tits are also plentiful, though often more brightly colored than their American relatives. Nuthatches, wrens, tree creepers, and dippers are very similar, and in a few cases — the winter wren and the northern tree creeper, for instance — the very same species are found in both North America and the Himalayas.

On warm days when the thermals rise or the winds of autumn begin to pull our thoughts southward, falcons, buteos, and accipitrine hawks sail over the ridges and canyons. On the forest floor one finds the camouflaged nests of the nightjar. Owls, from the tiny little scops owls hardly larger than your fist to the giant forest owls almost the size of an American great horned owl, hunt in the stillness of the night. Finches, sparrows, and grosbeaks frequent both the forests and the clearings, and are particularly common when the winter weather brings northern migrants south. Thrushes, robins, and redstarts contribute many species to the Himalayas and are present at all seasons.

Yet familiar as these were, many other North American bird families were completely absent from the Himalayas. We found no vireos, mockingbirds, tanagers, or blackbirds among the Icteridae, for instance. Other families had been replaced with species of almost identical appearance and habits but no true generic relationship. Hummingbirds, for example, are strictly confined to North and South America. In the Himalayas their place is filled by the sunbirds, which have the same bright metallic plumage, are small, with similar long delicate bills, and feed on flower nectar by hovering in front of the blossoms. Yet sunbirds belong to an entirely different family, indeed even a different order. An observant student can tell the difference immediately, for sunbirds, despite the remarkable speed with which they move their wings, actually beat them in the traditional up-and-down motion common to most birds and are unable to move them in the back-and-forth twisting motion on the upper axis as hummingbirds can.

Flycatchers exist in the Himalayas as in North America, but the American flycatchers belong to the family Tyrannidae, the Himalayan ones to the Old World family of Muscicapidae. Both have upright posture, wide bills, and occasional tail movements contrasting with their tranquil bearing. Both sit on exposed perches and make aerial sorties out after flying insects. But whereas most North American flycatchers are drab, plain-colored creatures, many of the Himalayan flycatchers are quite brilliant, such as the velvety blue-black large niltava or the sparkling rufous-and-blue beautiful niltava.

Himalayan warblers are just as difficult to identify as their American counterparts. Most of them belong to the Old World family of Sylviidae, and the bulk of New World Warblers to the Parulidae. There is one Asiatic genus, the *Phylloscopus* leaf warblers, that poses what is very possibly the most difficult field identification problem in the entire world of birds. This genus includes some fifteen Nepalese species, and most are dull green above, paler below, with a most confusing assortment of wing-bars, eyebrows, coronal streaks, and rump patches. Several species are so hard to tell apart that I refuse to rely on field observations and must have them in my hand before I am willing to identify them.

Perhaps most fascinating of all are several families of birds that would be completely new to an American visitor. These include the bulbuls (Pyncnonotidae), medium-sized birds with pronounced crests; the minivets (Campephagidae), brilliant red-and-yellow birds with slim bodies and long tails; and the flower-peckers (Dicaeidae), stubby, tiny birds that feed on nectar.

In addition there is one of the most incredible groups of birds in the world — the babblers (Timaliidae). These are particularly common in the eastern Himalayas as they appear to have originated in the Sino-Himalayan region. The greatest number of species is found there, and they seem to radiate outward in diminishing numbers across Asia.

The babblers demonstrate an extraordinary energy in their speciation, as if this one family were trying to produce all of the varied forms of birds known throughout the passerines. There are tiny gems of life that resemble traditional wrens; the scaly-breasted wren babbler is abundant in the middle-elevation forests of the Arun, is all mottled brown and buff, with a short tail, and lives a hurried life flitting back and forth among the moss and fallen branches of the forest floor. Then there are several species that are very much like true tits: Both the chestnut-headed tit babbler and the white-browed tit babbler have plump little bodies and short bills; they are highly acrobatic, cavorting in the brush and understory, prancing along the stems and twigs, and generally displaying all of the indefatigable bravery common to real tits.

The scimitar babblers, medium-sized birds with long decurved bills, look much like American thrashers. Shrike babblers have thick bills with a hooked tip similar to the bills of regular shrikes; the red-winged shrike babbler keeps to the top of the canopy and is a sluggish bird that finds its food of insects and berries as much by walking as by flying. The black-capped sibia, although a larger bird with a long tail and a variety of habits, always reminds me of a nuthatch in the way it climbs along the branches and trunks of trees, sometimes hanging on upside down, and searching for insects among the moss and bark. There are even

Collared pigmy owlet of the lower temperate forests

Nepal parrotbill breeds in the bamboo growths

nectar-eating babblers such as the firetailed myzornis, a gorgeous green-and-red bird that matches the colors of the rhododendron blossoms it visits. The tongue of the myzornis has numerous bristles on its tip that enable it to efficiently lap up nectar from the flowers.

Two groups of babblers are quite distinct and are the constant companions of any visitors to the middle-elevation forests of the Arun. The yuhinas, of which there are three common species in the temperate zones, are smallish birds with prominent crests; active and restless, they usually keep in small flocks that roam through the brush, constantly twittering as if discussing some important new gossip. The bamboo growths of the oak and magnolia forests harbor at least four species of parrotbills, curious little creatures with bills that resemble those of their namesake. Their heavy mandibles appear to be an adaptation to feeding on bamboo buds and are sturdy enough to quickly cut the sheaths on bamboo when searching for insects. Like yuhinas, parrotbills travel in noisy flocks that flow through the undergrowth like a stream of feathers.

The babbler family is perhaps best known, though, for its laughing-thrushes, a large group with at least fourteen representatives in the Arun. Most babblers are gregarious, and laughing-thrushes carry these social tendencies to the extreme; when not breeding they travel in large feeding parties, and during the winter I have seen more than a hundred individuals in a single flock. Some evidence even suggests that in a few species there may be communal breeding, with several adults contributing eggs and providing parental care for a single nest.

In general, laughing-thrushes are large birds, the size of true thrushes, with prominent bills and long floppy tails. They forage in the undergrowth, usually staying close to the ground, where they scurry along much like squirrels, their long tails bobbing up and down behind them. Most species are skulkers of the brush and are loath to fly, preferring to run and hop out of range when approached or, if pressed, leaping into the air in an awkward manner and sailing downhill until they disappear as quickly as possible back into cover. They share many peculiar habits with the other babblers, including the ability to scratch their heads by bringing a foot straight up — a trait almost unknown among the Old World passerines. Most European, African, and Asian passerines scratch their heads by dropping a wing and bringing the foot up and over the back of the lowered wing.

When feeding together laughing-thrushes keep up a continual conversation of chuckles, hisses, and soft squeaky notes. Their name, however, derives from their vibrant songs and calls, which in some species, such as the white-crested laughing-thrush, are reminiscent of human laughter. But the songs of most species consist of musical whistles composed in short liquid phrases. Typically, the birds of a flock sing together in unison, and a few laughing-thrushes practice the more complicated art of dueting, whereby two or more individuals answer each other in a precise manner so carefully timed that it sounds like the effort of a single bird. The leader of a flock usually begins calling and is soon joined by the others, to form a chorus in which the volume of sound rises to a crescendo with surprising energy and carrying power. As they sing, the birds often posture, with bills raised or wings flapping. The sound of a flock of black-faced laughing-thrushes calling from the shadowy depths of the magnolia and rhododendron forests is one of the characteristic and unforgettable experiences of the temperate zone.

Laughing-thrushes are notable for their participation in mixed-species feeding flocks, one of the most common phenomena of the middle-elevation forests. Except during the breeding season, the birds of these forests are seldom evenly spaced throughout the woods. Instead, they flock together, especially in the late fall and winter, so that you can walk several hundred yards through the forest with no sign of bird life, only to turn a corner and suddenly walk into a horde of birds that seem to overwhelm everything.

By any comparison with the lowlands, the middle-elevation forests are little affected by human interference. The village hunters who go after blood pheasants or serows take a small number of animals but really so few that it probably does not affect the breeding population to any great extent. We found that the most damaging impact came from the shepherds, who use the forests for grazing their sheep en route to and from the alpine pastures. Each summer the shepherds take their sheep up to the sunny slopes of the alpine region, where the lush growths of grass provide excellent forage. The trails through the oak and magnolia forests are cut wide for the sheep, and numerous small clearings are created by the shepherds throughout the forests to act as temporary pasture where the sheep can rest on their long journey. The total trip often takes six to ten days, depending on weather.

This repeated grazing is having a major ecological impact. In the alpine region, the increasing use of the meadows is affecting the species composition of the grass and in many places is causing severe soil damage and excessive erosion. In the forests, the sheep disturb the natural undergrowth and terrestrial flora; in essence, they vie with wild herbivores for the forest vegetation, and their sheer numbers along with human assistance make them overpowering competitors. Hunting, with the exception of gross commercial slaughter, seldom has irreparable effects on wild animal populations; but habitat destruction can and does markedly affect the success of individual species.

During my last summer in the Arun I happened to be studying a specific forest plot when a shepherd brought his flock there to graze temporarily before moving on to higher altitudes. I was greatly upset by the sheer amount of physical damage that they caused. The flock numbered about 35 animals, and they trampled more than ten acres of undergrowth into a wet mush. It was at the height of the breeding season and a great number of terrestrial and lower-story birds' nests were immediately destroyed. Like most shepherds, my visitor spent his free moments cutting foliage to create a clearing for the sheep. He pruned the tops of many trees to provide extra fodder for his sheep and to keep them from wandering. At night, he burned large piles of wood and brush around the clearing to drive away biting insects that bother the sheep. The clouds of smoke produced by the fires damaged arboreal plants, injured many nesting birds, and changed the behavior of all the local wildlife.

In my judgment such human interference has not yet destroyed the regenerative ability of the middle-elevation forests. Enough natural wildlife still remains to repair the damage being done by man and his domestic animals. I am not so confident about the alpine areas; the high-altitude ecosystem has a special fragility by virtue of its simplicity. It is particularly vulnerable to any human disturbance. And the terrible environmental destruction that has already occurred in the lowlands, with its powerful effects on weather patterns and climate, is having an immeasurable influence on the slopes just above. Thus, the middle-elevation forests constitute a narrow belt of superb wildlife, beautiful and rare, wedged between the devastation of the lowlands and the fragility of the highlands.

CHAPTER SIX

One Step from the Moon

> Snow's a bright, alluring cheat,
> Snow's a sprite with cloven feet,
> Snow's a soft, inviting thing
> With a sly and deadly sting,
> Snow's a fiend in fairy guise,
> Snow's a white-haired man who lies.
>
> — *Dance of the Bhuts*

FOR ONE WHOLE SUMMER, I wandered up and down the ridge of the Kasuwa or traveled across the high altitude valley of the Barun. The icy profiles of Makalu, Chomo Lomzo, and Chamlang were always in view, standing tall and thin in the clear heavens of the afternoon, or their snow cliffs aglow in the red light of dawn. Here and there wide meadows were covered, like a lush lawn, with new growths of alpine grass and a healthy sprinkling of bright yellow flowers. Clumps of rhododendron, somewhat past their peak of blooming but still holding thousands upon thousands of blossoms, lined the meadows like cultivated shrubs in a carefully planted garden.

The days were warm and sunny; blue skies stretched across the ceiling of the earth for I was generally above the altitude of the monsoon clouds that continued to pour their damp message from the Indian Ocean onto the valley below. Sometimes in the late afternoon I would be enveloped by fog — the cloudy top of the monsoon — but it passed quickly and much of the time I enjoyed the blessing of the sun. I even began to get a suntan and lose that clammy white feeling which had been with me during my monsoon work at lower elevations.

Pema was with me and I kept three porters, Thorbu, Urkan, and Laadee Bal, to help look for birds' nests and assist with the nets. At each camp, I would set up fifteen or so nets to catch those stealthy and secretive species which might escape my visual survey of the birds. A fresh supply of canned food from Kathmandu enabled us to enjoy a more varied diet than normal, and for over a month we reveled in corned beef hash, Vienna sausages, sardines, canned cheese, and most notably, one small but incredible can of brandied cherries, which I rationed out to myself every evening.

Even more importantly, there was time to roam where I wanted and take interest in whatever I might discover. Our first camp was at about 12,000 feet, on the ridge just above base camp, but every three or four days we would move camp farther along the ridge toward Makalu, eventually entering the Barun and marching right up to its base. In the mornings and evenings I took the tape recorder and explored the areas around camp, gathering the songs and calls of the birds. Most of the breeding species of these elevations were little-known creatures. Usually their songs were either a complete mystery or perhaps some garbled phrase written by a hurried ornithologist attempting to evoke with words the rich tonality, scale, and complexity of a bird's song.

The transliteration of animal calls into human sounds is, I admit, the only technique possible at times. But in Asia, where the birds are studied by many different people from varied linguistic backgrounds, the problems far outweigh the achievements. The white-collared blackbird was supposed to sing, according to an English ornithologist, "tew-i, tew-i, tew-o, etc., with variations." An Indian student of birds once told me it was more of an "ajari, batto, chanhari, repeated with emphasis on the to," while a German scientist once explained that it was definitely a "sprec-sii, sprec-sii, hund oiste!"

One day on the ridge I followed some extremely fluid notes to the edge of a tall grove of rhododendrons and, creeping around the trees so as not to scare off my singer, discovered this sorry-looking pied blackbird giving forth a melody as varied and full as that produced by a small orchestra. It was a stunning performance, one that rose and fell with symphonic theatrics, at times florid and richly embellished or, conversely, a soft and simple pastoral, but always brilliant. To reduce such a wealth to a meager "tew-i" or an abrupt "oiste!" is like the proverbial blind man describing an elephant by the feel of its trunk.

The problems of using transliterations encompass more than just the differences in native languages employed by individual observers but also include the fundamental disparity between the production of bird and human sounds. Birds have the remarkable ability to produce two notes or phrases simultaneously, and thus can literally perform two separate melodies at the same time. Unlike the mammalian larynx, with its single set of vocal cords, birds have a syrinx that contains two independently controlled sound sources. The mammalian larynx is part of the upper trachea, the familiar "Adam's apple"; but the avian syrinx is located at the point where the two bronchial tubes from the lungs join. Each contains an elastic membrane that can vibrate independently, allowing the bird in effect to have two separate instruments for sound production. In addition, the physical shape and size of the oral cavities and sound passages are so radically different between man and birds that the sounds produced by the two are bound to be different. Even the words uttered by trained myna birds, which seem to imitate the human voice so well, will reveal significant differences when examined by a sonogram.

The tape recording of animal vocalizations is one of the more recently evolved methods of gathering information about wildlife. Early workers were hindered by bulky and fragile recording equipment that generally gave poor reproduction. A bird's song has such a wide tonal range that it often surpasses the limits of the human ear, and at times its speed is so fast that a precise sequence of individual notes sounds to us like a single long slurred tone. The equipment for recording must be extremely sophisticated, yet small enough to be carried readily in the field. Fortunately, recent developments in electronic recording instruments have produced machines that are relatively compact and sufficiently accurate. The condensing directional microphone has been especially helpful, for it replaces the difficult-to-handle parabola of the past while still amplifying the faintest sound into a strong signal for the tape recorder. The person recording can now operate at a reasonable distance from his subject and confidently gather quality recordings.

Tape recording was initially employed solely for identification but now has developed into an invaluable technique for studying an array of important biological problems, from ontogeny and taxonomy to learning ability and heredity. Recordings of animal sounds are now required in the same way that comprehensive collections of museum skins and specimens were required in the past. We have come to realize that what an animal does is as important as its physical appearance. The tape recording of vocal behavior is an especially valuable way to gather data about an animal, for it forms a permanent record unhindered by human interpretation. Further, the data are organized in a quantitative way that is particularly convenient for study.

And of all animal vocalizations, perhaps the most exciting to study is that of birds. Unlike mammals or the lower classes of creatures, the diversity of birds and their songs provides a wealth of material for comparative analysis. At times, the ideas generated from the study of bird song can be applied to other creatures, even man. W. H. Thorpe has made the argument, "The idea that bird-song is often an expression of irresponsible joy or similar emotion is certainly not without some scientific justification and can, in fact, be supported by arguments which are far from negligible. It may indeed be true that songs of birds can be regarded as the first step toward true artistic creation and expression; and it so follows that birds were probably the evolutionary pioneers in the development of 'art,' certainly preceding by immense stretches of time the development of artistic activities by the human stock."

In a similar vein, P. Szoke has attempted to show that man probably copied his musical system directly from birds. His argument is based on the differences in the vocal apparatuses of man and birds. Unlike birds, man's vocal apparatus — his larynx, vocal cords, and oral cavities — are not forced by their construction to produce notes in a harmonic series of steps. But the syrinx of birds forces birds to use the natural series of overtones. Since bird song was highly developed prior to man's emergence, we cannot help wondering whether man merely borrowed his musical system directly from birds. It seems unlikely to suppose that he would arbitrarily adopt a system identical to that of birds when he had such a different range of abilities for sound production.

For my part, I can add that there is an uncanny resemblance between the vocal signals the hill tribe people of the Arun use when calling back and forth across the ridges and the calls or songs of endemic birds. In particular, there is a common phrase sung by villagers throughout the valley which closely parallels sounds of several local laughing-thrushes; it is a long wailing sound that rises and falls with cheerful energy. The villagers, of course, are singing to identify themselves and their location, as when telling friends who are farther up the trail of their imminent arrival. The acoustical properties of the song are good for conveying such information: The dominantly low frequencies of the song are of such a wave-length as to allow the two ears of the hearer to detect phase differences, and the repeated short syllables of the song as it rises and falls are excellent for providing clues for perception of sound-shadowing and time differences. Obviously, this could be a case of convergence, with both man and the laughing-thrushes using similar songs because of their ability to establish relative location. But the pattern and phrasing of the call used by the villagers so resembles that of the laughing-thrush that some imitation must be involved.

Perhaps the greatest reason for tape recording bird songs, though, is the sheer beauty of the songs. I can think of few more exciting and rewarding ways to spend one's time than wandering the alpine ridges of the Himalayas, enjoying the summer weather with its flowers and wildlife, while concentrating on the often mysterious and beautiful sounds of the birds. Sometimes, I spent hours following a single individual around, trying to capture the full repertoire of its calls as it flew back and forth among the blooming rhododendrons. Other times, I sat quietly and as patiently as possible at the edge of some meadow to wait for a short and fleeting call that I had heard before but never identified. My ears seemed sharper whenever I carried the tape recorder, and I could pay attention in a way I never had before to the slight variations and more subtle qualities of every song. I found it particularly gratifying to discover new sounds, and it became a great detective game to creep through the shrubbery following some new notes.

Many birds slow down their singing activity after ten o'clock, and I found it worthwhile to spend the middle of my day studying other aspects of bird breeding, especially nest construction and mating behavior. I spent much time searching for nests myself and also used the porters to locate nests. Like their vocalizations, the breeding biology of many alpine species of the Himalayas is very poorly known; there are numerous species of bird, for example, whose eggs and nests have never been discovered.

Such information is vital both to a general knowledge of the life history of each species and to the conservation of a species. Many bird species have very specific requirements for reproduction and it is only by knowing these requirements that we can insure their survival.

One day toward the end of June I discovered a nest of Gould's shortwing, an enchanting species whose breeding was unknown. It is a little creature with a chestnut back and breast, and the belly stippled with white, gray, and black, so that it resembles a clump of reddish moss casting a speckled shadow. Shortwings are, by tradition, secretive birds that prance around on longish legs in the gloom of the forest floor, but I found this species running bravely among the rhododendrons, climbing here and there, and occasionally mounting to the very top of a bush to sing or sun itself. I had looked for its nest for several weeks without success, but just after moving camp to a new location near Kongmaa La, I discovered a pair breeding within a short distance of my tent.

The nest was located about ten feet up on the wall of a rock outcropping that looked out across a meadow. It was quite well-hidden, covered with loose moss so that it blended in with the other moss and lichens scattered over the rock. There was a small opening near the top of the nest where one of the parents would stick its head out to watch me as I approached. It seemed so confident of its camouflage that it would not move until I was practically touching it. The nest itself was cup shaped, about five inches across by four inches high, and so situated beneath some overhanging moss that it had at first appeared to be a globe. Inside there was a marvelous construction of different layers: A loosely but carefully woven structure of grass lined the inside of the moss and, in turn, supported an inner cup that was plastered with mud and held the eggs. The rock walls of the outcropping were often quite damp, and the nest appeared a wonderful adaption to protect the eggs. Water is an efficient conductor of heat and poses a severe problem to any bird that nests in a damp habitat; I found many nests of other species, including those of the firetailed myzornis, that had been destroyed by the damp — their eggs wet and molding inside a soggy ball of grass. But the shortwing's nest remained dry; if the outer moss became wet, the loose grass cup would drain any moisture away while the inner plastered cup would hold the eggs high and dry.

The shortwing was vulnerable, though, to the other dangers of

Alpine scrub along the Barun Khola

Firetailed myzornis

breeding that I witnessed in the alpine belt. In general, I was stunned by the amount of nest predation I saw, regularly finding nests of many species in which the eggs were smashed and destroyed. Often, the parents were lingering nearby — wondering what to do. The predators included many species of mammal, such as martens and weasels, and also common bird predators, such as accipiter hawks, crows, and the black eagle. But everyone seemed to be in on the act, and many species of larger birds took advantage of the helpless nests, including the black-faced laughing-thrush, the white-spotted laughing-thrush, the yellow-billed blue magpie, the black-capped sibia, and the small cuckoo.

The predation was often highly sophisticated. One day I watched a pair of yellow-throated martens hunt in a coordinated fashion along the edge of a clump of rhododendrons. One of the pair would scurry along inside the trees making much noise while the other would walk quietly along outside of the clump at a suitable distance to observe. The marten inside the trees would eventually approach a nest and scare off its parents but because of the dense growth, it would be unable to see them leave. The marten that had been waiting outside, however, would have an excellent view of the fleeing parents and could pinpoint the location of the nest and both would then join in to feast on the vulnerable eggs or nestlings.

After a while, I had to warn my porters to be careful of approaching nests as even we became involved unconsciously. I discovered late in June that black-faced laughing-thrushes had learned of our interests in nests. Normally loud, boisterous creatures, these birds would now slide silently through the rhododendrons following my porters. If the porter stopped to investigate a potential nesting site, the laughing-thrushes would wait quietly nearby, and as soon as he had left, they would quickly rush over to the spot. There were several times when I would accompany the porters to a nest they had discovered the day before only to find the eggs had been crushed and bore the tell-tale sign of a small round hole, the size of a laughing-thrush bill, left in a shattered egg shell. From past experience, I knew that predatory mammals would behave similarly; they have learned that man often provides a free meal and when they come across his track, they will follow it down with the expectation of finding edible refuse at his camp. If he is an ornithologist, they can follow his trail to a nest.

Sometimes, I would spend an entire day stationed beside a single nest to record data about the parent's behavior or to photograph the young. I spent several days at the end of June at the site of a wood snipe's nest, another poorly known species. The wood snipe was formerly thought to breed at about 6000 feet in Assam, although this belief was based on a single egg discovered by a native collector who later brought it to an ornithologist. Since there was no on-the-spot identification of either the nest or the parents, this record was highly suspect. I found the wood snipe breeding between 12,000 and 16,000 feet in the Arun. Its behavior and breeding appeared to be similar to that of other snipe, such as the common species of North America.

Like the shortwing, the parents had an abiding confidence in their camouflaged bodies and nest, and I found that I could approach and photograph the incubating parents without disturbing them. At dawn and dusk, and sometimes in the middle of the day if there was fog, the snipe would perform an eerie nuptial display over a shallow pond formed by a depression on the ridge. The birds would fly in wide circles about 50 to 200 feet over the pond while uttering a harsh, nasal call — a sort of deep chilling laughter that seemed to inspire the moment with a demonic mystery. Often the light was so poor or the fog so dense that one could not see the birds, and their calls came echoing across the ridge like the voice of an incubus. They would also zigzag up and down or take long plunging dives while circling; these movements were accompanied by a whooshing sound which was produced by the feathers of either the wings or tail; I could not tell which.

At the beginning of July, I decided to move camp over the Kasuwa ridge and into the Barun Khola, for I wanted to explore the western areas around the Makalu glaciers. The trail at first led down from the meadows of the ridge and into the forests, mostly fir and birch, which lined the base of the Barun. We trekked for three days through these forests until they ceased, and we saw that we were in a wide U-shaped valley. Here the alpine scrub was noticeably drier than that found on the Kasuwa ridge; and I was surprised that the forest had continued up so high, to almost 13,500 feet. Obviously the steep walls and long valley of the Barun served to protect the vegetation and filter the effects of the southerly monsoon winds, a common phenomenon in many of the long inner valleys of the Himalayas. It was particularly interesting to notice the gouge marks on the almost perpendicular walls of the Barun; at one time, a glacier must have descended here to carve out the sides and bottom.

I spent the next several weeks working the upper portions of the Barun. Howard joined me in the middle of July, and together we marched to the present glacier at the top of the Barun. I had assumed that the glacier would be white — a jumbled mass of ice and snow, as so often shown in photographs of Himalayan mountains. Instead, its surface was dirty gray, covered with rocks and gravel that had fallen off the surrounding cliffs. Beneath was ice, but even it was stained dark by the debris. An occasional glacial pool was scattered here and there where melt water had filled up a crevasse or depression. Walking over the rocks of the glacier was extremely slow and tedious, and it took us almost three days to walk from the beginning of the glacier, at about 15,000 feet, to a camp spot at about 18,000 feet, where the glacier curls north around the western side of Makalu and offers a view of Everest and Lhotse Shar close by to the west.

We rested there for a day and then in the morning climbed up above camp on a spur of moraine that extended down from Chago, a sister peak of Makalu. After much heavy breathing we reached an elevation of 20,500 feet, a moderate but respectable elevation in the Himalayas. We found that our earlier months of living at high altitude served to acclimatize us somewhat, although we still got headaches after any heavy exertion. The terrain itself was unbearably simple — rock and ice, everything reduced to those two elemental substances in a vastness beyond belief. Climbing walls of snow leaped up around us. The glacier, with its massive seracs of ice, was spread out below but dwarfed by the impossible scale. The giant moraine ridge upon which we had climbed so laboriously for several hours was a full two thousand feet high, and yet the peaks around us extended another mile into the sky.

Sunlight seemed a hard substance, unlike the soft glow which illuminates the lower forests. It ricocheted among the slopes and there was an unnatural brilliance to everything, so that the world seemed to vibrate from the sheer energy of the sun. Even the sounds were different. Gone were the melodic songs of the birds and the varied noises of the insects. Human voices sounded louder by comparison, and the wind, echoing in the emptiness, had a hollow, ringing tone like water rushing down a naked

gorge. Above all, there was a strange and unfamiliar quality —
a growing recognition that we had entered a different medium
of existence, as if we had suddenly traveled to another planet
or descended to some great depth of the ocean. Footsteps seemed
an intrusion.

At first it appeared a sterile world, without life, but as we
overcame our awe of the scenery we began to discover many
living things. Hidden beside a boulder was *Stellaria decumbens*,
a low cushionlike plant that is the highest growing flowering
plant in the world. In the distance, I spotted the trim lines of a
red-billed chough flying past an icy crag, and far below, sailing
on thermal updrafts, was the bearded vulture gently maneuvering
in search of what, I am not sure. Completely incongruous were
several small white butterflies which suddenly appeared near
us, fluttering back and forth, delicate creatures to be flying over
such a terrifying land.

Mountains are known to produce very bewildering contrasts
in living conditions, and perhaps nowhere is this better empha-
sized than at the higher elevations of the Himalayas. This elevated world is one of the least studied ecosystems, despite the
fact that it is truly a biological marvel holding unique interest
for both scientists and laymen. To understand this world, one
must first understand the forces that cause it to be so different —
the factors of sun, wind, and air which tend to be forgotten as
part of lowland ecosystems. Here they are dominant forces ex-
erting a major influence on all life.

For a long time it has been fashionable to compare the bands
of vegetation that occur as one ascends the mountains with the
bands of vegetation that exist as one travels across the latitudes,
going from the equator toward one of the poles. The Himalayas,
because of their immense height, seem to confirm this analogy
better than other mountains, and it is true that one finds a regular and parallel progression of vegetation zones, starting with
tropical forests in the lowlands and gradually building to a frozen,
arcticlike environment at the summit. It is a useful concept in
that it immediately allows one to grasp the incredible range of
animals and plants found in the mountains.

But, like any other analogy, this one can be carried too far.
It breaks down in the alpine regions, and the popular image that
has been created of the mountain summits as merely high-altitude arctic environments is highly misleading. Some mountains

close to the polar regions do bear a similarity, but this is only because their proximity to the poles allows them to possess many of the same climatic attributes, such as severe winters of extended duration. Mountains like the Himalayas, however, which lie close to the equator, have an alpine ecosystem which is truly unusual. Makalu is less than 28° north of the equator, and her alpine region enjoys a much smaller seasonal difference in climate, and by comparison an extended summer. The arctic environment is dominated by the severe cold that is a function of the shape of the earth and the tilt of its axis; by the time the sun's rays reach the arctic they are weak and warm the air relatively little. But the atmosphere of the Himalayan alpine region is modified by the decreasing atmospheric pressure. The higher one goes above sea level, the less air one has above one's head, and thus the less weight, the less pressure.

This characteristic of alpine regions is of fundamental importance. The greatly attenuated atmosphere of high elevations causes a chain reaction of effects and influences on all other aspects of life. The magnitude of the decreasing pressure can be gathered from the fact that at 20,000 feet the total atmospheric pressure is only half that of sea level. The low density of the air readily permits the passage of the sun's rays without warming the air mass itself; thus, the cold of high altitude is the result of relatively less air being warmed. In turn, the rocks and soil of the high altitude, once warmed by the sun's rays, can lose their heat more rapidly, again without the air mass itself becoming warmed. I noticed this effect myself; standing in the intense heat of the sun, I would shed all of my heavy clothing and walk about in a thin undershirt at 20,000 feet. But as soon as I entered the shade or the instant the sun went down, the temperature would fall dramatically, usually far below freezing, and I would need to climb back into my parka. What was happening was that the air mass was never really warmed. Rather, I was feeling direct solar radiation and as soon as the sun disappeared the apparent temperature dropped.

The altered atmospheric pressure of high altitudes also affects the basic composition of the atmosphere. There is a gravitational settling of the heavier gases so that at high elevation air contains proportionally larger amounts of the lighter gases and proportionally smaller amounts of the heavier gases. Carbon dioxide, the principal gas required for plant metabolism, is relatively heavy

(1.97 gr./liter) and becomes extremely deficient at higher altitudes; while nitrogen, which is quite light (1.25 gr./liter), becomes more prominent. Animals at high altitude have to contend with a smaller proportion of oxygen (1.43 gr./liter — relatively heavy) compared to low elevations. It is not hard to envision how these changes in atmospheric composition would affect the abilities of all plants and animals to survive.

And there are other changes: The partial pressure of water vapor decreases with the decreasing density of the atmosphere. At high elevations, the air becomes drier; the aerosol content at 17,000 feet is less than one percent of that near sea level. Water droplets in the air serve to capture heat from the sun's rays, and their absence increases the coldness of the high altitude air. The shape and meteorology of the mountains produce frequent high winds, further increasing the rate of evaporation. Combined with the intense solar radiation, this extreme aridity causes an almost devastating desiccation that affects all alpine wildlife. From a personal point of view, both Howard and I developed raw, irritated throats from breathing the parched air. We found that clothes washed in the glacial pools would be dry within minutes.

The dust, moisture, and density of the air at sea level help filter off a great part of the sun's rays, acting as a protective blanket, but that blanket is much thinner at high altitudes. There is an increase of blue, ultra-violet, and ionizing radiations so that ozone is more prevalent in the atmosphere. Light reflecting off the snow and ice adds to the general intensity, so that after a while one imagines one is sitting in the very furnace of the sun. There is a tangible feeling of the sun's pounding down on your head, like a waterfall of energy, and even a blind creature would have no trouble detecting whether he was standing in the shade or in the sun.

The surface layers are dramatically affected. The intense solar radiation helps produce wide differences between air temperatures and the temperatures of objects exposed to the sun. The temperature of the soil surface, for example, can fluctuate widely. After staying below freezing for months on end, the soil temperature one day can suddenly soar to above 100° F. when the snow cover that has protected it throughout the winter melts. Because of the radiation of heat at night due to the thin air, the soil temperature can again drop far below freezing the evening of that same day.

The plants and animals living in this hostile environment show a heroic endurance to succeed against such odds. Often simple in structure and form, they invariably reveal some special adaption which permits them to inhabit what must be one of the earth's harshest environments. If any analogy is to be used, perhaps the most accurate comparison with the alpine world of the Himalayas would be the surface of the moon. The lunar landscape experiences similar wide fluctuations in temperature, an attenuated atmosphere, intense solar radiation, and extreme aridity. There is, of course, no known life on the moon. But if it did exist it would probably resemble that of the higher elevations of the alpine regions more than any other environment on earth.

The alpine region begins at the tree line — that point above which a grove or stand of trees does not exist. There are always scattered individual trees that proceed to high elevations, but they represent isolated vagrants and cannot be considered a true stand. In the Barun Khola, the three principal higher-elevation trees — the fir (*Abies spectabilis*), the birch (*Betula utilis*), and the large rhododendrons (*Rhododendron campanulatum, R. hodgsonii, R. grande,* and *R. barbatum*) — all cease at about 13,500 feet. This altitude corresponds to a mean monthly temperature for the warmest month, July, of about 50° F. It has been found that although the altitude of the tree line varies widely in the many mountain areas of the world, the tree lines always approach this 50° isotherm for the summer months. Intuitively we might suspect that winter temperatures were the controlling factor for the height of the tree line, but it now appears that it is indeed this almost magic 50° isotherm for the summer months.

In the Barun, there is an alpine scrub (continuing up to about 17,500 feet) above the tree line; this scrub is composed of dwarf rhododendrons, such as *R. setosum, R. anthopogon,* and *R. nivale,* and often several species of juniper, such as *Juniperus squamata* or *J. wallichiana.* These low bushes sometimes grow in a large mass covering an entire slope, but more often only dotting the terrain here and there like odd tufts of hair. At the very head of the Barun where the most arid conditions exist, other low bushes, such as *Ephedra gerardiana* or *Myricaria germanica,* can be found growing on the rocky moraine. There is a noticeable difference between this scrub growing inside the protected inner valley of the Barun and the moister scrub found on the more exposed ridges farther south in the Arun. The increased exposure to winds and rains depresses the tree line to 11,000 feet; the added moisture and lower altitude allows other species, like *Juniperus recurva* and *Rhododendron lepidotum,* to inhabit the scrub.

The absence of trees in the alpine region profoundly influences the remaining vegetation. The problems of resistance to wind, sun, and precipitation are dramatically increased. Typically, alpine plants are low ground-hugging species that lack much aerial growth. They are rarely annual plants because the conditions do not permit a seed to mature and produce seeds itself within a single season. Thus the alpine plants are usually perennial and are often of great age. Many have underground stems or rhizomes which sprout forth annually during the growing season; the new growth withers away during the winter, but the underground rhizome is protected by the soil. Certain cushion plants are perhaps the epitome of alpine adaptions. They are low, rounded balls that resemble a pin cushion and are common around 15,000 to 17,000 feet in the Barun. Similar plants have been studied in the mountains of North America, where it was discovered that they put out only two to three tiny leaves per year, growing only about a third of an inch in ten years. Their low profile helps protect them against the wind, and the dense leaves serve to trap air within them, creating a microclimate that is warmer than the surrounding air. Insects, attracted to the warmth, help cross-pollinate them, which is a major difficulty in this windy, freezing environment.

Other plants, for example, the sow's ear, *Saussurea tridactyle,* surround themselves with a dense mat of fuzzy fibers that perform a similar function of trapping and storing heat. The sow's ear looks like a gob of cotton and grows in the most difficult sites, such as among loose rocks on a moraine. Some plants have waxy leaves or dense, almost furry, hair on their leaves to help protect them; the latter adaption is characterized by the Himalayan edelweiss, *Leontopdium stracheyi.* Thus many plants have evolved methods of dealing with cold and desiccation from the wind. The primary limiting factor of alpine plants appears to be aridity — the absence of soil moisture. Precipitation is limited in the thin air, and, when it does fall, it is often in the form of either snow or ice. During the summer, after the sun melts the annual snow cover, a drought usually follows because of the quick run-off of water on the thin veneerlike alpine soils.

Most lowlanders tend to associate snow with the absence of

life, but in the Himalayas snow is one of the great comforts for living things. Snow at high altitudes usually sublimates directly into vapor instead of melting to form water, but wherever the snow meets the surfaces of rocks there is often some water. The rocks trap the sun's heat and melt the snow that touches them, providing a valuable source of moisture. Many plants have succulent roots — not particularly deep ones since thin soil does not favor depth — but superficial ones that are well adapted to capturing such melt water. Howard and I found many plants concentrated along the edge of snow fields where constant melt water was available, but plants were much less common in the center of the barren slopes.

Snow is also a great insulator. Within a snow bank temperatures rarely fall far below freezing, while in the air just above they can fluctuate widely. Snow thereby serves as protection for seeds and rhizomes during the winter when the air temperature might stay below −40° F. for weeks. A species of buttercup has cells that are so small and rich in nutrients that they resist freezing very much as antifreeze does; they can survive within a snow bank, but the extreme temperatures of the air would be too much for them.

The intense light of the high altitudes affects the color of the plants found there. The excessive blue and ultra-violet glare of the higher elevations prompts predominantly yellow, orange, pink, red, and white flowers. Only exceptional flowers are blue or violet. The former group of colors most powerfully attract flower-visiting flies and butterflies needed for cross-pollination, although most cross-pollination at high altitudes is caused by the wind rather than insects. As is well known, the vast majority of insect-pollinated flowers in lowland vegetation are visited by bees, flies, and butterflies; many lowland plants have sweet-scented flowers and there are a surprising number of ones that are night-blooming and are visited by moths. But at high altitudes practically no insect is about during the night — the cold prohibits it. The few active fliers are wholly diurnal and use the hours of brightest sunshine for their sorties. High-altitude plants bloom only during the daytime and characteristically lack the strong scents and nectars of their lowland counterparts. The high-altitude flowers offer only pollen to their insect visitors.

Many of the larger animals found in the alpine zone are merely transients using their mobility to escape the harshest conditions of winter. The Himalayan tahr, for example, normally lives at or below the tree line, but one warm summer day I saw three of them browsing on grasses, sedges, and buckwheats at 16,500 feet in the upper Barun. Although the animals I watched that day seemed complacent enough as they searched the high altitude moraine, I knew that if a sudden storm occurred they would retreat quickly to lower elevations and the protection of the trees.

We did not see any other large mammals during that trip, although the footprints of snow leopards were regularly found in the snow up to altitudes of 17,000 feet, and the local villagers who graze their domestic animals on alpine pastures say that wolves still exist at 13,000 feet in the Barun. Bears, such as the Himalayan black bear, apparently also frequent areas slightly above the tree line, for we also found their prints in the snow at 14,000 feet. It is likely that these records represent bears crossing the high passes for it is doubtful that they are consistent visitors to the exposed terrain of the treeless zone.

There are some mammals, however, that are residents. Most notable is the ubiquitous pika, a small creature that resembles a guinea pig. Actually related to rabbits, pikas burrow into the ground or live under rocks and piles of boulders. They eat leaves, berries, and flowers, and, despite the fact that rhododendron blossoms are thought to be poisonous, we saw them eating the flowers of *Rhododendron barbatum* several times. Inquisitive yet timid creatures, they run and hide when first approached and then if one waits for a while, they come back out to watch one's activities. During the winter, their homes are covered with several feet of snow and people have never been sure whether they hibernate or, like a beaver, stock their burrows with grass and leaves to feed on throughout the cold season.

One day I had the porters excavate a four-foot trench through the center of a pika burrow in order to discover what their underground homes were like. In the area we investigated, the ground was part of a depression on a ridge. There was a shallow pond nearby and the soil consisted of alternate layers of peatlike material or loam down to a depth of about four feet, where hard gravel and rock began. Looking at the exposed side of the trench, the ground was honeycombed with pika burrows, about two to three per square yard and stretching down almost three and a quarter feet in depth. Each burrow was from two and a half to six inches in diameter. Some tunnels traveled only an inch or two beneath the surface of the soil, making it convenient for pikas that might want to feed on the roots of the grass growing down into the soil. Several tunnels led toward the pond where, because of the relative elevation, they were filled with water, providing an underground source of drinking water for the pikas. But most of the tunnels were quite dry. Several contained copious quantities of grass and other vegetation that could have been a winter larder, suggesting that the pikas remained active throughout the cold season inside their network of tunnels. There was no other evidence to suggest whether they might hibernate or not.

Unlike arctic mammals, which often have white hair, alpine animals like the pika have dense, dark pigmentation as a rule. This is a protection against the intense solar radiation, high glare, and the action of ultra-violet rays. Dark pigments not only protect the deeper tissues, but are also serviceable in capturing heat. The dense hair is also a protection against the cold and desiccation. Narrow external nostrils help insure prewarming of cold air, and most alpine mammals have a high red blood-cell count, red cells of reduced size to facilitate movement through smaller capillaries, and generally more closely packed capillaries.

One of the most mysterious permanent residents of the high altitude zone is the wedgi. The first time I saw one I actually didn't *see* it. Out of the corner of my eye I noticed a sudden movement among the rocks and, turning quickly, saw just an empty field of rocks. I asked Pema, who was sitting nearby at the time, what it was and he explained, "Why, it's a wedgi, Sahib!" with that matter-of-fact expression that Sherpas use when teaching their slow-witted Sahibs.

This went on for a week or more at our camp near the Barun glacier. Something kept moving out there among the rocks, but I never seemed to be able to catch it in the act, and Pema was always ready with his "Another wedgi, Sahib." I began to assume it was some supernatural creature, like a dwarf or fairy, which only those born in the mountains can see. Finally, one day I happened to be looking in the right direction at the right time and there was the most marvelous little weasel, standing up on its hind legs, and staring at me with a thoughtful look as if, after co-existing together for such a long time, there should be no surprise in our seeing each other.

"A wedgi, right, Pema?"

"That's right, Sahib," Pema said while muttering something

beneath his breath which I expect was an evaluation of my claim to be a wildlife biologist.

These small Tibetan weasels hunt for rats and mice among the boulders of the high altitude area. We found them as high as 16,000 feet, although according to the villagers they descend somewhat in winter, and are even known to invade the villages during the coldest months to feed on chickens or village rodents. Apparently, they make dens in the shelter provided by overhanging rocks. Like the pika, they are dark brown in color and show many adaptions to the alpine region.

Of all animals, birds are perhaps the best adapted to the high altitudes. Their power of flight gives them great mobility so that they can take advantage of individual days of warm weather to visit the high elevations. They also have a highly efficient respiratory system which is, in effect, a pre-adaption by the entire class of birds to high altitude. The lungs of mammals take in air and expel it, using the dead-ended aveoli to exchange gases. But the structure of a bird's lungs and air sacs enables the air to flow through in a continuous unidirectional manner that is considerably more efficient. In addition, the arrangement of blood vessels allows a countercurrent of blood and air flowing in opposite directions so that oxygen exchange is further enhanced. The system of respiration in birds more closely resembles that of the gills of fish than the closed lungs of mammals, and birds are actually pre-acclimated to extreme altitudes. In an experiment with sparrows and mice, the dramatic difference in the abilities of birds and mammals was demonstrated. The two groups of animals, previously accustomed to sea-level atmosphere, were suddenly exposed to an atmosphere corresponding to about 20,000 feet; the mice became comatose, while the sparrows were still able to fly about and did not appear markedly affected.

Possibly the all-time record for the ability of a bird to fly at great heights was set by the bar-headed goose. George Lowe, a mountaineer, was climbing on the side of Everest and, upon reaching 23,000 feet, looked up to witness these birds flying directly over the summit of Everest at an altitude of over 30,000 feet. Not only were they flying at such an incredible height, but according to Lowe they were merrily honking as if out on a pleasant excursion — enjoying the harsh conditions with relish. It is now known that Lowe's observation was not unusual, and that the bar-headed goose regularly flies over the Himalaya's highest mountains as it migrates between India and its northern breeding grounds. Other species also fly at great heights; Wollaston, who accompanied the first Mount Everest Expedition of 1921, collected and observed, between 17,000 and 22,000 feet, both the painted and pintail snipe; at night, he identified the calls of curlews and godwits.

There are numerous birds that breed in the alpine region, some of which have been mentioned already, but also others that are found at even higher elevations. The white-capped redstart, possibly the greatest altitudinal migrant of the bird class, spends its winters on the plains of India and breeds at almost 18,000 feet, where it feeds on insects and the aquatic life of the glacial pools. Howard and I saw Himalayan snow pigeons breeding at 17,000 feet on a rock cliff above the Barun glacier; the snow partridge was found breeding at 16,200 feet on the walls of the Barun, while the Himalayan snowcock is said to breed as high as 19,000 feet. Most species descend below the tree line during the winter, although it is possible that the snowcock spends the entire year above the tree line.

Insects are common to all of the alpine zone, including ants, bees, wasps, flies, butterflies, beetles, aphids, leaf hoppers, stone flies, mayflies, grasshoppers, and so forth. Being cold blooded, they are forced to let their bodies fluctuate with the environmental temperature. Depending on the altitude and season, they become torpid at night or even during cloudy weather and must restrict their activities to periods of bright sunshine. When the sun suddenly goes behind a cloud, it is not uncommon to find bumblebees and butterflies lying torpid on their sides among the flowers that a moment ago they were busily feeding on. Most species seek special microclimates to extend their period of activity. The narrow cracks between rocks, for example, afford a retreat from chilling winds and the rocks radiate and trap heat even when the sun is not shining.

Many insects can tolerate cold to a remarkable degree. Moth pupae have been experimentally exposed to temperatures as low as minus 31° F. and have lived with no apparent harm. Often cold per se is not dangerous. While the oxygen deficiency of the very highest altitudes greatly hinders all mammals, cold-blooded creatures like insects can utilize the cold to overcome the oxygen deficiency, for it also lowers their metabolism. This lowering of metabolism prolongs development and growth; it is frequently accompanied by a general reduction of body size. Many insects of the alpine region require two to three years for a generation to complete a cycle, in contrast to the normal two to three generations per year in the lowlands.

Lawrence Swan has shown how certain wolf spiders use the numbing effects of the cold to their advantage. When the sun sinks behind the mountains or a cloud, the flying insects are immediately affected by the lower air temperature and are forced to seek shelter. But the wolf spider, dwelling close to the ground, which still retains some heat from the sun, is able to move about and capture the stunned insects. Further, Swan has shown that certain daddy longlegs (phalangid spiders) are able to run across the very surface of the snow when the sun is shining. The long legs of the spiders elevate their bodies high enough above the freezing temperature of the snow to enable their black bodies to absorb significant heat from the sun. (A black bulb thermometer, for example, will register more than 90° F. in the sun even when it is held less than one inch above the snow surface.) In essence, the surface upon which they stand could cause death and yet they are able to survive because of the special microclimate they dwell in just above that surface.

The evolution of alpine animals and plants has long fascinated biologists. Their studies have shown that some lowland creatures have specialized to produce populations which can exist at high elevations, but the bulk of the high-altitude Himalayan flora and fauna are highland forms that have evolved entirely at the high altitudes. Many of these forms apparently spread throughout the mountains during periods of glaciation, when the adjacent lowlands experienced a harsh climate of severe cold and served as pathways connecting separate mountain areas. M. S. Mani has shown that some alpine forms of the Himalayas are surviving species from an ancient age. In studying the insect fauna of the western Himalayas, he concluded, "They actually show closer affinities to the Tibetan and Central Asian faunal elements . . . There are also sufficient indications to believe that the insects of this region represent, at least partly, a geographic relic of the Pleistocene life of central Asia."

One question that has intrigued everyone who has studied the wildlife of the Himalayas is the status at the very top of the tallest peaks: Is there life, a permanent, year-round form, on the top of Everest? It seems remarkable that there are so many plants and animals at 15,000 or even 20,000 feet, but it seems utterly fantastic that there could be life at 29,000 feet — almost six miles in the sky and on the very edge of the earth's atmosphere. Some have argued that the alpine zone, if the term represented a region of life, would stop at about 19,000 or 20,000 feet, where the highest plants ceased, for above this there would be no basis for the food chain. Above that line, one would find merely a desolate and empty land of sterile ice and rock. But recent research findings have proved otherwise. M. S. Mani discovered that insects, "an increasing proportion of carnivorous species," could be found as high as he was able to explore. He also showed that "the upper wind currents blow up millions of minute insects from the lowlands and even the plains of India," and he suggested that this wind-blown organic material could form the basis for life. Like the bottom of the ocean, where life has been found to subsist on fallen organic debris from the surface, life on the highest mountains could subsist on life blown up from the surface of the earth.

Most recently, Lawrence Swan confirmed Mani's reports. He found that the highest plant, *Stellaria decumbens,* stopped at 20,130 feet, but that indeed there were many insect forms which existed year-round above this altitude and that they lived on wind-blown debris. He named this new community of life the aeolian zone, after Aeolus, the mythical god of the wind, and showed that it differed significantly from the alpine zone. While the alpine zone was heterotropic — like lowland zones, capable of producing its own source of organic material — the aeolian zone was truly autotropic and depended for its basic source of organic material on the powers of the wind. Thus, the alpine region would extend from the tree line to the highest green plant, while the aeolian region would stretch from the highest green plant to the summits.

Like all the other zones in the mountains, the alpine and aeolian zones have transition areas between them and the specific boundary of each varies in altitude according to the slope, aspect, and localized climatic factors. Not far from where *Stellaria* was found at 20,130 feet, the tongue of a glacier extended down to almost 15,000 feet, where it carried the aeolian zone with it. The daddy longleg spiders that Swan reported, for example, were actually operating in the aeolian zone, for they walked across the snow to feed on organic waste blown onto the glacier.

Open snowfields at 14,000 feet

Mt. Everest as seen from the headwaters of the Barun; note our camp
along the top of the moraine in the lower right-hand corner of the picture

Although at first it might seem that the concentration of wind-blown pollen, seeds, spores, dead insects, and miscellaneous plant fragments would be hopelessly small and support only a meager community, Swan argued that snow had the ability to concentrate the debris as it melted. In glacial pools at the foot of the snowfields, Swan reported finding large populations of a fairy shrimp, *Brachinecta* sps. Obviously, the same debris that falls on the snowfields must also fall on the snowless areas. It could be concentrated there in the cracks and crevasses where air turbulence is reduced and debris might settle out from the wind. This terrestrial phase is exemplified by such fleas as *Machilid thysanurans* and includes various mites, collembolans, anthomyid flies, and salticid spiders.

The suspicions voiced by both Swan and Mani were finally confirmed when a Mount Everest Expedition brought back samples of soil and snow collected from the very summit of the world's highest mountain. The samples had been affected by their difficult journey, but all contained microorganisms, proving that there is indeed some form of permanent life on the very top of the world. It seems incredible from any viewpoint and only serves to reaffirm the awesome potential of nature. In turn, man's egotism suffers another blow. He was not the first to conquer the highest summit. He was beaten there by some single-celled organisms so tiny they are hard to see with the naked eye. And while man stood but a moment on the summit before he had to rush back down to safety, these creatures call the place their home.

CHAPTER SEVEN

The Legacy of Chang Hua

> ...In many distant countries there are secluded
> places in the mountain districts which produce
> beeswax. These beeswax places are all abrupt cliffs
> and rock walls which are unclimbable ... When
> the bees leave not to return, the surplus hives and
> wax on the rocks are unlimited. There is a small
> bird in the shape of a sparrow. It comes in flocks of
> thousands to peck at [the wax]. Year by year it is
> like this without confusion. They call them wax
> honey birds, and call them spiritual sparrows for
> they are entirely unable to catch them....
>
> — *Chang Hua Chin Dynasty*
> ca 265–419 A.D.

FOLLOWING CLUES left some 1700 years ago by a Chinese
scholar named Chang Hua, I searched for the spiritual sparrows among the canyons and cliffs at the bottom of the Kasuwa
Khola. One day in December 1972, I investigated a small stream,
a tributary of the Kasuwa that cut back into the western side of
the Khola.

As I walked up along the stream, the steep forested slopes narrowed to form a gorge. The stream switched back and forth
across the gravel floor, forcing me to climb along the precipitous
walls or broadjump across the stream at the foot of the pools. I
found a cluster of serow tracks negotiating a convenient passage
between two large sand-colored boulders; jungle cat droppings
rested on the top of the tallest boulder, and I imagined green eyes

surveying their domain on a moonlit night. Checking his diurnal territory, a crisply tailored spotted forktail flew along the water's edge. Farther on, a spring of water flowed down the face of a rock outcropping high up on the side of the walls. I saw a troop of macaque monkeys there at the top, basking in the late morning sun — enjoying the warm rock and cold water after a damp morning feeding in the forest.

Turning a corner, I reached a huge cliff, over 300 feet tall, that blocked my way. Its ragged face of crumbling rock jutted out across the gorge to close off the gorge completely and form a box canyon. The cliff and canyon walls towered above, so that I felt myself in the very heart of the mountains. Green shade filtered through the foliage covering the walls and lining the rim at the top of the cliff. The stream was forced to take a wild sixty-foot leap over a constriction between cliff and canyon wall; the water plunged down into a shimmering basin gouged out of rock and kicked up a windy mist that sparkled in the sunlight. Raucous calls from a blue whistling thrush sang out above the constant roar of the waterfall, and the sweet scent of water and forest pervaded the air. The Himalayas are noted for their dramatic views, but surely this was one of their most captivating scenes. Unlike the lofty perch of a windswept ridge, here was an isolated private place, which enveloped the visitor with a different kind of Himalayan richness.

I climbed a spur of rock opposite the cliff to get a better view. There on the face of the cliff were several huge beehives; although there were no bees present — probably dormant during this winter season — I recognized the hives as belonging to the giant honeybee, *Apis dorsata*. They had the characteristic shape and construction of *dorsata* hives: Each hive was a single exposed sheet of wax hanging down from beneath a rock overhang or ledge; they were pocket-shaped and from a distance looked like a pale beard on a man's face. The largest hive was almost six feet across and four feet long. Others were much smaller. I could easily see the details of larval cells that covered the surface of the hive — a marvelous geometric design that stretched from the top to the bottom. As if on cue, as soon as I sat down to watch a small bird flew out from a shaded perch beside the lowest hive and landed near the top of it. He began feeding on the wax. It was a drab green, runty little creature, completely unimpressive at first glance, but I knew immediately that this was the object of my search, Chang Hua's spiritual sparrow — the orange-rumped honeyguide, as we now call it.

I marveled at the unique event that I was watching, for among the world's 8600 species of birds only the 15 members of the Honeyguide Family are capable of feeding on wax. Wax is an inert and indigestible substance by itself, but the honeyguide's intestines possess symbiotic bacteria that allow them to break the wax down into digestible compounds. Such a specialized feeding adaption is bound to affect other aspects of a species' biology, and I immediately became interested in studying this bird in detail. Suddenly it was not enough that I had documented the presence of the spiritual sparrow in the Arun Valley. I found myself wanting to spend the rest of the afternoon observing the honeyguide, and then, without really planning to, I decided to prolong my stay in the box canyon so that I could spend additional time watching the behavior of the bird. I came to call the box canyon the Honeyguide Grotto, and named the individual I was studying Chang Hua in honor of the ancient scholar.

While my reincarnated Chang Hua focused his activity around the beehive, I focused my life around him. I put up a small tent at the observation point on the spur and ate and slept there so as not to miss any of his daily activities. It was a beautiful laboratory to work in, for I could see Chang Hua anywhere on the cliff face. As so often happens when one is involved in a study of nature, the first major discovery I made was about myself. I realized that during the early months of the expedition I had been forced to study the avifauna as a whole, compiling species lists and dealing with life as a system of labels. I now knew that I wanted to concentrate, at least for a while, on a single species. Indeed, the Grotto offered me the chance to study a single individual, hour after hour, day after day. I became preoccupied with learning his daily routine, his patterns and their variations, his likes and dislikes, the problems of his individual existence. I realized a special need on my part to learn how one wild creature lives out his days.

During the next two years, I ended up spending almost four months in weeks scattered here and there through the seasons studying the honeyguide. I solved fewer mysteries about his behavior and biology than I created. I did, however, at least begin to answer that basic question of how Chang Hua spent his days.

During that first week in December, I learned that my Chang

Hua led a remarkably sedentary and parochial life. He had established a territory on the lower part of the cliff that centered around the single hive there. He defended this hive and his territory against other honeyguides who would occasionally attempt to feed on his hive. A second male honeyguide had established a similar territory around four hives located on the upper part of the cliff. This initial discovery suggested that the orange-rumped honeyguide differed considerably from other members of the Honeyguide Family. Several species of honeyguide in Africa have been studied briefly, and the reports have described honeyguides visiting beehives indiscriminately. The birds apparently travel widely through the forests and feed at hives for only brief periods before they move on.

But Chang Hua stayed within his territory more than 90 percent of each day for weeks on end. Possibly he stayed within his territory throughout the year. Besides an occasional territorial dispute, he enjoyed a quiet existence, for his territory provided him with all the requirements for his survival. The hive provided him with an abundant and readily accessible source of the wax that formed the major part of his diet. Two or three times a day he would visit the hive to feed for ten minutes or so on the exposed wax. Since wax is far from a complete food — lacking nitrogen, among other basic dietary requirements — Chang Hua would also feed on insects within his territory. From his favorite perch beneath the lower hive, he would make regular aerial sorties after flying insects, in the manner of a flycatcher. He acquired other necessary minerals and vitamins from his daily habit of feeding on vegetable matter, notably lichen and moss that he found on the cliff.

Also unlike the African species of honeyguide which have been studied, I never saw Chang Hua or any other orange-rumped honeyguide use the famous "guiding behavior" that is so well known and gives the family its name. The variegated honeyguide, for example, will literally guide certain mammals to beehives, where the birds will share in the spoils left after their mammalian helper opens the hive. Apparently, the bird will capture the attention of a passing animal, a honey badger, for example, with frequent calls and agitated flights; then in a regular progression the birds will gradually lead the mammal to the hive by flying back and forth in the appropriate direction. The mammals, including man, have learned of the variegated honeyguide's habit and are quick to pay attention to its signals. The behavior appears to be an adaption to the difficulty of feeding on the typical honeybee's nest, which is built in an enclosed place, like a tree hollow or termite mound. Most likely, the birds cannot open the hive themselves and need a stronger assistant if they are to gain access to the wax. By contrast, the *dorsata* hive hangs naked on the cliff and is completely accessible to the orange-rumped honeyguide. Chang Hua needed no help to feed on his hive.

Altogether, I was impressed, if not envious, of Chang Hua's lifestyle during my first winter's observation. He would wake late, sitting on his roosting perch until nine or ten o'clock, and then quietly, as the sun rose to warm the Grotto walls, fly over to feed for a while on the hive. The middle hours of the day consisted of an occasional nap or preening activities at his perch. Again in the evening he would feed on the wax. There might be eight or ten aerial sorties after insects, and an occasional short walk among some promising lichen on the cliff face. Even the infrequent territorial disputes were mild encounters; Chang Hua would quickly drive out any invading honeyguides without need for any physical violence. His lifestyle was completely different from the haunted, almost furious hour-by-hour hunt after insects that warblers must endure as they flit back and forth constantly, trying to keep up with their rapid metabolism.

Early in my study I realized that Chang Hua's unusual territorial behavior afforded me a unique opportunity. Field biologists seldom have the chance to observe their study subjects continuously. Far more often, the study subject travels widely through difficult terrain or occupies a territory in a dense forest so that it disappears from view regularly and their observations are limited to brief encounters. They must piece together the behavior of the subject on the basis of intermittent contacts, and they are always faced with the nagging suspicion that an important aspect of its biology has occurred while they were absent. But Chang Hua's position on the cliff and his parochial habits allowed me to watch him continuously from dawn to dusk. I decided to make a minute-by-minute account of his activities, writing down the precise times he would feed on wax, make aerial sorties after insects, or the time and duration of his territorial disputes. I evolved a system called "continuous days of observation" or DCOs, making my notes as complete as possible so that later in the study I would have comparative data for investigating seasonal changes in his behavior or would be able to extrapolate additional information about his energy expenditures and use of time.

Such avid notetaking consumed most of my time, although I still had odd moments in which to wonder about more subjective matters. While Chang Hua would quietly preen on his perch for several hours I could not help asking myself what he thought of me. Did he return any of the intense interest and curiosity that I showed in him? What did he make of the sudden appearance of my observation blind or of my furtive late-night visits to his territory?

Such questions do have scientific importance in that a biologist is always responsible for assessing his impact on the behavior of his study subject. But I know that I asked them out of a different rationale. I simply wanted to know something of the inner workings of Chang Hua's mind, rather than just the external aspects of his behavior.

I suppose I must answer that Chang Hua had little more interest in me than he did in the trees that grew around my observation blind. He seemed complacent and at ease with my presence as he sat on his perch with his shoulders back and his head held high. While scanning the area around my observation blind he would look right past me as if my existence counted little in his purview. His eyes would be in constant motion, looking by me for some unknown matter of interest that would trigger his attention and cause him to cant his head back and forth or twist his body on his perch for a better view. My fixed stare — universally an important signal among animals — never forced him to stop his gazing back and forth. We dwelt in two different worlds, and although they might occupy the same physical space they were separate and divorced from each other in a way I could not even define. I wondered if this boundary was not the ultimate study of field biology.

During other slow periods I merely enjoyed the surrounding forests. The greenery cascaded and rippled down the slopes like a silent waterfall. The stream, glistening in the bright sun, tumbled and pooled its way down over the rocks toward the river. Everything seemed, on the one hand, to be pushing and straining upward toward the sun, and, on the other, to be plunging and sprawling its way downhill with the weight of the earth. Once a serow passed through the clearing on the slopes directly across the stream from the cliff; it moved slowly, pausing to look at me and examine my tent without any air of fear or worry. Another day a lone langur monkey, an old male, slept just above my tent. I came to know a pair of dippers quite well, for they fed at the foot of the waterfall each day. Extended field research offers the opportunity to cease being a visitor and become a participant in the wilderness.

My administrative responsibilities with the expedition kept me from returning to the Grotto until late April. As soon as I reached the cliff that spring, it was obvious that the situation with Chang Hua had changed dramatically in several important ways. The bees were active and now covered the hive in a swarm so dense that the hives appeared almost black from their innumerable bodies. Each individual bee is quite large, almost the size of the small finger on a man's hand, and yet there must have been thousands upon thousands covering the surface of the hive like blades of grass on a lawn. They made a constant motion over the hive, animating its surface with primordial energy, as if the hive itself was a single creature, breathing and pulsating.

The bees now actively defended the hive against predators, including the honeyguides. Chang Hua was still there defending the lower territory, but whenever he made an attempt to land on the hive the bees started attacking him, those closest extending out their stingers while holding on to the hive with their front legs, and others flying over to hit him forcibly.

Other predators, such as the large vespid wasps, also approached the hive. They attempted to feed on the larvae and young bees by flying directly into the hive. As they approached, the bees responded by sticking out their hindquarters armed with their potent stingers. The bees closest to the invading wasp did so first, and the neighboring bees followed suit as the alarm spread through the hive. This produced a curious rippling motion across the surface of the hive, resembling the motion of a wave created by dropping a pebble in still water. The bees stuck out their stingers in a series of ever-widening concentric circles.

As a result, Chang Hua had difficulty feeding on the active hive and preferred to feed on isolated bits of comb that had fallen from old hives or pieces of comb that were still attached to the cliff where old hives had once been. Chang Hua would fly down to the base of the cliff where several such pieces were lying

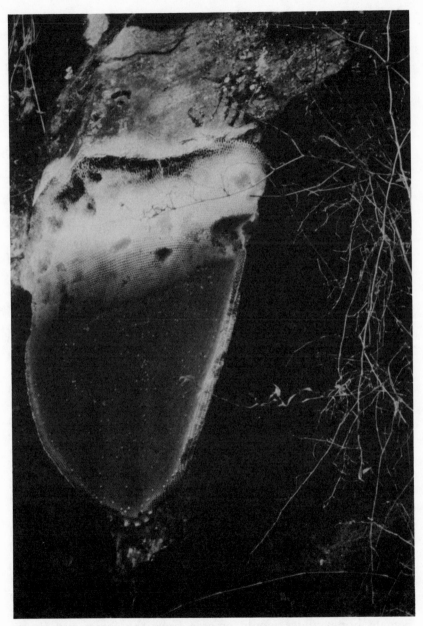

The dormant hive of the giant honeybee; Chang Hua is sitting on a branch just below and to the right of the hive

about; the upper male fed on pieces caught in the vegetation and cracks of the upper part of the cliff. This new feeding behavior presented me with the opportunity to capture Chang Hua, something that I had wanted to do since I had first started the study.

It is imperative that the field researcher be able to positively identify the individuals that he is studying. Many large mammals have distinct features that enable easy field identification, but because of their close feathering and small size, birds are almost impossible to separate with any certainty. Thus, the ornithologist must use a system of wing tags or leg bands to mark the birds that he is observing, which requires capturing them unharmed in order to attach such markings. The previous December I had tried every technique I could devise to entice Chang Hua into my nets but no amount of trickery was successful.

Fortunately when I returned in April the intense activity of the bees allowed me to trap Chang Hua easily. A team of scientists visiting the expedition under the auspices of an American museum was down at the Grotto when I first arrived; they were studying the mammals of the Grotto. The leader of the team, Doug Lay, suggested the simple idea of hiding all pieces of comb except one and placing a mist net right beside this remaining piece so that we could drive the feeding honeyguide into the net. With the assistance of Paul Sherman, a member of the team, in a short time we had Chung Hua in hand.

After weighing and measuring him, we marked him with a red plastic wing tag placed near the axillary of the wing, where it acted very much as a feather would and caused no discomfort or harm. The brightly colored plastic tag could be seen from a distance and positively identified Chang Hua. Later, we could use other colors of wing tags to mark additional individuals, such as invading males, females, and the upper-territory holder.

Another major change in Chang Hua's behavior was revealed in my first few hours of observation that spring. Not only did his territory now provide him with his basic food requirements, but his control of the lower hive and comb pieces also provided him with an abundant supply of joy! I discovered that his drab exterior concealed one of the great lovers of the bird world: Female honeyguides would emerge from the forest and fly directly toward the fallen piece of comb where, just as they began to feed, Chang Hua would fly down to them and through a series of postures invite their participation in copulation. In my first day of working with Chang Hua I witnessed eight separate copulations with possibly as many different females.

The study of birds often reaches its most exciting and stimulating point during the mating and breeding activity. It is then that the greatest demands are placed on individuals as they strive against predators, weather, and changing food supplies to accomplish the arduous task of reproduction. Mating behavior also holds special interest for the biologist because of its important ramifications on the evolution and adaptions of species. Obviously the crucial point in transferring genetic material between generations occurs at mating, and simple logic dictates that whatever influences mating behavior can significantly influence the genetic make-up of future generations and thus the very development of the species.

Among wild animals, monogamous mating systems are by far the most common, and ornithologists have estimated that over 90 percent of all bird species practice monogamy — that is, one male mating with one female, as the robin does. Polygamous mating systems, which include the three major divisions of polygyny (one male mating with several females), polyandry (one female mating with several males), and promiscuity (indiscriminate male-female mating) are so rare that biologists actively seek them out to study. Like the exception that proves the rule, such aberrations are often the most productive ones to investigate for they sometimes provide special insights into the mechanisms by which all systems operate. How, for example, does a polygamous mating system evolve? What feature of its environment or what aspect of its behavior causes it to adopt such a wayward system? No creature is completely frivolous in its behavior, and, if one looks hard enough or studies a creature long enough, usually specific factors can be identified as contributing to the basic behavior patterns.

Chang Hua's multiple copulations with several different females indicated that he was practicing a polygynous or possibly a promiscuous mating system. I realized that a special opportunity was at hand to study mate selection behavior in a most unusual species. I immediately began to organize a research program for the spring season.

First and foremost was the need to mark females who visited Chang Hua's territory to determine how many mates he had and how often he copulated with each. With that done, I could then visit other cliff-bee sites nearby to determine whether any of Chang Hua's mates were frequenting other males. I also wanted to mark the upper territory holder to keep track of his behavior and gather comparative data demonstrating whether Chang Hua's behavior was typical of orange-rumped honeyguide mating. Very quickly, a host of questions and problems presented themselves to me, and I outlined a program for studying Chang Hua's spring activities.

Meanwhile, the team from the museum left, and by May 4 Pema and I were alone to work on Chang Hua. The monsoon would be coming in a few weeks and the other members of our expedition had returned to Kathmandu for a brief vacation. I, too, was anxious to take a break from field work but knew I could not leave Chang Hua at this decisive time.

I asked Pema to set up a camp in the forest, away from the stream so that we would be safe from any monsoon flooding. Near the mouth of the canyon there was a small, flat shelf of land that supported a mature forest where the oaks grew to full height. Really no clearing was needed, and we simply parked beneath several enormous old oaks whose high leafy arms blocked out the sun and left a smooth carpet of ferns on the forest floor. Pema, with the help of Jetta and Pasang (two porters whom I kept on to help supply us with food from the village), erected a field kitchen using the wide buttress of one particularly huge tree. Beneath the kitchen tarp they fashioned a sturdy bamboo table to hold our assortment of cooking pots and supplies; as usual, the cooking fire was placed in the center where it would be protected from the rain. My tent was put up some twenty feet away on a small mound so that it would stay dry. Pema and the porters chose to sleep beneath the kitchen tarp where they would be close to the fire.

Most nights I would sleep at our forest camp but would always awaken early so that I could be in the observation blind at the Grotto before dawn. Pema would bring my lunch to the blind, and I would return to camp in the late evening when the long shadows of twilight illuminated the forest path. It was certainly the most enjoyable commuting to work I have ever experienced. In the morning I was always in a hurry, but on the way back to camp I would stroll slowly.

I remember one particular walk, when I noticed for the first time the unusual quality of forest acoustics. Unlike an open field where the sounds of the birds increase and decrease in volume with regularity as you travel by them, the forest interior was like a series of separate auditoriums. Each section of the path presented its own music, for the trees and understory vegetation served to muffle and isolate the sounds. The niltava flycatcher performed a melancholy chant at the beginning of the trail, and then suddenly, as I turned around a tree toward another section of the path, I met the bustling racket of a feeding flock of laughing-thrushes. Farther on, I came into another chamber created by the trees, where I heard the faint melody of a yellow-bellied fantail. The curious part was that I could retrace my steps to revisit any one auditorium and hear each performance again.

Another evening, I was delayed on my return to camp by a conspicuous *Pnoepyga,* or streaked wren babbler. I stopped to investigate the situation, for whenever this shy creature is conspicuous something unusual is going on. The *Pnoepyga* is one of the Himalayas' drabbest creatures — brownish above, dirty buff below, with some streaking and scaly marks. Quite small, it is hardly three inches tall and normally is impossible to spot as it creeps in the most modest fashion among the mossy fallen trees and ferns of the forest floor. It has a seemingly nervous habit of incessantly flicking both wings open simultaneously — not as if about to fly off but as if it were trying to catch its balance. Certainly it should not be so worried for it does not have far to fall. Some ornithologists argue that many species of redstart constantly flick their tails up and down, open and closed, to scare insects out of concealment and procure themselves a dinner. There might well be a similar method in *Pnoepyga*'s madness.

The *Pnoepyga* normally moves so silently in its terrestrial world that its whereabouts are usually revealed only by its call note or the quivering strands of vegetation left after its passage. The call note itself is peculiar and in keeping with its general demeanor. The call has been most accurately described as "nothing so realistic as an ill-mannered person loudly sucking his teeth." A pitiful creature in a way, it is probably a master in its own right, ruling the bottom three inches of the forest. The individual that I met that evening was certainly acting like a ruler, for he danced and cavorted in open view as if parading for his subjects. I suspected that a nest was nearby and so fol-

lowed him about until, after a half-hour's search, I found a glob-
ular mass of moss and rootlets lodged in the crack of a decaying
stump. The moss on the stump spread down over the nest, cam-
ouflaging the nest so well that I had trouble even finding the
small opening — one slightly darker spot in the variegated shade.
Inside were three white oval-shaped eggs; careful not to disturb
or damage anything, I took a few notes and then walked back
to camp.

During the early days of May I spent much of my time marking females that visited Chang Hua. Pema helped me, and together we would set up the net beside the single piece of comb
and wait patiently until a female arrived. Usually the female
would head directly for the comb piece and begin to feed, but
Chang Hua would quickly spot her and fly down to her so that
he interrupted her feeding. He would perch in a bush or on a
rock nearby and utter several rapid "cheets" as he vibrated his
wing tips and tail feathers up and down, exposing his yellow-
orange rump in the process. Most often, the female responded
by flying off a short distance to land on another rock, where she
would droop down on the rock, lying limp and almost lifeless,
with her wing tips relaxed at the side to expose her yellow-
orange rump patch.

Such a droop is admittedly a rather exasperating response for
most males, but Chang Hua would become even more excited
and proceed to dance around her, making several circuits as he
pranced with his head held high and his tail raised up in a noble
fashion. Copulation would follow shortly, and then Chang Hua
would return to his favorite perch up on the cliff while the
female would return to the comb piece and resume feeding. If
the female had not been marked yet, now would be the time
when Pema or I would approach her and drive her into the nets.
Within a minute or two, we would have her weighed, measured,
and tagged, and would release her. Although our interruption
did not seem to bother the birds much — indeed the females
often stayed nearby or returned to feeding — I limited my detailed notetaking for DCOs to days when we did not capture
birds, so that such interruptions would not bias my data.

Gradually we marked more and more females and began to
learn something of their habits. Typically, each female would
visit Chang Hua many times during the course of about a week.
Some females visited regularly for over a month. On more than

one occasion, Chang Hua mated with the same female several times within no more than a half hour. Once Chang Hua was visited by two females, and, after mating with one, he mated with the other, and then returned to the first female and re-mated with her. I also observed Chang Hua not responding to some females, but in all cases when this occurred with marked females, it was one that Chang Hua had regularly mated with a week or two before. Conversely, I witnessed cases in which females refused Chang Hua, and again these were birds with which Chang Hua had previously mated. When he tried to mate with one female who had visited him many times in the past, she flew off; Chang Hua followed her and attempted to mount, but she would have nothing to do with him and dragged him around as he clung, helplessly trying to relieve his passion while riding piggyback.

This early data suggested that the orange-rumped honeyguide was indeed polygynous. The marked females came into Chang Hua's territory alone and, with one exception, ignored the upper-male territory holder, who seemed to have his own contingent of visiting females. I spent several days watching activities at a neighboring cliff-bee site about one kilometer away, where a third male orange-rumped honeyguide held court; he also had his own contingent of females, and I did not observe any of Chang Hua's marked mates visiting him. It appeared that the females had formed a loose relationship with individual males and would repeatedly return to copulate with (and feed on the comb pieces of) only one particular male.

An even more important discovery emerged from comparing observations at the different sites: In all cases it appeared that females were attracted into the territories by the wax and not by the resident male. The males never offered any displays or vocalizations to the females until after the females had arrived in the territory, and usually after they had begun feeding on wax. For their part, the females would fly directly toward the comb when entering the territory and would respond to the terri-tory male only after he had approached them. Thus, the wax seemed to be not only the primary focus of the male's territory, but also the primary focus of the female's interest. In essence wax is the motivating force that brings the sexes together, and it is the male's control of wax that determines his reproductive success. Wax became for Chang Hua a secondary sexual character and played the same role for him that an elaborate song does for a thrush or the brilliantly colored feathers do for a bird of paradise.

In comparing Chang Hua's mating system with that of other birds I realized that he was practicing a unique form of resource-based polygyny — "resource-based" in the sense that Chang Hua's polygyny was centered around an important food resource, the wax. This system is considerably different from other forms of polygyny, such as those found in the arena systems practiced by the prairie chicken or the ruff. In those systems, the males congregate at traditional sites or arenas where they compete among themselves for the "best" position; females are attracted to these sites to mate with the males, but the arenas are not associated with any important food resources and are merely traditional plots of land known by the individuals of the species.

Chang Hua's mating system was also different from that of other species of honeyguide as reported to date. A few of the African species have been studied in the wild, and they have been described as practicing a loose form of polygyny or possibly promiscuity. Apparently, the males establish "stud posts" from which they utter elaborate songs to attract females for copulation. But Chang Hua's all-purpose "cheeting" was not used to attract females into the territories and would be hard to construe as a song. In addition, the "stud posts" of African honeyguides are not associated with any specific resources but are merely lone trees or prominent positions in the forest.

The only known parallels with Chang Hua's mating practices are found in certain species of hummingbirds. In the Anna hummingbird, for example, the males control a food resource of flowering bushes and trees around which they establish territories; the females, like Chang Hua's mates, visit the territories to feed on the nectar and in the process mate with the resident male territory holders. Like wax, the nectar resource is apparently easily defendable by males and is of vital importance to the species as a source of food. Thus this similar mating system is found in a species with very specialized feeding habits.

Now, with the broad parameters of Chang Hua's mating system known, a new series of questions arose. Chang Hua and perhaps a few of his mates appeared to have a plentiful supply of wax, but what about those males that did not own territories? During May I managed to trap and mark 17 females who were

Chang Hua wearing his bright wing patch

Swollen monsoon stream near the Grotto

copulating with Chang Hua. If I assumed an equal ratio of male to female honeyguides, and there seemed no reason not to, this would mean that there were at least 16 males who lacked a territory and thus a readily available source of wax. Where were they and what did they do for food? Were they merely wanderers in the forest who managed to live on a different diet — a seemingly unlikely hypothesis if one half of the population was so dependant on wax!

Also, now that the honeyguides were mating it meant that they were soon going to begin laying eggs; where did they lay them? Many of the African species of honeyguide are known to be brood parasitic: Like cuckoos, they lay their eggs in the nests of other species and thereby cause the unwitting foster parents to bring up their deserted young. Several African species of honeyguide are reported to have made a peculiar adaption to brood parasitism. The young nestling honeyguides are born with a special tooth, actually a cartilaginous sharp point that extends down from their upper bill; the baby honeyguides instinctively use this tooth to pierce the bodies of other nestlings in their foster home. Thus, the baby honeyguide is the only nestling left alive and the foster parents devote their entire efforts to the growing honeyguide. Such a strongly developed pattern in the honeyguide family suggested that the orange-rumped honeyguide was also brood parasitic.

One day in mid-May a new variable was added to my study. I was sitting on the slope across the stream from the Grotto searching for evidence of nonterritorial males, when a mist came in. Then it started to rain. The clouds, formerly bright and cheerful, became dark brooding shapes that moved slowly through the trees like gray elephantine spirits. Suddenly I felt on a subconscious level that something had changed. That night the porters said the monsoon was near.

The monsoon, despite its size and importance, is a poorly understood phenomenon. According to one theory, it is caused by a dynamic depression that forms over central Asia at the end of April. Wet equatorial air that has soaked up moisture from the Indian Ocean is drawn north by this depression and leaves a trail of rain and winds across the face of the Indian subcontinent. As the warm humid air meets the foothills of the Himalayas, it is forced to ascend the slopes to the cooler higher altitudes and precipitates further rain and storms on the mountains. Another theory holds that the monsoon is actually triggered by a jet stream in the upper atmosphere that for most of the year flows east to west over the plains just south of the Himalayas. Sometime in May, this jet stream is sucked north by the Asian depression, and it jumps over the mountains in one sudden leap to flow across southern Tibet. This abrupt shift in upper air pressure causes the dramatic bursting of the monsoon that many people mention; it begins suddenly, the thick clouds rolling north with gathering speed to slam against the mountains and unleash their winds and rain.

In the Grotto the rains began as if hiding their intention. We might have an afternoon of showers and then there would be several days of clear weather before another overcast day. I worked harder, realizing that my time was limited. I continued monitoring the situation with Chang Hua at the Grotto but also spent several days at neighboring sites to study other male honeyguides. In particular, I worked at the Graveyard — as I had named this cliff-bee site after it had provided me with two close calls. One day I was setting up a net to trap the resident male honeyguide and had to climb the cliff in order to position the net near a piece of wax attached to the rock. Suddenly, the ledge I was standing on gave way and I found myself standing in the air; I fell some 10–15 feet before I was pulled up tight with a back-wrenching yank by a rope I had fortunately secured myself with. The Graveyard cliff, like the Grotto cliff, was composed of rotten rock and loose debris that were extremely dangerous to climb over. The increasing rains made the cliff even more dangerous, for the rocks and dirt, saturated with water, would unexpectedly fall out.

Shortly after this experience, I returned to the Graveyard with Pema; we made it up the side of the cliff all right, reaching a ledge that offered a good view of the birds, but on the way back down Pema kicked out a large boulder by accident, and it came tumbling down toward me. I had nowhere to go but out, which I did, leaping through the air like a wounded sparrow. I had the luck to fall into the top of a tree not far below and by that time was excited enough — my stomach was still back up with Pema — that I made a lunging grab at the branches. I somehow managed to find a hold, although the momentum of my fall carried me beyond so that I ended up holding on upside down. I could see Pema looking down at me, wondering what on earth was the matter and why I had jumped so suddenly. He scrambled down to rescue me, and we returned to camp without saying much to each other.

Despite such difficulties, the work at the Graveyard helped me finally begin to answer the mystery about the nonterritory-holding males. I had noticed at the Grotto that frequently several males were lingering around the periphery of Chang Hua's territory. Occasionally they would attempt to feed on Chang Hua's wax but were quickly repulsed; they also tried to sequester females that were coming into Chang Hua's territory and would attempt to stop them with mating postures. But they were rarely successful, for the females seldom cooperated. From these observations I suspected that perhaps each cliff-bee site was surrounded by peripheral males that maintained semipermanent residence on the edge of existing territories. I decided to test this hypothesis at the Graveyard.

After some maneuvering with ropes and poles I managed to get a net up across the face of the Graveyard cliff. In a short time I captured the resident male honeyguide and, after marking him with a wing tag, placed him in a temporary holding cage. Within a very few minutes, a new male appeared at the Graveyard territory and proceeded to defend it against other honeyguides and to copulate with incoming females. In every way that I could tell, this new male acted as if he were the resident territory holder. After about an hour of watching him, I decided to capture him and pulled the net back into position. I quickly had him in hand, and, marking him as I had the first male, I placed him in a holding cage. Again within a brief time, another new male appeared at the territory and proceeded to take up position as if he were the resident territory holder. I watched this third male for several hours but, finally, because of the lateness of the day, captured him also. I carried all three males away into the forest to a point about halfway between the Graveyard and the Grotto before releasing them. The next morning when I returned to the Graveyard I discovered that the first, and original, territory holder was in residence. A careful perusal of the surrounding forests revealed that at least one of the other males was still nearby maintaining a peripheral position.

Thus, at least during the mating period, there appeared to be a floating population of males that lacked territories themselves and were relegated to maintaining indefinite positions around existing territories. They probably did not contribute much to future generations because the females would not respond to their advances, but their peripheral position at least enabled them to be ready if a resident male were injured or disappeared. Resident males would never let peripheral males feed to any extent on the wax supplies, and so I still wondered where the peripheral males acquired wax. Possibly they fed on the wax of one of the other species of honeybee found in the oak forests of the Arun; there are two common species which build traditional hives inside tree hollows or other enclosed places.

The most perplexing problem remained: Where were my honeyguides laying their eggs? I worried greatly about solving this problem, for the increasing rains made observation more and more difficult. Chang Hua was also changing his daily activities. On one DCO conducted in late May I discovered that almost all the mating had stopped and that Chang Hua had begun to leave his territory for unusually long periods of time. He was now absent almost 40 percent of the day, and I wondered if he was not assisting the females in some way. Surely the females had laid their eggs by this time, and maybe Chang Hua was participating in the work at the nest — if they built their own nest — or he was helping to decoy foster parents — if they were brood parasitic. On the other hand, since many birds molt shortly after mating, Chang Hua's absence might have been related to the process of regrowing feathers. There was no sure way to understand the significance of Chang Hua's absence unless I first learned about the eggs.

Chang Hua's behavior was not the only thing that was changing. The freedom of the Himalayan spring with its warm sun and clear skies was gone. There was a new pattern to the day. There might be a slight pause just after dawn, but the rains would start up again shortly thereafter and come down in a heavy drizzle throughout the morning and afternoon. The heaviest rainfall was at night. Thick drops pounded on my tent with a monotonous sound that at first aided sleep but quickly grew to be a constant annoyance that made even the tent a dismal retreat. The trails were slippery and treacherous, and traveling through the undergrowth was a soggy adventure.

In desperation I asked Pema to hurry to the nearest village and bring back as many men as possible to help me search for the honeyguide's eggs; perhaps I would have some luck with more men on the job. Pema managed to bring back over a dozen local villagers who promised to help us for a few days. But the men were anxious because the increasing rains were causing floods along the Kasuwa and if they were not careful they would be cut off from their village. At first, we attempted to follow female honeyguides as they departed from the Grotto; I set up a network of men through the surrounding forests, and I hoped by yelling back and forth we could communicate the direction of a departing female and follow her to the eggs. But the first hour's work revealed the impossibility of this plan. The tiny green females were lost to sight as they traveled high in the green canopy of the forest; the mists and dripping rain muffled the villagers' voices, so that within a short time the network broke up over the slope and everyone was somewhat confused and lost.

My only other recourse was to use the men to search directly for nests in the odd chance that we would find either the honeyguide nest itself or the nest of foster parents. I divided the men up so that they would cover the surrounding slopes in an orderly fashion. We found many nests and I was busy checking out each promising site; I asked the men to mark each nest they found and then report back to me so I could accompany them to the nest later to examine it personally. But as the days passed the men grew tired of the work and we still had not found a baby honeyguide. The vegetation was now covered with leeches and the men began complaining bitterly about the working conditions; gradually they began leaving, returning in groups of twos and threes to their homes. The hope of finding the honeyguide's nest seemed to be dissolving in the increasing downpours.

Finally, by June 5, I became resigned to not finding the nest; the work with the honeyguide had gone incredibly well despite this final setback. My birthday was on June 6, and I decided to honor myself with a special celebration. Of course after eight months in the field a rather ordinary birthday celebration by normal standards would seem special to the primitive tastes and basic hungers I had been acquiring as a matter of survival. I thought that the best possible present to myself (and the men) would be to close our camp at the Grotto and return to base camp for the night; I dearly wanted to rediscover the feeling of a clean bed and indulge in our larder of canned food there. I sent Pema to scout out the trail back up to base camp and gave orders to the remaining men to begin getting our equipment ready for traveling the next day. But when I went to check our rain gauge for a final time I discovered that it had rained a record 13½ inches. Pema returned after only half an hour, soaking wet and discouraged, and he reported that the Kasuwa stream was now so swollen by the heavy rains that it was impossible to ford. It blocked our only way to base camp. We had stayed too long in the Grotto.

My sleeping bag was now continually damp and perhaps even moldy, but, as I argued to myself, who can smell in an aquarium? I had asked Pema to cut a wide trench around my tent to drain away the water, but it didn't really help. I finally managed to keep the tent floor somewhat dry by building a special platform of bamboo and lining the inside of the tent with plastic. I had to dry out my camera equipment and binoculars each evening, placing the lens along a log by the fire while I had dinner. The moisture on the lens would disappear only slowly, sometimes taking an hour or more. Half a load of potatoes went bad from the damp, and I asked Pema to hang up all our food supplies in cloth bags over the cooking fire. We no longer had to carry water from the stream but merely put out buckets. I could no longer feel the leeches biting and would learn of their presence only after feeling the warm blood flowing. That evening I found several stringy blood clots in my hair and asked Pema to help me cut it as short as possible.

With no hope of reaching base camp on my birthday, I decided to spend the day in the forests. The increasing rains had prompted everything to new life. The orchids had started blooming in abundance, especially a delicate yellow species with red veins trimming its mouth. The forest itself was luminous, giving the impression of humid wealth. Leathery oak leaves glistened in the canopy, and there was a wet sheen on the laurels in the understory. The ferns lining the forest floor were tense and upright, supported by a new turgid pressure. In a way, it was difficult to perceive any one plant as separate. A depthless space provided by the mists gave a uniform and diffuse lighting. The vegetation had a composite effect. The branches of the canopy were confused with the vines that hung down in wide arches through the understory. Moss covered everything, green and dripping.

The sounds were also special, different. The birds seemed to sing louder than before, as if they were competing with the sound of the rain, and there was a mysterious new quality to their songs. It was impossible to see through the mists the creator of any one call. Trills, throaty clicks, resonant booms, strange ephemeral flutings, formed a varying melody punctuated by the croaking of the tree frogs. And always there was the background sound of dripping. That evening, nocturnal flying squirrels sang eerie gurgles and laughs from the canopy.

My birthday party was a success of sorts. Coming down to the kitchen from my tent, I found the setting looked pretty melancholy. A light rain dripped through the aging holes in the tarp and a wind blew a fine spray in on our fire. The smoke from wet wood mushroomed up beneath the tarp, flowing upward around the edge. Light from the flames leaped out to illuminate leafy ghosts in the forest around us. Pema slaughtered the last of our chickens, one of four we had brought to the canyon with hopes of having fresh eggs. The only one that ever laid an egg was, by mistake, the first to be eaten. The chicken for this evening had the tangy tough meat that was a tribute to the hardy breed that survives the village dogs. We had fern shoots, and, as ever, the staple was rice. Pema found a last can of peaches, which we had for dessert.

One of the porters had some local brew which he offered around. This noble potion gave some spark to the party, and thus emboldened, we spent the evening discussing the tradition of a birthday. Pasang sat hunched on the ground beside the fire, his wool tunic open exposing his kukri. His narrow eyes smiled warmly as he argued that the whole idea of a Sahib birthday was foolish. He considered it a lame excuse to begin drinking, which, after all, is a God-given right to be exercised without the need for any explanation. He said he had no birthday and did not remember the specific date of his birth. The villagers only remember the day of the week they are born on and its relationship to the full moon. If one believes in lunar astrology, which they do, I suppose it would be a far better way to calculate things.

Just before I went back to my tent, Pema told me that although he liked the work and found it easy, he was having difficulty. "Down here I think too much," he said. "Up on a high ridge, where I can see the mountains, I do not think all the time. It is bad to think all the time."

After being born and growing up in the high alpine areas, a

forest at the bottom of the valley must be a very depressing place for a Sherpa. Still, it puzzled me. We saw the natural world in such different ways. My men were bored, and rightfully so, while I was absorbed with the beauty and complexity of the forests, the wildlife, and especially the honeyguide.

For the next three days I spent my time either at the Grotto conducting observations or on the surrounding slopes searching vainly for a nest site. The situation at the Grotto had changed little. Chang Hua was still absent a disproportionate amount of time. The rains continued dense and unyielding, making it impossible to observe the birds or walk up the steep slopes. I couldn't help realizing that meanwhile I was missing out on important activities higher up the mountain. My entire program for studying the breeding biology of other birds required that I move up in altitude with the passing of the seasons. The birds at the Grotto were past their peak, while four thousand feet above, a new set of birds was just beginning. I really could no longer work profitably in the Grotto and felt the days pass agonizingly by.

Even our forest camp was now in danger. One night a large limb from the canopy broke off and, with a frightening sound, fell a few feet from my tent. The thick arboreal growths on the limbs had absorbed the rain, increasing their weight many times, until the strain was too much for the tree. Pema explained that often large trees are uprooted when top heavy with monsoon rains.

I felt that regardless of the outcome we had to make a dash for base camp. I had been waiting for a break in the rain that might allow us to ford the stream, but that possibility seemed less and less real. Finally, I went out to examine the Kasuwa myself. It had become a raging torrent and was living up to its reputation among the villagers as one of the most vicious and dangerous rivers of the entire Arun watershed. Like the blood vessels of a living monster, the waters appeared to surge with a pulsating rhythm. Swimming across was impossible. The current was too swift, and enormous boulders came crashing down, shoved and pushed by the violent waves. The boulders made a groaning sound as they smashed along. Smaller rocks produced a higher-pitched pinging noise as they ricocheted off each other. Large trees had been swallowed up, and their scarred trunks bobbed in the murky currents like corks on a gale-driven sea.

Standing alone in the rain I felt small and inconsequential. I could see myself trapped in the Grotto throughout the monsoon, the victim of the natural forces of the Himalayas. Pema came over to where I was standing, and we discussed the prospects for getting out. There was a possibility that men could make it without loads, by going up through the forests on the Grotto side and crossing on the ridge over to base camp, but that would mean leaving all of my equipment in the Grotto to be destroyed by the rains. I needed the equipment for my research, and to leave it behind would mean abandoning hope for any further work that summer. The only alternative seemed to be to build a bridge, and that would require getting a man over to the other side of the Kasuwa. The distance across was too great to throw a rope and have it catch on the other side. I asked Pema if he was willing to try to go up through the forest to the ridge, cross to the opposite side, and descend to the Kasuwa again on the far shore. He kindly agreed to try — although he had as much desire to get out as I did — and left that afternoon with a porter. He thought it would take him a full day to make the trip. I felt better as soon as he had left. There was a certain relief in action, any action which displaces time and consumes thought. We were at least doing something.

My stay with Chang Hua ended on June 13, my last day of observation. He was gone from his territory almost half of that last day, doing what I know not. I did not see any copulations, but once a marked female came in to feed. It was sad to say good-bye to him and not to know more about his life; there was too much left to learn. Late the next afternoon, Pema appeared, waving through the mist on the opposite shore of the Kasuwa. With the perpetual Sherpa smile, he was laughing at the way the Kasuwa was tearing apart a fallen tree caught between submerged boulders. The shattered limbs vibrated in the current with a sullen tension, and I could imagine myself or one of my men caught in a similar fashion. We immediately chose a site on the shore where tall rocks perched over the waters and set about building a bridge. After several attempts, we managed to get a rope across between us and Pema and then, dragging over a larger rope, fixed a strong line. With this established, we could push and drag long poles across and, after several hours of work, managed to arrange six poles that might support our weight.

Pema then tied himself to the rope, and, as I belayed him, he crossed the bridge over to our side. I was nervous watching him; he slipped twice and ended up crawling on his belly. The extent of our interest in leaving the Grotto could be measured by how encouraging this sad performance seemed to all of us. One by one the men tied onto the line and crossed. Pema and I then divided the equipment and supplies up into small baskets, tying them securely to the line, and the porters hauled them across. Pema finally crossed back and without any hesitation, I followed in acceptable style — belly down, hugging the poles tightly, a ribbon of mud forming from head to foot.

We climbed slowly up to base camp, tired and worn thin by the excitement. The trip would have taken only a few hours during the dry season, but we had to walk late into the night and reached camp completely exhausted. I looked back toward the Grotto canyon, where mists swirled around in a large eddying motion through the trees, hiding the cliff; the mists had certainly hidden other secrets from me.

The local villagers say I will never find the nests and eggs of the honeyguide for they don't exist. They, too, like the original Chang Hua, call the honeyguide a spiritual sparrow. Somehow, though, I intend to keep trying, and I have promised myself that I will return to the Arun someday to discover the answer. I am compelled to learn more of the honeyguide's intriguing behavior.

I am grateful to the original Chang Hua for his wisdom and perception in describing this dull-looking species among the many spectacular animals harbored by the Himalayas; unfortunately, modern man's interest in natural history is often confined to those large, colorful, or dangerous beasts that are dramatic enough to secure his attention in a stimulus-saturated world. The less spectacular species are usually ignored, sometimes even in the wildlife and conservation sciences. And in Asia, where our knowledge of the wildlife is so limited, such creatures remain relatively unknown or sadly forgotten.

CHAPTER EIGHT

The Night of the Abominable Snowman

> Oh yes! We have many kinds of wild animals in
> these forests. There are bears, and musk deer,
> and yeti, and pandas, and leopards, and civets,
> and monkeys, and many, many more.
>
> — *Arun Villager*

WITH NONCHALANCE and an almost staggering glibness, a Lumdumsa villager answered my question about the kinds of animals to be found in the local forests. It was part of an interview that we gave to experienced hunters to determine the extent of their knowledge about the wildlife. Most such exercises were duly informative, enjoyable, and, after a while, actually boring in their repetition. But here, suddenly, without prompting of any kind and with an unbearable confidence, this man included the yeti as just one more species to be found in the Kasuwa! The yeti, that mysterious, unknown, and monsterlike creature of radioactive excitement for all Westerners, was mundanely relegated to the status of a panda or a leopard — neither more nor less interesting.

Truth is a hard thing to come by in people, no matter what their background, and there are few statistical techniques for weeding out the unintentional elaboration, the white lie, or the unsaid thing. I came to put much faith in the answer this hunter gave, as much because of the context of the question, as because

of his unflinching expression. Often, if I asked directly about
the yeti — sometimes as soon as I would mention it — the hunters
would either become cautious and unresponsive, or launch into
an obviously corrupt and grotesque tale in which the yeti had,
if not supernatural powers, then at least the intelligence and
abilities of man. In one story I remember, the yeti used fire to
cook his food and spoke a dialect of Tibetan popular in the northern regions of the valley.

Some villagers have heard of the foreigner's fascination for the
yeti, and they are quick to take advantage, trying to please their
way toward a few extra rupees by demonstrating to the Sahib
their widespread knowledge of yeti lore. But they do the same
with many other wild animals, and hill people love the tall tale.
Lubricated with chang and warmed by a campfire at the end
of the day, I have heard village hunters tell stories about bears
that could travel great distances instantaneously, or hold a threatening grudge toward a specific individual and come out of the
night, as if a transparent spirit, to seek a murderous revenge. All
people fictionalize their wildlife, and there are certain truths,
about both animals and men, that can be explained only by such
a license. Still, Kipling's Bagheera does not mean that black leopards are any less real.

Reports of the yeti have come out of the Himalayas for almost
two centuries. There is an eighteenth century drawing of the
yeti in a Chinese manuscript on Tibetan wildlife. The first Westerner to have published an account of the yeti was apparently
B. H. Hodgson in 1832. Since then, over forty mountaineers,
naturalists, and explorers, including such reputable gentlemen as
N. A. Tombazi, Sir John Hunt, W. H. Tilman, Sir C. K. Howard-
Bury, and Dr. Norman Dryhrenfurth, have reported sighting the
yeti or its footprints.

Several expeditions have been made to the Himalayas specifically to look for the yeti, as, for example, the London Daily Mail
Expedition in 1954, or the several Slick-Johnson Expeditions during the early 1960s. The World Book Encyclopedia Expedition of
1960–61, led by the renowned Sir Edmund Hillary, included a
team of zoologists from a prominent American museum who
searched for evidence in the Everest region. All have come back
with evidence of one kind or another, and the evidence has always
been highly controversial.

The recent reports include a well-documented sighting of footprints by a Polish Expedition in 1974. In the summer of that same year, Lhakpa Sherpa, a young girl from the Khumbu Valley, was attacked by a yeti while tending a herd of yak and zhum. According to the official report filed by the Nepalese Police who investigated the incident, the girl was sitting on a big rock near a stream when she heard what she took to be coughing. She looked around and saw a huge black-and-reddish-brown, monkeylike creature with large eyes and projecting cheek bones. The creature grabbed her and carried her to a nearby tributary of the stream; she was released, shocked but essentially unhurt. The yeti remained in the area for thirty minutes or so, during which time, in an irrational demonic rage, it killed two of her yaks with punches, and broke the neck of a third.

The primary question concerning such reports has always been the reliability of the witnesses. Accusations buzz like flies around the decomposing heap of the evidence. The natives, after all, are not to be trusted because of their limited knowledge of zoology. Among the foreigners, perhaps some were excellent mountain climbers, but how qualified were they to examine spoor or interpret visual sightings? Were they tired or in some way affected by the high altitudes? Did the powers of suggestion from a lengthy history of yeti lore convert otherwise explainable circumstances into confirmed yeti reports? Are the reports outright hoaxes, perpetrated for publicity or fame?

None of these accusations appears valid, given the personalities and accomplishments of the witnesses. Local villagers require no great scientific training to describe the appearance of an animal. Many of the Westerners are respected public figures with illustrious careers who would have nothing to gain from further publicity. Many are competent naturalists and mountaineers familiar with the wildlife and field conditions in the Himalayas. Typically, their own first reaction to their discoveries has been to explain them in terms of exotic fauna, altitude sickness, or atmospheric aberrations; and it is only after discounting such possibilities that many witnesses were willing to suffer the abuse and doubt that accompany the reports of a yeti.

Certainly some of the reports are questionable, being too vague and having too few details to make any concrete decisions. But there is also the inescapable logic that even if all the reports are inaccurate except one, that one constitutes proof that the yeti does exist.

By now, the reported cases of yeti sightings or spoor number in the thousands; yet each year new reports receive prominent and conspicuous mention in the popular press. There seems no end to the yeti lore, nor to its universal appeal. For a hypothetical creature of ifs and maybes, the yeti holds a disproportionate part of the public attention. Everywhere, it touches a sensitive nerve, as if there were something there we were trying to remember, or forget. If, for a moment, we put aside the question of its zoological reality, the yeti as a phenomenon makes an intriguing statement about man.

Obviously, the interest, in part, has to do with the very mystery and controversy surrounding the yeti. It captures the imagination in a way that only a manlike form can do. The immediate sensation that it creates is a welcome counterpoint to the grim reality of war, famine, and politics that normally consumes our media. Flashy tabloids treat it as a Frankenstein monster incarnate — the Abominable Snowman. Movies make it into a vivid nightmare, something to frighten the audience and enhance box office receipts. While the institutions they work for maintain a dignified silence, inside the mausoleums the scientists endlessly argue the pros and cons for its existence.

In part, also, the interest has to do with the creature itself. If there really is an unknown anthropoid of the yeti's description alive today, it must be a close relative from our distant and forgotten past. Man's foremost interest is man, and the yeti would be the most significant zoological and anthropological discovery of the century, offering comparative insights into our own development, behavior, and prehistoric society. It would not be just another fossil ape, but a living breathing creature that we could study in the flesh.

The greatest part of the fascination, however, has to do with what the yeti represents emotionally. The yeti is the ultimate ancestral myth. In today's science-oriented society, people who depreciate myths as superstitious inventions are guilty of a kind of scientific superstition themselves — the belief that science can explain the universe. We have gone from a mythological explanation of the world that was comprehensible to all, to a scientific explanation of the world, phrased in terms of quantum mechanics and the theory of relativity, that is comprehensible only to the most isolated specialist.

Myths are the public dreams. They are the display panels of

the human psyche and represent the vehicles of communication between our collective conscious and unconscious. The gnawing interest in the yeti might be that it touches on one of the most sensitive aspects of man's involvement with the universe: What makes him unique? What separates man from the animals around him? What is man? The yeti, half man–half ape, raises this elemental question in a more than allegorical way, while science has only confused the distinction; and the layman has been left in a vacuum of nonsense definitions about tool using and social communication.

Possibly, the yeti holds the answer for that distinction and will set to rest, once and for all, our agony of self-evaluation. Indeed, the yeti might be so serviceable to our emotions and science that we should hope that it does exist.

Prior to the expedition's entering the field, Jeff and I had made as thorough as possible an examination of the evidence for the yeti's existence. The literature was extensive, scattered in both the most obscure and most prominent scientific journals, and it included several books wholly devoted to the subject. It became an absorbing pastime for us, something to occupy evening hours when we were too tired to study more exacting subjects. We were not at all serious about actually finding it, and although we mentioned the possibility to several sponsors, we fully recognized its real unlikelihood. Oddly enough, sponsors often wanted to talk more about the yeti than our scientific or conservation goals. Having not yet traveled in the Himalayas, or come to know her people, it was a subject that one could be playfully serious about. From the narrow streets of civilization, it seemed altogether too incredible, too fantastic, and too much fun to be ignored.

Based on the various eyewitness reports, a detailed description of the yeti can be constructed. Its body is stocky, apelike in shape, with a distinctly human quality to it, in contrast to that of a bear. It stands five and a half to six feet tall and is covered with short coarse hair, reddish-brown to black in color, sometimes with white patches on the chest. The hair is longest on the shoulders. The face is hairless and rather flat. The jaw is robust, the teeth are quite large, though fangs are not present, and the mouth is wide. The shape of the head is conical, with a pointed crown. The arms are long, reaching almost to the knees. The shoulders are heavy and hunched. There is no tail.

One of the most remarkable aspects of these descriptions by the various eyewitnesses is their consistency; each one describes essentially the same creature. Those reports that can be considered reliable do not depict strange colors, unusual growths of hair, fangs, extraordinary proportions, or any of the likely elaborations that one would normally associate with a monster story. Rather, the reports show an uncanny zoological expertise in their portrayal of a creature that is exactly what a scientist would expect.

The behavior described in the visual sightings is even more familiar to the scientist. Recent field studies in Africa by George Schaller, Jane Goodall, Dian Fossey, and Vernon Reynolds have built a substantial body of data on the natural behavior of wild apes. Local villagers and Western observers could not possibly anticipate these findings, and yet they describe the yeti's behavior with details that are easily recognized as displacement conflicts, aggressive posturing, and social interactions as we now know them to be typical of wild apes. The reports seem too good, too accurate, not to be true.

Although the sightings must be taken on faith, the photographs of yeti footprints contribute concrete data. The most noteworthy discovery of footprints was made by Eric Shipton and Michael Ward during the 1951 British Mount Everest Reconnaissance. The prints were made on a thin layer of crystalline snow lying on firm ice, indicating that little erosion or melting had occurred. The photographs are exceptionally clear and sharp, thus enabling definitive comparisons to be made.

The yeti's foot is large, some twelve and a half inches long by seven and a half inches wide, with the heel nearly as broad as the forepart. A conspicuous humanlike arch is absent. The great toe, or hallux, is quite large, with the second toe the longest and relatively thin, while the remaining three toes are short, stubby, and united toward their base. The hallux is separated from the second toe in an opposable manner, that is more like the thumb on a human hand than the big toe on a human foot, and suggests a more primitive condition than that of modern man. These photographs have since become the "type-specimens" of yeti prints.

Possible identification of the yeti footprints as those of a known creature ranges from bears, snow leopards, wolves, eagles, and langur monkeys to the barefoot man. Shipton's yeti prints are too large, the hallux is too opposable, and the heel is too

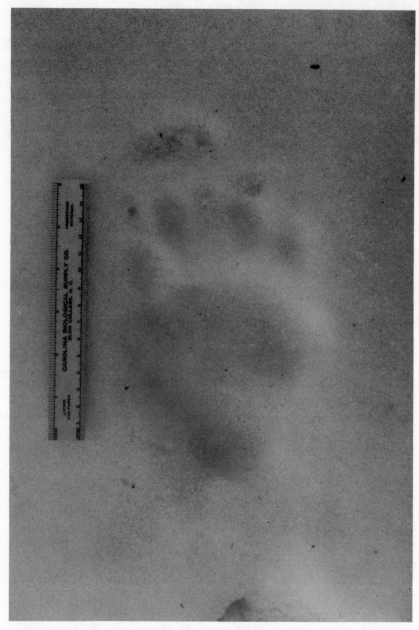

Typical footprint of a bear as left in snow; probably made by the hind foot of a Himalayan black bear

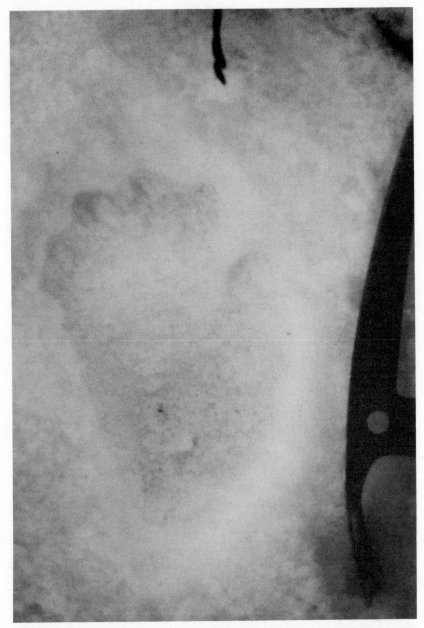

One of the yeti footprints left in the snow outside our tent at Kongmaa La

broad for us to accept a human foot as its author. The prints are also too large to be that of any known species of monkey; the entire musculature is different, and the width/length ratio of, for example, a langur foot is on the order of 25 percent, while the yeti print is more than 60 percent, making even a giant monkey foot too narrow to be considered. Hypotheses that entertain the possibilities of snow leopards or wolves (which have nearly round prints) and eagles (which have four narrow toes arranged in a palmate structure) are really more the property of the sensational press than a serious investigation.

Bears, because of their size, habits, and habitat, are the most likely candidate. Several forms of bear are known to inhabit the higher Himalayas, including the "blue bear" (Ursus arctos pruinosis), the "red bear" (Ursus arctos isabellianus), and the Himalayan "black bear" (Selanarctos thibetanus). During the expedition's stay in the Arun Valley, we encountered numerous bear prints which the local villagers would occasionally identify as yeti prints. But the prints of all three forms of bear invariably showed the equally sized, *symmetrical* arrangement of toes typical of the group. In contrast, Shipton's yeti prints show distinctively larger and smaller toes, arranged in a characteristic *asymmetrical* pattern. Further, bear prints typically have a narrow, drawn-out heel, while Shipton's photograph shows with exceptional clarity a broad, rounded heel.

Shipton's photograph is in fact so detailed that the movements of the foot can be ascertained. Like the hominid foot, the prints have the deepest impression along the outer side of the back of the heel, where the foot first touches the ground; the next deepest impressions are along the inner side of the hallux, which is used to propel the foot forward. Such details are known from criminological studies and strongly suggest that, like man, the yeti uses bipedal progression, that is, walks on two rather than four feet. Shipton himself commented that the series of yeti prints he discovered appeared to be made by a creature walking bipedally.

Bipedalism in the yeti seems to have aroused the greatest controversy and is a source of disbelief among skeptics. It is often thought by the uninformed that bipedalism is unique to man among the primates, but, in fact, it is by no means rare among apes. Gibbons, the most arboreal of the apes, consistently walk upright when on the ground. Adriaan Kortlandt found that the chimpanzees he was studying walked bipedally for 10–15 percent of the distance they covered. George Schaller has shown that gorillas occasionally revert to bipedal progression for short distances when traveling through wet vegetation, apparently to keep their hands dry.

Bipedalism is not even a recent adaption of the apes. According to David Pilbeam and Elwyn Simons, "The Miocene apes and their Oligocene ancestors probably showed a high degree of trunk erectness and doubtless spent much time walking or running bipedally either in trees or on the ground." A particular bit of damning evidence against the skeptics has been discovered by Sydney Britton of the University of Virginia, who found that captive chimpanzees he was studying walked bipedally when there was snow on the ground, probably to keep their hands from getting cold. In careful analysis, it not only seems possible, but altogether likely that an ape who frequents the high snows of the Himalayas would be using bipedal progression.

Another point of serious controversy between the advocates and the skeptics has been the supposed yeti scalps. Several monasteries in the Khumbu Valley are known to keep what are purported to be yeti scalps. The expedition that was sponsored by the World Book Encyclopedia managed to borrow one from the Khumjung monastery. It was taken directly to museums in Paris, London, and Chicago, where zoologists examined it carefully, comparing it to the skins of known Himalayan animals. The verdict of the experts: a fake made from the skin of a serow.

This judgment was a terrible disappointment to many believers in the yeti. They realized that photographs and even the most detailed reports might never establish anything. Only a solid, incontestable piece of evidence, such as teeth, bones, or skin, would resolve the question. That the first piece of "hard" evidence examined at a museum should turn out to be a fake was a shattering blow to many.

But the verdict was not unanimous. Dr. John Hill at the British Museum pointed out that the hairs from the Khumjung scalp had a simian quality despite their gross resemblance to serow hairs. Comparing the granules of pigment in the hair, he detected a symmetrical arrangement quite different from normal serow pigments. In addition, ectoparasites from the scalp were also strangely different. According to Hill, the mite ectoparasites recovered from the scalp were unusual in respect to their sculpting of the cuticle, the arrangement and conspicuousness of hairs, and the size of limbs. Such mite ectoparasites are normally very host specific, and it would be highly unusual to find nonserow mites on a serow skin. Either the serow population in the Khumjung area had unique ectoparasites, or the scalp was not serow.

Also, the very identity of the scalp was in question. In their excitement in getting the scalp out of Nepal to where it could be tested, the scientists from the expedition failed to mention some important qualifications. The scalp was known to be at least several hundred years old, and none of the Sherpas alive at the time could, realistically, vouch for its authenticity. In fact, several of the Sherpas had insisted from the beginning that the Khumjung scalp was a fake, made in imitation of the real yeti scalps found at other monasteries to enhance the reputation of the Khumjung monastery. Such a scalp was considered a powerful talisman by the villagers, and a necessary item for the religious ceremonies and spiritual powers of any monastery.

In reviewing yeti literature, it becomes increasingly obvious that the biases of the scientists involved, rather than any inductive logic, determine the interpretation of the data. Responsible authorities operating with the same evidence reach completely different conclusions. One notable scientist who visited the Himalayas stated flatly that, based on his discovery that known animal tracks can be melted by the sun into facsimiles of yeti footprints, "the yeti does not exist." Not only is it a doubtful accomplishment to recognize that snow melts, it is also a serious insult to logic, ideally the tool-in-trade of the scientist, to assert that an unknown thing does not exist.

Comparison of the evidence for the existence of the yeti with accepted scientific ideas reveals the even deeper dilemma of the fine distinction between empirical evidence and fact. Fossilized material is a significant part of modern scientific dogma, used in supportive arguments for everything from systematic evolution to the ecology of dinosaurs. But fossil records are the rock molds left after bone material dissolves and, in that sense, are analogous to the snow and mud molds left by the yeti's feet. By studying a few fragments of fossilized bones, paleontologists are able to construct a specific account of an extinct creature's general morphology, ecology, and behavior. These accounts are highly theoretical constructions, yet we still rely on them. The yeti, by comparison, has been seen, for lengthy periods, on numerous occasions, in many different areas, by dozens of people. What is it that makes us so reluctant to credit the reports of the yeti? Even at this late date, we seem to be hindered by a conservatism and parochialism that do disservice to the potential of science.

Any creature existing today must have had ancestors, and it may be that the antecedents of the yeti can be found among the known fossil forms. Numerous possibilities are mentioned in the literature, including *Oreopithecus, Australopithecus robustus,* and *Homo erectus,* but one in particular, *Gigantopithecus,* seems especially likely. Remains of *Gigantopithecus* have been found in the foothills of the Himalayas, not far from where many of the modern sightings of the yeti have occurred. Other remains have been found in Kwangsi Province of southern China, indicating an extensive range throughout South Asia. The dating of this material is as early as nine million years ago, and as recent as 500,000 years ago, or middle Pleistocene age, which would make it a contemporary of *Homo erectus.*

Gigantopithecus's size and shape are what make it such a likely candidate, for it closely resembled the description of the yeti as given by eyewitnesses. Based on the remains discovered so far, it was a large ape, and undoubtedly had the large jaw and teeth mentioned in yeti descriptions but, also like the yeti, lacked conspicuous fangs or elongated canines. Also, the large mandible of *Gigantopithecus* meant extensive jaw muscles. In apes, this is often associated with a tall sagittal crest, which is required as an attachment point for these muscles, and would exactly duplicate the pointed head so consistently mentioned in the sightings of the yeti, and observed in the scalp. In contrast, man has a relatively weak jaw, few jaw muscles, and thus, their attachment is confined to the side of the head; there is no sagittal crest, but rather the round smooth surface that marks the human skull.

There are ecological reasons to support *Gigantopithecus.* It probably came in contact with evolving man in India, and there would have been strong competitive pressure between them. A basic principle of population biology, the Competitive Exclusion Principle, states that whenever two allied forms have a similar range, niche, behavior, and ecology, one will invariably gain a selective advantage over the other and soon displace it. The less successful form either becomes extinct or is forced to migrate.

During the middle Pleistocene age, man had already learned about fire and had an extensive use of stone, bone, and wooden tools. *Gigantopithecus* was found in association with a mixed habitat — forests, open areas, and areas transitional between the two — indicating sufficient behavioral flexibility to invade new habitats, such as those of the higher mountains. While man would have been a powerful, almost overwhelming competitor against such allied forms as *Gigantopithecus, Gigantopithecus* would have had available to it a mountain range well known for its ability to isolate populations of animals in its steep valleys where they would be protected from outside competition. There is no valid reason to believe that the Himalayas could not harbor a population of relict apes as they do harbor populations of other relict species.

Gigantopithecus was originally discovered by G. H. R. von Koenigswald when he encountered unusually large anthropoid teeth in a collection of "dragon bones" in a Chinese pharmacy in Hong Kong. On examining the material, he explained that, "despite its large size, *Gigantopithecus* has more 'man-like' teeth than any living anthropoid ape." Other researchers interpreted the teeth to mean a truly phenomenal size for *Gigantopithecus,* weighing up to 600 pounds, and possibly nine feet tall when standing erect. Koenigswald felt that "It strikes me that we had best suspend judgement on the whole matter [size] until the missing limb bones themselves have been discovered. In any case, *Gigantopithecus,* whose teeth are larger than those of the gorilla, is likely to have had a larger cranial capacity as well."

Since cranial capacity is often correlated with intelligence in the early stages of man's development, it seems likely that *Gigantopithecus* might have been an exceptionally intelligent ape. Koenigswald felt that *Gigantopithecus* probably had a cranial capacity corresponding to that of early man. Consequently, although there is still much disagreement, *Gigantopithecus* is usually placed somewhere between the pongids (or ape forms) and the homids (or human forms). First hailed as the missing link, the yeti is doubtfully a living form representing a transition between ape and man, but if it is a *Gigantopithecus* descendant, it probably does constitute an evolutionary offshoot that still possesses characters common to such a form.

How would *Gigantopithecus* have fitted into the Himalayas? It is a valuable question in that it helps dispose of two common misconceptions about the yeti: 1) that the yeti is a resident of the harsh climate of the perennial snows; and 2) that it seems unlikely that a large primate could hide from the numerous investigators for such a long time.

My experience in the Himalayas suggests to me that a yeti-*Gigantopithecus* would not inhabit the snowlands. It would favor the dense vegetation of the steep valleys in the middle-altitude zone. The yeti is encountered in the snows because, like the mountaineers who discover its tracks, it uses the snowy passes as routes from one valley to the next. The topography of the Himalayas forces any animal traveling across its country to use the limited number of gaps, ridges, and passes as roads from one area to the next.

A creature like *Gigantopithecus* could easily survive in the lush forests of the valleys. The succession of vegetational zones on the steep slopes provides a diversity and abundance of plants, and a complex small mammal fauna including rats, mice, voles, moles, and pikas, that would offer a large ominvore a more than ample supply of food. Numerous large mammals already enjoy the rich conditions and maintain sizable populations. In the mountains of Africa, gorillas are known to inhabit areas at altitudes of up to 12,800 feet. A large primate would do equally well in the Himalayas.

The yeti would have little trouble escaping detection in these dense forests. In many places, the vegetation presents a nearly impenetrable wall. The thick, compacted undergrowth of bamboo, rubis, and rhododendron greatly constricts one's ability to hear, see, and move, so that a large mammal could easily hide nearby and remain unnoticed. Even the irregular topography contributes places to hide. In the best monster tradition, the yeti could disappear among the numerous gullies, canyons, cliffs, rock shelters, and varied slopes. The slopes fold back and forth upon themselves to include a prodigious amount of land.

In addition, these forests are seldom visited by people. The mountaineers hurry to and from their icy peaks and keep on the main trails to facilitate transport of supplies. The villagers are primarily agriculturalists and pastoralists who have little purpose in exploring the forests; those villagers who regularly hunt are also the ones with stories about the yeti, but they are a small minority. Surprisingly few naturalists have spent any length of time anywhere in the Himalayas, and even they usually keep to the trails. As in mountain country throughout the world, the trails follow the natural signposts of the topography, the ridges and streambeds. The vast area of slope is virtually isolated.

Further, the ability of large mammals to escape documentation by science is infamous. The kouprey (*Bos sauveli*), a large wild bison, was not discovered by Western science until 1936, when the first specimen was identified inside the Paris Zoo. This animal favors the open woodland and savanna areas of Cambodia, where the terrain and vegetation leave him highly visible. Other creatures, such as the mountain gorilla, pigmy hippopotamus, and giant panda, were all known from village reports and yet remained unknown to science for years.

Finally, adding to the difficulty of discovery, the yeti is probably nocturnal. Like many other large mammals that suffer from man's disturbance of the wilderness, the yeti has probably developed the habit of hiding and sleeping during the day, and confining its traveling and feeding to nighttime. Many elephant populations of South Asia have adopted this same strategy.

Thus, the sum total of evidence demonstrates that although by no means do the traditional zoological data required for naming a new species exist, there is no zoological, paleontological, or ecological reason to suppose that an unknown anthropoid does not exist in the Himalayas. In fact, a significant body of data suggests there does.

In December 1972, Howard and I decided to make our first research trip to the high altitudes. Chosing Kongmaa Laa mountain as a site, we wanted to use this trip to investigate the winter conditions of the ecosystem. We joked about the yeti before we left, warning our compatriots that they should join us, for it would be the first expedition trek to "yeti country," the alpine ridges north of the Kasuwa. Jim and Karen declined, saying they were busy at base, but Jeff said he would accompany us at least part way.

We left base camp in the Kasuwa Khola on December 14. The first days were a slow trek through the upper temperate forest. Later we encountered heavier snows, which made traveling difficult and Jeff and our porters turned back. On the 17th, accompanied by two Sherpa assistants, Howard and I emerged on a high alpine ridge connecting to Kongmaa Laa. The weather was beautiful, with a clear sky and warm sun. The icy summit of Makalu dominated the horizon to the northwest. In the late afternoon, we discovered a depression in the ridge at about 12,000 feet, a flat place with firm snow that would be suitable for camp.

The area was small, less than half an acre, a completely clear snowfield unmarked by animal prints. The slopes on the side of the ridge were precipitous, falling several thousand feet to the Barun River on the north and the Kasuwa River on the south. We made camp, pitching two light tents, had dinner around an open fire, and retired just after dark. The evening was calm.

Shortly before dawn the next morning, Howard climbed out of our tent. Immediately, he called excitedly. There, beside the trail we had made to our tents, was a new set of footprints. While we were sleeping, a creature had approached our camp and walked directly between our tents. The Sherpas identified the tracks, without question, as yeti prints. We, without question, were stunned.

We immediately made a full photographic record of the prints before the sun touched them. Like the conditions Shipton had encountered, the surface consisted of crystalline snow, excellent for displaying the prints. These conditions were localized to our camp area and were the result of the effects produced on the depression by the sun and winds of earlier days. The prints were clearest in the middle of the depression, directly beside our trail, where some ten to fifteen prints, both left and right feet, revealed the details of the toes and general morphology of the creature's foot. Some of the right footprints were actually on our previous trail, making them difficult to interpret. Other prints of the right foot were distinct.

The prints measured approximately nine inches long by four and three-quarters inches wide. The stride, or distance between individual prints, was surprisingly short, often less than one foot, and it appeared that the creature had used a slow, cautious walk along this section. The prints showed a short, broad, opposable hallux, an asymmetrical arrangement of the toes, and a wide rounded heel. These features were present in all the prints made on firm snow. Most impressively, their close resemblance to Shipton's prints was unmistakable.

We then proceeded to explore the rest of the trail left by the creature. By the direction of the toes on the clear footprints, I determined that the creature had come up the north slope. I investigated these prints first, following the trail back down the slope. Because the north slope received less sun, it was covered with very deep snow, and the tracks consisted of large punch holes in the snow revealing little detail. I descended several hundred yards, but the heavy snow made walking impossible, and I was forced to cling to the slope with my hands. The creature must have been exceptionally strong to ascend this slope in these conditions. From a vantage point, I could look back down the trail, which continued toward the bottom of the valley in a direction generally perpendicular to the slope, but there seemed little advantage in climbing farther down, and I returned to the top of the ridge.

From our camp, the tracks continued out onto the south slope, but here the increased exposure to the sun had melted most of the snow, and there were bare patches of rock and alpine scrub which made following the trail extremely difficult. We walked farther up the ridge toward Kongmaa Laa to get a view of the trail from above, and discovered what appeared to be the prints of the same creature coming back onto the top of the ridge. They crossed back and forth several times. Here, the ridge was covered with low bushes, which enabled deeper snow to accumulate, and again the prints were confused punch holes. The trail then went back down onto the south slope, and we attempted to follow but lost the prints on the bare rock and scrub. The slope was extremely steep, and searching for the prints was arduous and dangerous. We realized that whatever creature had made them was far stronger than any of us.

We considered the possibility of a hoax perpetrated by our Sherpas, but discounted it, realizing that the Sherpas were not capable of making the full trail of prints we could see from the top of the ridge. They would not have had the time. We also doubted their ability to make prints which were so consistent with each other and which so closely matched the yeti footprints that we were familiar with from photographs.

We sent word with one of the Sherpas down to the other members of the expedition, and Jeff came up to the ridge later with plaster of Paris so that we could make casts of the prints.

During the next three days, we kept a careful watch for the possible reappearance of the creature. We made a new camp farther up the ridge, and spent the days examining other snowfields. At night, taking advantage of a bright moon that clearly illuminated the surrounding slopes, we watched from the front of our tent for possible nocturnal activity. There were no further signs.

*

Upon reflection, there are several aspects of this incident which contribute valuable information to the controversy about the yeti:

1. The circumstances eliminate the hypothesis that all yeti prints are a function of melting by the sun or wind erosion. We know that the prints were made during the night of the 17th, or very early on the morning of the 18th. We photographed them before the sun touched them. We knew wind had not affected them, since a comparison of our own footprints made on the morning of the 18th with our footprints made on the 17th showed little, if any, distortion.

2. The prints are not referrable to any known fauna of the area. During the expedition, we devoted special efforts to examining all large mammal prints made in snow; we noted possible variations produced by different snow conditions, terrain, and activities of the animal (i.e., running, walking, et cetera); a photographic record was made whenever possible. From comparisons of these photographs with the photographs of our yeti prints, we feel we can eliminate with assurance the possibility that the yeti prints were made by any known normal animal of the eastern Himalayas.

3. The prints support the hypothesis that the various yeti reports refer to one species. The prints are very similar to those photographed by Shipton, differing only in being smaller, with a shorter hallux, which probably indicates an immature male or a female. Sexual dimorphism — a difference in size between the sexes — is known from *Gigantopithecus* and many other primates, and could easily account for the stories from villagers about different species of yeti.

4. The prints support the hypothesis that the yeti is an anthropoid. Dr. George Schaller, who spent a year in the mountains of Africa studying a free-ranging population of gorillas, commented after examining the plaster casts of the prints made on the 18th that they "demonstrate a close resemblance to those of the mountain gorilla."

5. The arrangement of the prints supports the hypothesis that the yeti uses bipedal progression. The prints demonstrated a left-right-left-right pattern, with no overlapping and no indication that more than two appendages were used in making a lengthy series of prints.

6. The weight of the creature that made the prints was less

than or equal to the weight of an average man. My footprints (I weighed approximately 185 pounds, including winter clothes and boots) were slightly deeper, suggesting that the creature weighed about 165 pounds.

7. The circumstances support the hypothesis that the yeti is nocturnal.

8. The creature displayed some inquisitiveness, since it made a detour along the ridge in order to enter our camp and pass between the tents. From careful examination of the terrain, it appeared likely that the creature approached our camp by following a natural spur up the ridge to cross from the Barun to the Kasuwa Khola at a point which would enable it to avoid the heavier snows farther up the ridge. Although it is possible that the creature saw our camp during the first hour of darkness when the campfire was burning, it seems more probable that, given the angle of the slope, it did not know our camp was there until it was almost upon it. The point at which it reached the top of the ridge was some 20–30 yards east of the camp, but rather than turn back or cross the ridge at that point, it turned west to walk along the ridge toward our camp, finally passing between the tents. It is possibly significant that the creature appeared to be an immature, based on the size of its feet.

9. The presence of its tracks supports the hypothesis that the creature inhabits the forested regions, using the snowy passes only to cross from one valley to the next. The tracks came from the heavily forested valley of the Barun and, instead of going in the direction of the higher snowfields, crossed the ridge and continued toward the forests of the Kasuwa and Iswa Kholas.

10. The tracks of the creature suggest that the yeti is exceptionally strong and well-adapted to traveling across Himalayan terrain. At several points along its track, it walked directly along the branches and limbs of the rhododendron bushes, using the displacement ability of the vegetation to support its weight above the deepest snows. I have seen, in their tracks, that both snow leopards and bears frequently use this technique.

11. The prints lend credibility to the general theory concerning the yeti. Their resemblance to the numerous footprints previously reported, some of which occurred decades ago and more than a hundred miles from Kongmaa Laa, suggest a uniformity of data strongly indicating the existence of an unknown creature in the Himalayas.

Based on this experience, I believe that there is a creature alive today in the Himalayas which is creating a valid zoological mystery. I do not want to mince words or argue definitions, but I am not saying that I believe in the Abominable Snowman. I am saying that there is a real and unresolved enigma concerning a creature that walked by my tent one night. It is possibly a known species in a deformed or abnormal condition, although the evidence points toward a new form of bipedal primate. Or perhaps an old form — a form that man once knew and competed with, and afterward forced it to seek refuge in the seclusion of the Himalayas.

Even though I am intrigued with the yeti, both for its scientific importance and for what it says about our own interests and biases, I would be deeply saddened to have it discovered. If it were to be found and captured, studied and confined, we might well slay our nightmares. But the mystery and imagination it evokes would also be slain. If the yeti is an old form that we have driven into the mountains, now we would be driving it into the zoos. We would gain another possession, another ragged exhibit in the concrete world of the zoological park, another Latin name to enter on our scientific ledgers. But what about the wild creature that now roams free of man in the forests of the Himalayas? Every time man asserts his mastery over nature, he gains something in knowledge, but loses something in spirit.

CHAPTER NINE

And Every Shepherd Tells His Tale

Man's history can be briefly told:
A few short years of washing gold,
(Or struggling with some other toil),
A wife or two with whom to coil
Upon the floor on chilly nights,
A few quick looks at thrilling sights
Viewed from a lofty mountain peak,
And then Nirvana's peace to seek.

Work, woman, food, a laugh or two,
The catalogue is far from new,
And work's the one that means the most,
Regardless of your rank or post.
'Tis your Nirvana on this earth,
And how you treat it proves your worth.
Know well your task, then onward press
To brilliant failure or success.

— *From the Tibetan*

AS THE EXPEDITION PROGRESSED I realized that of all the
animals and plants in the complex ecosystem of the Arun
Valley perhaps the most important to study was man. Unlike
the other creatures, man fills more than one niche, can be found
in every habitat, and has an unregulated pattern of growth. Man
is often the dominant force that determines the fate of all living
things, including himself. Thus, I began spending as much time
as possible with the local people, trying to learn something of
their habits and of their relationship to the surrounding wildlife.

I interviewed them regularly, not as a prosecuting attorney cross-examining a witness, but as a sympathetic student of their lifestyle. I say this trying to maintain the role of a scientific investigator. In fact, I warmed to them immediately and found great joy in their friendship. The mountains are a large, lonely place.

Among the hill people I came to know best were those of the village of Lumdumsa. Like most villages, Lumdumsa contains several ethnic groups, including Rais and Chetris, but the majority of people call themselves Sherpas; and it is true that many have immigrated from the Solu Khumbu Valley where the term most properly applies. The Lumdumsa and Khumbu Sherpas share the tradition of having originally come from Tibet, and both have the same wild desolate bearing that echoes the harsh wastes of the high plateau.

Lumdumsa was for us an outpost of humanity, being the nearest settlement to our base camp. It had that young, lean, raw look found at the edge of any civilization. The prosperous villages at lower elevations, with their carefully shaped terraces and solid upright houses, were like fatted lambs by comparison. Lumdumsa was composed of scrub and rock, and the makeshift houses were a collection of hand-hewn boards with odd cracks that let the sun in and the smoke out, and the sounds of field sparrows intermingled with the cries of newborn babies.

According to village elders the first homestead was less than 50 years old and the village had never numbered more than 25 separate households. These were spread over the irregular slopes of Kasuwa Khola. Everywhere one looked, the village was conspicuously poor in a pioneering sense and represented the displaced children from kinder, more hospitable places. There was a general feeling of urgency — of the immediacy of the struggle to stay alive. Even the dogs seemed hungrier. They seldom joined in the evening chorus of wails and barking so common at other villages. They preferred to spend their time hunting rodents in the fields or searching for fallen grain beneath the floor boards.

Our primary friends and contacts in Lumdumsa were Pasang Larkba and his family. I first met him during the reconnaissance when we camped in an open field above his house late one evening as the mountains closed in around us. As ever, the inevitable group of children and young women crowded around our camp, a giggling mass of sniffles and smiles. Pasang sud-

Lumdumsa children

denly appeared in the midst of them, sitting on his haunches
with one arm round a young boy and as curious and entertained
as everyone else. His face bore the deep lines of age, some 50
years or more, and yet was young in its expression, as if capable
of all the unrestrained joy and wonder that every other child in
the crowd possessed. He drew my attention specifically because
he did not stand out in that group of children. It is a paradoxical
trait of certain hill villagers that they maintain the aspect of the
young in the body of declining years. They have the faces of
men who live in the present, not busy trying to secure the future
or retrieve the past.

We did not talk and I did not see Pasang again until a month
later, when we negotiated with him about storing some of our
supplies at his house. The expedition needed a place to keep
certain supplies and equipment that would be convenient for
our trips to the lower portion of the Kasuwa. He came to base
camp and wandered among the tents, bemusedly studying our
foreignness until Pema pointed him out to me. I went over to
him and, with Pema translating, tried to explain our requirements and to ask him if he was interested. He was barefoot, and
dressed in a short baggy tunic and a gray grease-spattered down
vest that had come from some previous mountaineering expedition and had obviously seen several owners before him.

Pasang had an infectious way of smiling and would repeatedly
nod his head in agreement even before my questions could be
translated into his language. It was as if the words of the conversation meant little and all that was needed was a mutual
pledge of faith; he would protect and guard our belongings if we
would insure his salary as custodian. I had no idea of how or
exactly where our things were to be stored in Lumdumsa, while
he, I am sure, had no knowledge of how many supplies or how
long they were to be stored. It was enough that we had looked
each other in the eye and that everyone knew an agreement had
been made. He seemed impressed that we should so honor him.

During the course of the expedition Pasang's behavior was ex-
emplary. We did not lose so much as an ounce of rice or a
single spoon from the things we left with him, and there were
many men working for us who did steal. His honesty created in
me a special affection for Pasang. He would speak to me a great
deal more frankly and openly than would other men in our
employment, whose remarks were cautiously worded to inspire

admiration and avoid offending. Pasang was too old to pretend.

I stayed with Pasang whenever my work took me to Lumdumsa. His house was set to one side of the village, near a gully where the eroded rubble of rocks and gravel let only harsh twiggy brush grow. The roof was made of boards and the sides of the house were constructed of crudely woven bamboo mats. Inside, there was one large room with a single partition near the rear to block off an area for storage. Ears of corn containing next year's seeds hung from the rafters, and strips of what appeared to be goat's meat were lying on a mat in a corner. Chamjii, Pasang's wife, kept a low fire going all day in a small pit set along the far wall. There were no windows, so that even during the day the inside was dark and shadowy, providing a kind of privacy in its dimness. Smoke from the fire, captured in the windless space, formed a sooty cloud, and it was uncomfortable to stand for long because your eyes began to weep. On entering the house one was drawn naturally down toward the fire.

I have heard it argued that hill villagers have such smoky houses because of their failure to invent the chimney. But that is too pat an answer and the chimney is too simple a device to be ignored so consistently throughout the hills. I once asked Pasang why they had none, and he told me it was because they liked the smoke. "It feels good," he said, and I wondered what he meant.

Perhaps foreigners are tired of the polluted air of crowded cities and long for the clean skies of the mountains, while the villagers are tiny figures in a vast landscape, longing for signs of their fellow man. Clean air is an abundant commodity of low value to those who live in the Himalayas. Fire is uniquely a human invention, and the smoky interior of a house connotes a man-made environment as nothing else can — shelter, fellowship, safety. The emotion is as important as the reality and the senses have greater power than the intellect.

Pasang became my teacher about many things. I was anxious to learn the language and so communicate directly with the natives, but my own staff, especially Pema, saw it as a threat which would undermine their position as translators and break the bond that tied me to them. Pasang had no such vested interests and criticized my mistakes openly with a peculiar gleeful laugh, turning his back so as not to embarrass me, and in such obvious amusement that I was happy to bring him the pleasure.

He taught me that villagers have no words for "please" or "thank you." They have expressions or phrases that can be used in an elaborate formal sense to express the original meaning of these terms but nothing that corresponds to our glib, constant use in passing salt and pouring tea. My staff had encouraged me to use *dhani bhat* when they saw that I needed such a term, but each time that I used it in Lumdumsa Pasang would start into another fit of laughter. He explained that *dhani bhat* is reserved for the most crucial circumstances, such as following your lifesaving rescue from a river. When he serves rice in his house, he said, it is his position as host that demands him to do so and is a basic responsibility to all and any guests, with no need to depreciate the event with a *thank you*. If I was so set in my manners that I needed a filler of some kind I could use *tik chaa*, a grunting phrase that means "OK" or "fine" or just "hello, I'm still alive."

I also learned from Pasang about some of the complexities of the local language. By comparison, English is a technical language that excels especially in its verbs. The idea of "push," for example, can be expressed by a wealth of words, each conveying a slightly different nuance: *ram, cram, shove, drive, propel, thrust, prod, poke*, et cetera. Such versatility is extremely useful in discussing the exact movements of a machine. The Lumdumsa language has its wealth in a different area. Like many tribal societies, kinship relations are very important, and a *nu* is a father's brother's son while a *changbu* is a mother's brother's daughter. I began taking notes from Pasang about the names of forest vegetation, but was soon overwhelmed not only by the individual terms that applied to almost every species around Lumdumsa, but by the varied terms that applied to the same plant depending on the season, the age of the plant, the condition of its fruit or flowers, and so forth.

As my ability in language developed I found that I became more comfortable in Pasang's presence and somehow blended in better with his household. Perhaps my growing communication skills enabled Pasang to see that I was a rather ordinary man beneath my Western clothes and manners. Or maybe it was just that the strangeness wore off with the passing months. Whatever the reason, I was no longer the center of attention and could learn something of the normal routine that made up their lives.

Pasang's wife ground corn or barley each day in a small stone mill that she turned by hand. Three or four hours of milling were required to produce enough flour for a large meal. The upper stone weighed 40 to 50 pounds and moved slowly against the lower stone, which was slightly larger. It was a tiring, laborious process. Once on a trip north I had seen the water-driven mills of the Kar-Bhotias. These small but efficient structures completely eliminate the need for hand milling and are quickly built with the most basic skills. I asked Pasang why he did not build one for his wife; there was a nearby stream, he certainly had all the knowledge and materials required, and his wife was getting older. He replied, "We have always done it this way and we always will. The water mill is the way of the Kar-Bhotias and this is the way of Lumdumsa Sherpas."

Chamjii, his wife, was listening and nodded in agreement as if my question had been silly. She became my *ama*, or "mother," as I called her during my visits. While Pasang served as host and with grand gestures would offer the first cup of chang, it was Chamjii who prepared the meals, quietly and efficiently, or with a watchful eye filled my cup as it emptied. She was an older woman, it was hard to guess exactly how old, and maintained the traditional dress of a black skirt, colorful embroidery, and always a necklace or two of silver coins. She had a special sense of the importance of simple things and attended to my needs in a way that Pasang, joking and enjoying, never noticed.

After forty years of marriage, Chamjii and Pasang were like two wheels that over the years of turning against each other become a matched pair. They knew each other's habits so well there was little need to talk. Gestures were enough to explain it was time to fetch firewood or prepare the cooking fire. One would hold the bowls while the other served the rice with a speechless precision as if their movements had all been minutely planned in advance. They knew enough of each other not to expect too much or offer too little.

Once, Chamjii told me how their house had burned many years ago. With a sad expression she brought out a small pile of artifacts, twisted lumps of metal that were the only things left by the flames. She pointed out a shiny object that had once been a piece of jewelry given to her by her mother and a tarnished nugget that had once been a silver spoon. She talked to herself as much as to me, using a mumbling, melancholy narration. Pasang sat beside her, quiet and supportive.

One of our visitors was an American microbiologist who stayed with the expedition for a few weeks, and we had occasion to stop at Pasang's house one day, seeking shelter from a rainstorm. Pasang was not there, but Chamjii offered us some tea and a place by the fire. She was busy making rakshi, a distilled liquor made from chang, and had set up the clay pots and metal funnel over the fire to boil off the alcohol from the chang, condense it, and finally collect the potent product. The microbiologist was completely taken aback; he could not quite believe that in this roadless land without wheels, a village woman should have such a technological knowledge about the process of distillation. Chamjii, I am sure, could not quite believe that a Sahib should be so interested in such a simple business as making rakshi.

By chance, Howard and I stopped at Pasang's house on the night of the annual celebration of his father's death. There was to be a large party, with much food and drink, to pay tribute to his father's spirit. Pasang invited us to participate, pointing out that it was an auspicious event, and an important lama from Seduwa village would be coming over to lead the prayers and offerings. Social gatherings in Lumdumsa had a natural exuberance, a sense of fraternity and rejoicing in and because of the presence of others. We were tired but quickly accepted Pasang's invitation.

The first guests arrived just before dark, heralded by a flock of children who suddenly filled the room with lively conversation. Chamjii began making *dhildo*, a mushlike cereal made from millet, and the other women, arriving in several groups, helped her stir the cereal as it cooked or began handing out cups filled with chang that they had brought. By the time the first men arrived it was so dark that they were bearing torches of split bamboo to light the way. All wore their best clothes, and there was much joking and talking.

Chamjii served each guest an enormous bowl of *dhildo*, a huge lumpy glob of paste the size of a melon, which was consumed with obvious relish. People sat down on the floor to eat, crossing their legs beneath them in the Asian manner or squatting on their haunches. The woman across from me propped her bowl of *dhildo* on her pregnant belly and with great deliberation dipped her fingers into the paste to grab a handful which she carefully stuffed into her mouth. She seemed to rock back and forth with delight, finally licking her fingers clean in a thorough way. All concentrated on eating, and a satiated lull pervaded the now crowded room, which was slowly heating up from the warmth of so many bodies in such a small space.

The arrival of the lama changed the tone from a social gathering to a more formal occasion. In truth, he was not a lama in the sense of having received formalized training or of being attached to a monastery. He was really a local *dhami*, a medicine man, who lived in his own home where he combined the life of a farmer with his role as doctor, priest, and perhaps psychiatrist. Lumdumsa villagers preferred to call him a lama, though, as it added to their own prestige.

His clothes and manner set him apart from everyone else. He wore furs and animal skins, with a strange peaked hat on his head. He entered the house slowly, as if he wanted everyone to pay attention to him, and sat down beside a small altar that Pasang had built near the partition. A small boy followed him, carrying a large drum which was then hung from the rafters. Chamjii offered the lama some food, which he refused, and drink, which he accepted, quickly swallowing several bowls of chang. A prayer book was brought out, and while the lama read the boy started pounding the drum, making a throbbing sound like the pulse of the night.

A wild and uncertain feeling came over the gathering. The room was so full that every corner was packed tight, and the faces were lit in flickering animation by the cooking fire. The lama, in a deep rich voice, read the prayers out loud, so that they formed a continuous chanting background which he occasionally interrupted by blowing long wailing notes on a conch shell. Every now and then someone rose and walked over to the altar to make an offering. Some offerings were simple flowers laid beside the candles, and others were the traditional rancid butter and juniper boughs which were burned in shallow dishes. The guests stood for a moment in front of the altar, as if reciting something to themselves, and then bowed down on their knees to pay full tribute. The other people in the room continued their low lively conversation but carefully watched out of the corners of their eyes the process at the altar.

Meanwhile I was getting more and more inebriated from the chang. I began nibbling on some of the *dhildo*, which normally I would never do, as it tastes much like warm ashes and sand. Then suddenly, sometime just past midnight, I realized that the room was quiet. Chamjii, who had been sitting by the fire whis-

A local "lama"

pering among a group of older women, was quivering and slowly shaking back and forth, as though in the throes of a mild convulsion. Everyone stopped and watched her. She started moaning softly and rose to her feet, her eyes closed, and danced about, trembling and wavering, as if entering a trance. Even the lama stopped reading and the boy ceased drumming. After some minutes, Chamjii fell to her knees, prostrating herself before the altar, and screamed once in the loudest possible voice. She buried her face in her hands and was quiet.

I didn't know what to think. At first I assumed she was ill and was ready to rush over to her when I looked around and saw that no one else was moving. Their faces bore expressions of patience and satisfaction, not concern. The whole room was still, as if time itself had stopped. Chamjii started speaking in a high falsetto voice, part singing, part hissing, part calling. She talked to no one in particular. Pasang went over to her and knelt behind her back. He answered her long statements with a sonorous phrase, "Ush ahhh, Ush ahhh, Ush ahhhhhh."

I could not understand what she was saying, for the words were ones I had never heard before. I asked the man sitting next to me and he said she was a *lhawa*, a spirit caller. He gave me a rough translation, explaining that the words of Pasang's father were being spoken through her body. "You who travel through the clouds of night and know my enemies well. Let their fields dry and their houses burn. Run from this place before the dawn strikes and make their chickens sick."

The meanings were varied. She warned of an evil spirit who had lately inhabited a tree near the stream where people daily fetched water. All should be careful not to damage the tree and thereby incur the wrath of the spirit. Later, she spoke of the coming weather and a hardship of landslides which would damage several fields on the northern rim of the village. She talked for about half an hour, and then as quickly as she had entered the trance she bowed her head a final time and became quiet, conscious. Chamjii rose to her feet with a great effort as if exhausted from a heavy load. She went back to tend the fire and acted as if nothing had happened. She looked cold to the touch, like a Himalayan snowfield resting beneath moonlight.

This was the only time that I ever saw Chamjii exercise her psychic powers. I asked her about them later, and she said that they came from her father, who was also gifted as a medium.

She said she was happy to have such powers, for they helped her people against the invisible forces which caused so much affliction and mindless calamity. That night I felt more than ever that the realities of a hill villager are different from our realities. The differences in our worlds go beyond structure and organization. Their ghosts and spirits are quite as real as our atoms and photons, and they play just as important a role in their lives. Their intellectual abilities equal ours but merely encompass a different range of human ideas and experiences.

I stayed on at Pasang's house for the next several days, I guess, because I needed time to understand what had happened that night. Our tents and field gear were at a high-altitude camp, and Howard and I had come down to arrange for new food supplies. We decided that I would wait in Lumdumsa until our rice and salt arrived, while Howard would return to camp and continue working. Normally when I stayed in Lumdumsa I slept in my own tent, but now I had none and Pasang kindly invited me to sleep inside their house.

Himalayan villagers have different sleeping habits from ours. We shelter ourselves away inside sleeping bags or blankets that provide sufficient warmth for the whole night. Pasang and Chamjii could not afford the luxury of such expensive items and so relied on a combination of food, fire, and each other to survive the winter nights. Immediately after the evening meal, Pasang said, they can go to sleep quickly because of the warmth produced by the food in their bodies. As the hours wear on and their bodies cool off, they huddle close together to tap each other's warmth. Every member of the family, and even guests, will lie one next to the other like a litter of kittens. Finally, though, they wake from the cold in those last hours before dawn and so tend to the fire, passing the remaining time half dozing, half sitting up and talking. Their nights have a rhythm which is lost to us in our nylon shells.

The eating habits of the villagers are also different from ours. I discovered that I have rather narrow tastes in food compared to the comprehensive appetites of Pasang and Chamjii. Usually their diet was composed almost exclusively of *dhildo;* they would eat two large meals a day, one around ten o'clock in the morning and again just before retiring in the evening. But when other things were available, any animal or vegetable matter was considered fair game. Wild mushrooms, nettles, plant tubers, goat's blood, bats, beetles, and so on were readily eaten and obviously enjoyed. I remember that one night Pasang ate a partially cooked chicken foot we had discarded in the brush. It was a grisly sight, for the foot had been cut off just above the joint and all that remained were scales and nails. Pasang bit off a toe and then slowly, methodically, chewed up the nail, tendon, and bone before tearing off another digit. It was tough stuff and he had to grind his teeth to chew it up. The sound was enough to cut my appetite for a week.

The villagers have their own kind of medicine. One night at Pasang's house a villager came in complaining of terrible back pains. He refused my offer of Western medicine and sought the advice of Pasang, who examined him for a while by massaging his hands. Pasang then sent for the lama who had been with us the night when Chamjii had gone into her trance. The lama came later in the evening and, after a lengthy conversation but no real physical examination, explained that the villager's pains were caused by a particular bad spirit dwelling in a nearby cliff. Apparently, three years earlier a man had fallen to his death on the cliff and, because he was a poor man, his family had not hired anyone to pray over his body or provide him with a proper burial. The lama said that the spirit of the man still wanders, lingering there at the cliff and displeased by his improper and premature death.

The lama then treated the sick villager in a small ceremony beside the cooking fire. He first held the villager's index finger while saying a quiet prayer and consulting his own personal god to ask which treatment would be appropriate. The lama burned about a tablespoonful of butter and some acrid-smelling herbs which he drew from his waist cloth. This would appease the forest goddess who would then help send away the bad spirit. Next, the lama walked outside with the villager and tossed a few grains of rice out among the bushes. This made the bad cliff spirit come to the surface, the lama said, for such shadows are always hungry — not because they can eat but because they remember having eaten when they were flesh and blood.

A few minutes later, the lama returned to the cooking fire and, gathering a few strands of grass, rubbed them in the ashes of the fire until they were dry and gray colored. Holding the grass in his left hand, the lama stroked the villager's head and body several times with a downward motion while chanting a loud prayer. This was to brush the spirit out of the villager and into the ash-covered grass. The spirit was attracted to the grass because he could remember the warmth and comfort of a fire. The lama tied the grass into a large knot and, screaming at the top of his lungs, threw the knot into the fire, where it immediately burst into flames. The bad spirit was forever destroyed, the lama said, and it would travel with the smoke away from the villager. The next morning the villager reported that his back pains were gone.

Most villagers do not wear shoes, and I have always wondered how they run across the sharp rocks and stone-covered trails without hurting themselves. They develop heavy calluses on their feet, sometimes so thick that they seem to serve as shoe soles. They dislike walking through snow or water for it alternately wets and dries their calluses so that they break open, sometimes in deep cracks extending to the soft tissues, which begin to bleed.

One night during the monsoon Pasang complained of a foot infection. It appeared to be a fungus growth to me, something he had probably picked up from the soggy trails around the sheep herds. I offered him some fungicide, and he quickly took the shiny metal tube of medicine and put it into his pocket. He said the fungus itched terribly, and I could see where the calluses were sloughing off on one side. He treated his foot by taking a hot coal from the fire and holding it directly against the calluses near his toes, literally burning the infected area, and causing a nauseating smoke to rise. Later that night, he also put salt on the infection. He probably kept the fungicide to himself so that he could use it to barter for things he needed more.

Western medicines were greatly appreciated by the villagers, and Howard, as medical officer, gave freely of his spare time to help villagers wherever we went. He came to be known as a good "outside doctor" by the villagers because he could readily stitch up a wound or provide antibiotics to cure an infection. However, when it came to serious internal problems, such as an ulcer or tuberculosis, there was little Howard could do with his limited supplies and during the short time he could stay in any one village. As a result, the villagers preferred their "inside doctors," like the lama, who with ceremonies and natural medicines

tended to the sick and dying. The hill people have an elaborate
medical science that incorporates wild plants, animal parts, and
a variety of techniques that are foreign to the West. I have seen
them effect cures that are truly remarkable and have erased any
skepticism within me about the value of at least some portions
of their science.

I spent much of my time in Lumdumsa talking with Pasang
and others about the wildlife of the Arun. Many villagers are
very accomplished biologists who are familiar with the habits of
most species. For instance, one night I talked with a man about
the breeding of birds, and without prompting he gave an authori-
tative lecture on the manner of bird breeding and the way certain
species time their breeding according to the availability of food
supplies. He pointed out that seed-eating species usually breed
later in the spring so that their young will emerge from the nest
at the height of the seed production, while insect-eating species
often time the emergence of their young with the high point of
insect activity that occurs earlier in the season. He pointed out
the rule's many exceptions and deviations, and in general provided a comprehensive insight into this phenomenon that is well
known among traditionally trained ornithologists.

Pasang once told me about cuckoos and the way they parasit-
ize the nests of other species. His facts were both precise and
accurate. He was even familiar with the specialized behavior
known about some species in which the baby cuckoo, shortly
after hatching, pushes all other eggs out of the nest. This behavior appears to be innate and enables the young baby cuckoo
to survive alone and thus receive all of the food brought by duti-
ful foster parents. Pasang did a marvelous imitation around the
cooking fire, pulling his coat up over his back so that he resembled the awkward body of a baby cuckoo, and then dancing
about and pushing backward against the other men until he had
shoved everyone away from the fire. He loved the story and
dragged it out so that the telling took more than an hour.

On another evening he described a strange encounter he had
with frogs and barbets when he was young. The red light of
dying embers cast soft shadows on his weathered face as he told
of how, during the course of three days, he had seen a large
black frog turn into a barbet. Barbets are squat chunky birds
that on profile do have a peculiar resemblance to frogs. On the
first day, Pasang said, the prominent bump on the back of the

frog slowly became a bill and then the head of the barbet appeared. On the second day, the flesh at the sides fell away, exposing feathers; and finally, on the third day, the bird was free and flew up into a nearby tree. The story was fascinating for me in its parallel to the normal morphogenesis that frogs undergo in changing from tadpoles into adults. Interestingly, Pasang knew of the nests and eggs of most species of barbet in the surrounding area, and yet he also firmly believed this story.

We talked about many of the birds and mammals in the Arun, and I was constantly surprised by the extent of specific knowledge that Pasang and his friends possessed. They had their own names for everything, of course, which took a while for me to decipher. Occasionally, they would confuse two similar-looking species as one species, or they would divide a single species with dimorphic sexes into two species. But in general they were aware of 80 percent of the birds and large mammals that were found in the nearby forests.

Pasang also had an understanding of what was happening to the land itself. He was particularly concerned about the condition of the pastures for his sheep and water buffalo. He said that today the pastures were poor in comparison to the fields when he was young. Rich growths of grass had flourished in the warm sun and monsoon rains, wetting your ankles on a dewy morning's walk. Now there was only a green-brown tinge over the scattered rubble and debris of the hills.

The herds had grown but not as fast as the demand for wool and meat, and each year more and more sheep used the same area. The succulent species of grass were eaten early in the season before they had a chance to ripen and seed. The pastures now contained only the toughest kinds of grass, grasses that the sheep were not fond of and that grew low to the ground, clinging tenaciously to the rubble. These grasses were the only ones that had a chance to seed, but they did not hold the soil well. Each year the streams were brown with the earth that belonged on the pastures. He said that the soil was now so barren that he doubted the good grass would ever grow again.

It made him sad. His face looked tired and his arms hung limply at his sides. He said he was worried because he could only foresee a worsening situation in the years to come. Soon there would not be enough grass for all the sheep. Soon the herds would have to be reduced. There were many young men in Lumdumsa and each wanted to have a large family and own many animals. Last year fighting had broken out at one pasture when two young men had argued over whose sheep would use which area. The rights to use different pastures in the forests and alpine areas were constantly in dispute. How could you control it, he said, when the young men ignored tradition and were desperate to find whatever forage they could for their animals? He did not want the government to intervene. He said he was an old man, as old as the pastures, and like them he would soon die. He said it was not his problem.

Listening to his story I realized that Pasang had a basic understanding of ecology. He knew, perhaps more simply but employing the same concepts that biologists use, that there was a fundamental relationship between the sheep, the grass, and the soil. He was aware of the symbiosis between natural forces and living creatures, and of the pervading influence of man. His story touched on the varied problems of species replacement, nutrient depletion in the soil, and erosion. He saw the difficulty when land, for example, the pastures, was considered to be communal property. Each individual having access to the property will naturally tend to maximize his own share without regard for the rights of the whole group.

Pasang could speak eloquently about such topics. He had a way of cutting through to the gist of the matter and had certainly seen enough of life to know what was really happening. At times, when the evening hours grew late and Chamjii began dozing, we talked about the cultivated fields and how their productivity was declining. Of firewood and how it was getting increasingly hard to find. Or of the young men and how they were getting anxious and hungry. He saw, it seemed to me, that there were great changes taking place in his village and in the land.

Once, and only once, Pasang talked about the village in Khumbu, where he was born, and of the conditions then. He said all the men wore pigtails at that time and the women always wore their traditional dress. There had been much work in the fields, and as a young boy he had gone with the older men of the village on trips to Tibet, where they traded goods. There had been almost no money and few outside wares were available. But everyone had something to eat.

He had left Khumbu in his teens and had come to Lumdumsa

to marry Chamjii, whose family was from this area. He was very upset with the new world of ideas and values that accompanied the rising Sherpa affluence — the product of expedition salaries and the mountaineering business. On the one hand, Pasang enjoys the new clothes, aluminum cooking pots, and little things that he can buy for Chamjii with the money that the expedition gives him for storing our supplies. But he also mourns the passing of the old ways. Few men wear pigtails anymore. The young men crop their hair because they feel it is more acceptable to the Sahibs and the government officials in the valley.

I believe that mountain people, isolated in their high valleys, gather much of their strength and the qualities we so admire from their sense of community. Perhaps more than lowlanders, they are sensitive to cultural changes and know that a new aluminum cooking pot costs more than "X" number of rupees. It costs a tradition of homemade earthen pots that had the personality, and thus the reminder, of who and what they are and where they come from. Mountain people are accustomed to harsh periods and changing conditions, but these new changes are of a different kind. Pasang said that he could easily do without the aluminum cooking pots.

Through Pasang I met two men in Lumdumsa who became invaluable friends and left an indelible impression on my mind. The first was Thorbu, my prized porter. I hired him whenever he was free and after getting to know him seldom went on a trip without his aid. His chief attribute was his incredible strength, willingly and readily given to all endeavors. He was tall for a hill villager, some four to five inches above the other porters, and he could regularly carry almost twice as much as any other man. At most, I would guess that he weighed 160 pounds, but he could lift several hundred pounds with ease and would carry on his back a load of 260 pounds for an entire day. On one occasion, while working some distance from any village, I needed to move camp in a hurry but could find no porters to help. Thorbu somehow managed to carry four loads all by himself that day; I'll never understand how.

Thorbu also had his affection for vices that in his enthusiasm he made seem the key to his strength. He loved women, of all kinds, tribes, sizes, and dispositions. Wherever we went he would be the first to discover a lonesome miss. And his affairs were conducted in such a charming and inoffensive manner that they never harmed the reputation of either Thorbu or the expedition. His ability to drink was also phenomenal. Few would dare keep up with his pace and none seemed able to consume more. He would disappear from camp most evenings and the early hours of the morning would find him staggering back, singing loudly and completely dissipated. Yet, by breakfast he would be bright and sober and ready to do whatever we asked of him. He became so much my favorite that I taught him special skills so that I could keep him on in camp even when we didn't need porters to carry loads. He was my insurance policy against the mountains and whatever fickle weather or disastrous floods they might produce.

Thorbu was, frankly, fearless. Crossing bridges, clinging to narrow trails, climbing a rotten tree to examine a bird's nest were his fortes. Whenever we had to cross the main bridge at Paksinda he would end up carrying the loads of those porters who refused to risk the swaying bamboo. Once, a porter started carrying a load over the bridge, but halfway across his knees suddenly gave out and he stumbled, dropping his load so that it caught in the side bracing of the bridge. Thorbu climbed out by holding onto the bridge upside down and finally managed to untie the straps holding the man to the load. The man hurried across to the other side while Thorbu heaved the load up onto his back and, struggling, pulled and dragged it the rest of the way across. That load contained my mist nets and was so close to dropping into the river and washing away my hopes for spring research that I felt forever in Thorbu's debt.

Throughout the spring and summer of 1973 he was with me and when I left him at Tumlingtar that fall for a brief vacation in Kathmandu I asked him to meet me again in a few weeks. I remember his standing at the corner of the airstrip gleefully eyeing a local Rais girl and strutting about with his pockets full of expedition rupees. When I returned after three weeks he wasn't there, but I attached little importance to it — out of sight, out of mind. He had gone back to Lumdumsa, they said, to see his family and relatives. I did not see him again until a week later when I had almost reached base camp. He came round a bend of the trail, crouched over and withered, like a cripple.

While I was gone Thorbu had received a terrible injury. He

had gotten into a heated argument with a relative who, they told me, was jealous of the amount of money Thorbu was making with the expedition. The night after the argument the relative had come again to Thorbu's house to pursue his anger. He found Thorbu drunk after a long bout with chang; Thorbu was staggering and helpless. The relative started hitting Thorbu with his fists and Thorbu tried to fight back but fell to his knees. The relative then took one of the large kukris that they use for slaughtering sheep — its blade more than two feet long — and struck twice while Thorbu was lying on the ground. The first blow landed on Thorbu's back, cutting a savage gash across the shoulder bone, severing the muscles, and extending from near the top of his shoulder down to below the middle of his back. The second blow landed on the side of Thorbu's head, slicing his ear in two, and cutting open the cheek to expose the inside of the mouth.

Thorbu's friends, desperate to stop the bleeding and save his life, had bound the wounds up with cloth and used the local practice of covering the bandage with rodent feces. The nearest doctor was in Dhankuta, almost six days away, but eight men managed to carry him, like a giant bag of rice, in only four days and five nights. They rotated the load, each man carrying him for an hour or so, and the others running alongside. Still, by the time the doctor saw him the wounds were too old to be properly sutured. The doctor cleaned the exposed wounds, gave him some antibiotics, and sent him back home. Despite the blood he had lost, Thorbu was able to walk the last half of the trip.

Once a very handsome man, Thorbu's wounds greatly disfigured his face. The hearing in the injured ear was destroyed and the wound on his face did not close properly. A small duct drained from his mouth to the outside so that the salivary gland secreted its juices through the cheek. Whenever he ate, drank, or smoked a cigarette, he had to hold a rag against the side of his face to catch the flowing salivary juices. He would wring out the rag after each meal. His wounded shoulder hung noticeably lower than the other, and when I met him he was still suffering greatly from infection. I gave him more antibiotics to break the fever. For a long time, he wore a scarf across his face so that others would not stare.

His disposition was, of course, changed. Much of his old cheerfulness was gone, and the daily discomfort from his wounds produced a constant grimace. He was tired from the pain, and yet he remained optimistic about being able to work again. He promised that soon he would be able to carry a heavy load, perhaps not as much as he had once carried, but at least a standard expedition weight. He bore a grudge against his relative and swore in a quiet way that he would murder the man if they should ever meet. The police had taken the relative into custody for a while, but rumors said that the man had paid a bribe and was now living in a distant district.

A few months later I happened to look into Thorbu's eyes and saw that his view of life was different from mine. It was more than a Buddhist belief in reincarnation and the irrevocability of karma. He had taken the injury, like a heavy load, as his lot in life and was neither disappointed nor disillusioned.

Pasang brought Urkan to me and recommended him so highly that I hired Urkan to work in the kitchen and help Pema. I liked Urkan immediately because he was eager, quick to learn, and still young enough to be relatively malleable. He did not have Pema's developed tastes. Indeed, Urkan was only 17 years of age and his mind seemed open to all possibilities. He was not the shy inexperienced type but rather had the boldness of an "I can do anything" philosophy. He was careful in his manner to avoid mistakes, and when he did ruin a pot of soup by leaving the cover off so that it tasted of ashes he would apologize so sincerely that I had to excuse it. A pot of soup was a small price to pay for the attentive and enthusiastic assistance of so willing a worker.

Because this was his first expedition he had much to learn and followed the Sahibs around, anxious to digest any information that might further his position. I often assumed the role of his teacher and taught him how to pitch a tent and make his first leavened bread. At the beginning he was merely a kitchen helper relegated to washing dishes and serving coffee, but as I came to rely more and more on Pema's help with the ornithological research, Urkan slowly assumed complete charge of the kitchen. He learned how to cook most of the standard Sahib trail dishes, how to choose and set up a correct camp, and how to organize the porters.

Like Pema, he had the ability to watch the proper procedure for doing something once and thereafter to imitate it to perfection. Also like Pema, he seemed more intelligent than the other porters or Sherpas. But it was a curious kind of intelligence. He would carry out the most complicated tasks, such as setting up the meteorological instruments, without ever understanding the reasons for doing certain things in certain ways. It was not curious that he did not understand Western meteorology, but it was curious that he would not ask, as if there was a limit to how much he wanted to know of the Sahib's ways.

There came a time when I realized that he was teaching me more than I was teaching him. His inventiveness saw solutions to problems that were beyond me. He devised a way of packing the tents so that the poles would not bend, fashioned a small oven out of plates that baked the bread better, and managed to pack the loads so that the jars of jam and peanut butter did not break. He did not pretend to know better but simply did things in so obviously superior a way that I felt foolish making any recommendations after a while and left him to run the kitchen however he might want.

I visited his home in Lumdumsa once and discovered that he was indeed wiser in some things than I. Although ten years younger than I, he was already married, had two children, had built his own house, and had successfully cultivated his crops for several years. While my birthright had given me the opportunity to explore the world and know things and places he would never see, I felt terribly young in contrast to Urkan, naïve in the most worldly way. He had already achieved the real goals of human existence — home, family, food. I might be able to identify birds with expertise, but I was hopelessly young in real terms. Being a Sahib has an artificial quality, a fragile emptiness, in comparison to being a young porter who earns his money with his back and then runs home to sleep with his wife.

I remember making our last trip down. Howard and I had been working in the high-altitude areas between the Barun and Iswa throughout the late fall, and in the final week of December we started the long trek out for Tumlingtar, Kathmandu, and America. We were exhausted from our work and the isolation had grown over the months until we were slightly dizzy. Lumdumsa would be our first contact with the world, and there we would find our mail and learn of events at home. Lumdumsa offered a few days of hospitality, with fresh faces and new foods.

On that day we carried ice axes and light packs so that we

could race along ahead of the porters. The trail led over Kong-maa Laa, then followed the narrow ridge between the Kasuwa and Iswa, to finally wind through the heavy forest and emerge at Lumdumsa. As we descended, jumping from stone to stone, taking long sweeping strides along the flat sections, and using the power of gravity to pull us homeward, we passed through increasingly familiar places. The memories sparked a quicker pace. Here was the stream that had served as the first friendly landmark after an afternoon of wandering lost in a heavy mist; the water tasted better for the memory. Here was the forest, cold and damp as usual, hidden from the sun; but it meant that we were less than three hours from the village. The last knoll above Lumdumsa was the steepest, and we abandoned the traditional cutbacks, caring less about our knees than our stomachs, and leaped down the slope like mating frogs.

The first sight of Lumdumsa — homes, fields, people — was unbelievably wonderful. What a difference from our initial re-action during the early civilized days of the expedition, when it appeared such a sorry place! We headed straight for Pasang's house and, finally admitting the weariness in our legs, we slowed down to relish the last minutes. We stumbled awkwardly on swollen knees but still tried to hold our heads high so we could make a proper entrance. Let a man assume the title of Sahib, and he immediately exhibits the worst in human vanity, vacil-lating between the cartoon emotions of demanding authority for his rank or begging sympathy for his dubious heroics. Even the villagers like to play the game, though, and Pasang greeted us with an outrageous and obviously make-believe look of pity and concern. Ah, we were home for the night and wallowed in the luxury of it all.

Howard and I sat on the earthen wall of the terrace above Pasang's house, slowly untying our boots and leaning back against our packs to breathe the humid smell of farmlands and domestic animals. Clouds formed along the far Topke ridge, shattering the evening light into rays and raising a wind that raced in odd angles across the slope. Around us stretched the patchwork ap-pearance of scrub and fields where Pasang was wrestling his meager living from the land. Suddenly he appeared with two bowls of chang. We asked him about our mail and he ran back inside to bring two bulky canvas bags.

We opened them in a leisurely way, dividing up the letters,

Lumdumsa

telegrams, a few small packages, and almost four months of old issues of a popular American news magazine. We had been away a long time. We slowly sorted, or rather fondled, our respective mail, but soon a group of children came around to gape at the breathless, disheveled Sahibs. Such a large group was too much for me right then, and I feigned the need to relieve myself, in hope of some privacy. With exaggerated motions I walked away from the crowd toward a small gully. Fortunately no one followed me, with the exception of a hungry dog anticipating his favorite meal, and I found a small platform on the top of a ledge to read my mail.

News from home was the typical entertaining chitchat of events and happenings that were so real I could almost touch them and yet were impossibly distant in time and space. Picking up the first of the news magazines, I read about the crisis of an oil shortage, the threatened world economy, and the austerity measures being adopted to conserve the dwindling supply of the world's petroleum. Sitting there, perched on top of a Himalayan ridge, the idea of an oil embargo was as strange as anything I could possibly imagine.

It seemed incredible that there was another world out there with problems and aspirations that were so different from those of this Sherpa village. There was no oil shortage here, indeed, not more than a few gallons of kerosene could be found in the whole village, and that was a luxury reserved for the prestigious use of lamps. Pictures of oil tankers, Arab sheiks, idle factories, offered the greatest possible contrast to the plunging slopes around me where a few rock and wood houses sent up puffs of smoke indicating rice cooking, people talking.

Lumdumsa was as untouched by an oil embargo as Mars would be, as real as the birth of a child or a full belly beside a warm fire. Lumdumsa was not affected in even the most minor way by whatever might happen out there. I felt comforted and sensed a kind of independence in Lumdumsa that was the basic root for humanity. The people of Lumdumsa had their own place in the sun, and it was of their own making. If something frightful should happen, a nuclear war or the reciprocating effects of mindless pollution, these people at least would endure and survive. They would hardly notice the fall of the skyscrapers and the weeding over of the superhighways. They, like the mountains, had no vested interests in our world.

It then seemed to hurt, in a biting kind of way, to realize that they too were vulnerable. One expects skyscrapers to fall — it is implicit in their construction. They will be replaced when obsolete or forgotten if our inventions should fail us. But we have always counted on there being people like Pasang to begin again, and now, even Lumdumsa was showing signs of falling. Their place in the sun was getting drier and drier as they dug deeper into the soil.

CHAPTER TEN

A Place in the Sun

God will be pleased if people keep things beautiful.
— *The High Lama of*
Thyangboche Monastery

WHILE ONE PART OF THE WORLD calculates the cost of a reusable space shuttle, another part wonders whether there will be enough food to feed its people in the morning. During my stay in Nepal, evidence accumulated to indicate that a major ecological disaster is looming over the Himalayas.

"If the present trend continues unabated," S. J. Rana, a Nepalese authority on development, warns, "the degradation of the mountain environment may eventually cause irreversible damage to the mountain ecosystem of Nepal."

A Swiss observer, A. Schild, explains, "The general assumption is that the ecological balance is deteriorating, that the fast increasing demand for all basic resources can less and less be met from local resources, or in other words: The development of the hills is largely a negative one."

A United Nations FAO advisor, R. Finder, states emphatically, "A critical point has now been reached where more agricultural land is being lost to erosion than can be gained by the opening up of fresh land. If something drastic isn't done, this whole country will wash away in another generation."

"As a result of centuries of overuse, and now misuse," Mervin Stevens, a FAO expert on soil and water conservation, concludes, "square kilometers of land are being turned to desert."

A few years ago such prophecies of disaster would have been labeled irresponsible and inaccurate, but today a growing majority in Kathmandu recognizes that something is desperately wrong in the hills. Reports are filtering in from all sectors suggesting that a serious environmental problem threatens not just the welfare of the animals and forests, not the mere economic development of the people, but the fate of the nation itself. It is a problem of such magnitude that precise measurements of its dimensions are impossible. It is a problem of such scope that it promises to affect the lives of all Nepalese, from the poorest farmer to the richest merchant. It is a problem which endangers the very survival of man in the Himalayas.

The symptoms of the problem must already be familiar to the reader: massive deforestation throughout the lower hills; widespread erosion on denuded slopes and frequent landslides in heavily abused areas; a large human population dependant on agriculture and still practicing primitive techniques of planting and harvesting; an excessive number of domestic animals that are overgrazing pastures and competing with a dwindling number of wild herbivores; unpredictable and radical changes in the natural composition of the fauna and flora; and so on through a hundred minor examples. But symptoms do not describe the nature of a disease any more than the motion of an airplane explains the principles of flight.

The feverish alarm spreading through Kathmandu is based on a broader understanding. This illness has its roots in the most basic relationships between man and his environment. The diagnosis is most frightening because it is the land itself that is afflicted. Like a hidden cancer that grows unseen for years finally to erupt and devastate the patient overnight, this cancer of the land has grown imperceptibly through the centuries.

Prior to man the hills were, of course, completely forested. It is easy to imagine what the original landscape looked like. A broad expanse of mixed forests and grasslands, sliced here and there by shimmering rivers, spread across the flatlands of the Terai. Verdant hills climbed through a constantly changing green terrain; each ridge, each slope, was covered with dense stands of oak, laurel, castanopsis, or pine. Even the icy peaks emerged from shoulders of fir and rhododendron.

A natural balance had been worked out between the climate, the topography, and the forests. Into this equation were calculated the moisture-laden winds of the monsoon, striking the highest wall of mountains in the world to cause precipitation levels of unbelievable proportions. One factor of the equation weighed the intense erosional processes of weather against the tectonic forces of the growing mountains. Another factor balanced the organic processes of the forests to manufacture soil, resist erosion, and provide a fertile living place for diverse wildlife. It was an equation which occasionally accepted imbalances — a sudden landslide or sporadic flooding — but in general there was a basic pattern of stability.

The first farmers of Nepal doubtless practiced slash-and-burn, or swidden, agriculture. Swidden agriculture is not in itself damaging to the environment when conducted by small populations, and indeed, was self-limiting in that it would support only a meager number of families. A plot of living vegetation was cut during the beginning of the dry season; the tops of the trees were lopped and the lower branches were cut so that the foliage would dry as the season progressed. Then, just before the coming of the monsoon, the field was burned by lighting the dry foliage, effectively clearing the land. Crops were planted for two or three years, but the fertility of the shallow mountain soil quickly declined so that the field had to be allowed to lie fallow for at least ten years to enable the regrowing secondary vegetation to replenish the soil. The cycle was repeated as farmers were forced to move constantly from one slope to another, seeking fresh soil. They would revisit previously used areas only after a suitable fallowing period. A new environmental balance was reached between the consumptive uses by man and the natural regeneration of the soil by wild vegetation.

Later, the swidden farmers discovered that through terracing, rotation of crops, and especially wet-rice cultivation, they could increase the productivity of a plot of land and use a single plot for extended periods. These innovations in agriculture spread north from their centers of origin in India and Southeast Asia and caused a revolution in the environmental balance of the hills.

Terracing on the steep slopes required enormous inputs of human labor, but once a flat piece of land was constructed the farmers could use the more efficient technology of plows and harrowing devices drawn by domestic animals. More important, the terraces created a natural system of dikes and retaining walls that trapped the monsoon rainfall for wet-rice cultivation. Wet

Most terraced fields are designed for wet-rice cultivation and consist of a small platform surrounded by a tall earthen retaining wall

Unfortunately, such terraces are subject to erosion and are often swept down the slopes by the heavy monsoon rains

rice thrives when partially submerged in water and has almost twice the productivity of dry-rice cultivation. When the silt-carrying waters are retained, their nutrients and organic matter settle out to refertilize the soil. Careful rotation of different crops enabled a regular progression of productivity. The use of domestic animals provided manure to further fertilize the soil. For the first time, the hill people could establish permanent settlements around selected plots of land. Forests were cleared and terraces spread across the lower hills as bazaars and villages flourished.

For a while, quite a long while, the economy of the hills prospered. The population expanded rapidly as the farmers found that they had a surplus of food. Immigration from neighboring countries occurred in increasing numbers. Cottage industries, such as weaving, leather tanning, mining, wood carving, and paper manufacturing, developed as the resources of the land were made available to the people. The herds of domestic animals multiplied as the forests were turned to pastures. The cultural and religious values of the hill societies matured as the people found the wealth to build temples, support a priesthood, and devote energies to community projects. A land ethic evolved predicated on each village's protecting its territorial rights to surrounding forests and land. Agricultural practices became ritualized as social customs. For generations, the people enjoyed a rich harvest from the land.

But this new environmental equation was unbalanced by the demands of a constantly expanding society, and it was unavoidable that the population levels would eventually catch up with the carrying capacity of the land. At the turn of the century, the population of Nepal hovered around 3 to 5 million people. By 1950, it had soared to some 9 million, and then within the span of a brief twenty-five years increased to over 12 million. The technology of wet-rice cultivation and terracing, despite its earlier success, was now hopelessly inadequate to support such a huge population. The economy of the land began to falter as the people made impossible demands on its resources. The hill farmers began encountering the basic limits of the land to provide.

After all, there was a fixed amount of land to begin with. The bulk of the mountains consists of snowbound wastelands, precipitous slopes, or flood-ravaged riverbeds that are beyond the realm of practical use. In the Arun Valley, for example, all land above 7000 feet is unsuitable for agriculture since the dense monsoon clouds do not permit the passage of sufficient sunlight for healthy crops. The deep V-shaped valleys, a natural product of the forces of mountain building, make the terrain too steep to cultivate along most rivers. The only productive land lies in a narrow band along the middle levels of the slopes. Only 14 percent of Nepal's total land area consists of arable land, whereas by contrast, India enjoys over 50 percent and Bangladesh over 60 percent arable land. At present, Nepal has one of the highest man-to-land ratios in South Asia — almost nine people are forced to subsist on each hectare of arable land.

In addition, the hill farmers discovered that there were special problems caused by the steep terrain. The technology of wet-rice cultivation was better adapted to its place of origin, in the plains. The canals which channeled water to the rice terraces formed natural routes for gully erosion on the angled slopes. Terracing as adapted to growing other crops had similar hidden dangers; the maize terraces, for instance, were constructed without a raised bund and generally inclined outward to prevent water retention — a necessary condition for high maize yields but also a prime condition for excessive sheet erosion. And no matter how hard the hill farmers worked the mountain soil it would never be as fertile or as rich as the deep alluvial soil of the plains. A depressingly large amount of good land was destroyed, its nutrients leached out, and its soil washed downhill by the monsoon rains.

The hill farmers began fighting a losing battle with soil erosion. A healthy forest provides a layer of leaves and other organic matter to produce a relatively porous soil. Such soil can accept heavy downpours since it has a high infiltration rate and readily absorbs rainfall. Aided by a covering of protective vegetation, it has a correspondingly low run-off rate. But when the hill farmers began clearing the forests permanently to construct terraces and pastures, the land suffered the direct abuse of the monsoon.

The denuded soil quickly becomes compacted. The high kinetic energy of raindrops falling on naked ground breaks up the soil and carries it away down the slope. Exposed to the sun, the bare soil overheats and then drys out, causing a further destruction of organic matter and again reducing the ability of the soil to hold water while increasing the evaporation of moisture.

Increased run-off produces increased erosion. It has been estimated that if heavy rains double the water flow, scouring capacity is increased four times, carrying capacity thirty-two times, and the size of the particle carried sixty-four times.

In a conservative survey of the Arun Valley it appears that

over 20 percent of the land once devoted to productive pastures and terraces now lies barren and infertile because of erosion.

The secondary effects are as bad, if not worse. The increased run-off of rainfall will temporarily exceed the capacity of downstream riverbeds and cause flooding; much good land along the river in the lower part of the valley has been swept away by recent floods. Excessive erosion can also reduce the support for slopes and cause landslides; entire villages have been forced to relocate when their agricultural fields were destroyed by a single disastrous landslide. Finally, the absence of infiltration into the soil depletes the ground water and leads to a drying up of springs. In many places, such springs are an important source of drinking water and mandatory if villages are to be built high on the slopes where there are better soils for cultivation. Soil erosion has become the most pressing problem for the hills, surpassing all other concerns in its importance to the future survival of the people.

But there are other concerns. Traditionally, all the fuel needs of the hill people were met by firewood, with no alternative sources, such as peat or coal, which are commonly found in other parts of the world. Because of the rugged terrain hindering the transportation of any goods in large quantities, each village was forced to supply its own source of firewood. Acquiring sufficient firewood was little trouble in the days when forests dominated the landscape; later, as the forests were cleared for fields, most villages designated a specific woodlot located nearby as a convenient source of fuel.

Unfortunately, the villagers adopted rather wasteful techniques of wood consumption during the days of forest abundance. As long ago as 1931, one observer noted that the average hill family consumed one whole tree trunk annually solely for construction; massive timbers were used around windows and doorways and for roof construction. A recent survey indicates that in the eastern hills about 70 cubic meters of valuable wood is logged per house per year, although less than 20 cubic meters would suffice if properly utilized. This rapid consumption, combined with the expanding demands for heating and cooking fuel, has resulted in a serious depletion of all village woodlots. But when the villagers look for new sources of firewood they discover that because of the widespread clearing for fields and pastures the nearest forests are several hours' walk away.

Today, many villagers are forced to devote inordinate amounts of time to collecting and gathering firewood. Much wasteful construction has stopped, and now almost 90 percent of wood extraction from the forests is directly for firewood, but the demand for firewood has grown with the population and there is tremendous pressure on all reserves. Ten years ago it might have taken an hour or two to gather sufficient firewood for a day's use, but now most families are forced to spend eight hours or more scavenging for a similar quantity. In essence, one member of each household must spend full time seeking fuel.

Firewood has ceased to be a renewable resource and is being cut at a rate that surpasses any possibility for regeneration; the shortage of firewood is becoming a crisis for the villagers as desperate as the shortage of arable land. Some authorities suggest that at the present rate of forest consumption Nepal will be totally denuded by the turn of the century. What happens then doesn't matter — all the rice in the world is useless if it can't be cooked.

The herds of domestic animals provide a third factor in the environmental degradation of the hills. Livestock has always been a prized possession. Cows were kept for their symbolic reasons in the Hindu religion; sheep and goats were used for certain religious practices. Water buffalo were an important source of milk and proteins and, like oxen, useful for the cultivation of the soil. Sheep and yak provided wool for the production of cloth. Various animals, large and small, were used to help carry goods across the mountain trails. Perhaps more important, manure from all animals was an invaluable source of fertilizer, and the development of large herds was one of the few ways of capital investment in a bartering economy.

The breeds of domestic animals found in the hills were inferior to normal standards. They represented low productivity compared to the amount they ate, but this was of little consequence when the resources of land and forests were plentiful. Widespread areas of forests were clear-cut to make pastures. Much standing forest was grazed indiscriminately, and fire was frequently used to promote the growth of grass. Leaves and twigs were lopped from trees in woodlots to provide fodder. During the dry season, the livestock ate stubble and weeds off the terraces. In general, most farmers did little to assist their animals beyond herding them from one pasture to the next; the cultivation of pasture or fodder specifically for the animals was never

practiced, because an abundance of vegetation seemed readily available.

But now the livestock compete with man for dwindling natural resources; as herbivores, they represent a higher level in the food chain than vegetable crops and thus a less efficient use of land. The lopping of trees to gather fodder disrupts the regeneration processes of the forest. Forest fires, purposely set to promote grass, rage out of control to burn innocent land. The use of stubble and agricultural by-products for fodder removes organic matter that should stay in the fields. The increased cutting of forests for fodder means that firewood is harder and harder to find, in turn causing the very dangerous practice of using animal dung for fuel, which further deprives the soil of valuable nutrients. All arable land is needed just to produce human food; the increasing cultivation of wheat during the winter reduces the grazing area formerly available to cattle, making forest grazing even more prevalent. Land of higher elevation that is unsuited for agriculture is used for pastures, but the extensive overgrazing there destroys the watershed for lower-elevation cultivated fields.

At present the number of domestic animals far exceeds the capacity of the hills to support them. Not only must the land provide for over 12 million people, but, according to a recent census, it must also provide for over 10 million cattle and buffalo, 4 million sheep and goats, 18 million poultry, and some 320,000 pigs. Many animals are seriously undernourished, and their reproductive rate is declining as newborns starve to death. The lack of a proper diet reduces the ability of the animals to ward off illnesses, and epidemics are becoming common among the herds. It seems obvious that a hundred emaciated and ailing animals are inferior to even ten healthy ones, and yet the hill people persist in maintaining large herds for cultural and religious reasons. As with the problems associated with firewood and wet-rice cultivation, the people long ago adopted rather wasteful land-use habits and seem incapable of altering their behavior.

In a chain reaction, the problems compound themselves. Each field is used for more and more crops, despite the diminishing returns. To increase productivity, the farmers dig deeper and deeper into the soil, increasing the exposure to erosion. The people must look to higher elevations for new land, which, by virtue of its climate and slope, is less productive. Areas of increasingly marginal quality are used — remaining forest tracts,

A village of the upper Arun; notice the extensive forest clearing above the village and the prominent erosion scars

crests of ridges, rocky gullies, and the sheerest slopes. The farmers revert to swidden agriculture on such land, but the initial yield is poor, so the proper fallowing period is eliminated, and the land is destroyed in the desperate search for food. When the forests are cut for firewood and fodder, the quality of the watershed diminishes along with the future productivity of the land. A dangerous spiral of tragedy is setting in — as the demand grows, the labor per yield increases, but the total per capita yield decreases.

Obviously the population pressure is the accelerator that is driving the spiral downward. The manner of population growth dictates an increasing proportion of young families who, like their parents, demand the traditional rewards of homes and children. Parents who raised their children successfully on a limited plot of land must now divide that same land among their children and expect each child to raise a family on this even smaller share. The children must either use intensive methods of cultivation which permanently damage the land or seek new lands elsewhere. The society is composed of more and more transient people who have little regard for appropriate conservation steps to preserve land. Short-term planning becomes the overwhelming concern as people fight for even tomorrow's meal.

The Nepalese have a lengthy tradition of seasonal migration. The hill people have gone abroad since at least 1861, when they fought with the British as mercenaries. Young Nepalese men were present on many battlefields during both World Wars. Most hill families have a practice of sending some members of the household to the lowland bazaars each year to acquire special supplies, such as salt and brassware. But now, many people are taking extended leaves for two, five, or even ten years at a time to earn cash. In part, this is a result of the increased use of money instead of barter in commerce. In part, this is because of increasing indebtedness incurred by the return to subsistence-level economy. Many now find themselves encumbered with debts caused by sickness, marriage compensations, and socially important ceremonies. They must go abroad to find the cash to pay back profiteering money lenders.

Since the 1950s, however, there has also been a major increase in permanent migration. Many people are now abandoning their homeland solely to find sufficient arable land. In 1951, less than 4 percent of the population left their homes to settle elsewhere;

by 1961, the rate rose to almost 6 percent, and at present over 10 percent of the hill people leave the mountains to find a new living. In some areas of the hills, including portions of the Arun Valley, more than half of the migration is directly the result of landslides. Some people go abroad to India, Bhutan, and Sikkim; others move about within Nepal.

Most migrating families look to the Terai for new land within their own country. The forests of the Terai remained largely untouched prior to 1925; there followed a brief period of sporadic cutting for the Indian timber market, but the prevalence of malaria protected the Terai forests from widespread use. When this disease was eradicated in the early 50s, the government attempted to organize a program of gradual settlement but quickly found itself overwhelmed by a flood of desperate families.

The relatively empty Terai offered fertile flat land, convenient transportation, and the prospect of industry. From 1964 to 1974, government officials distributed 77,700 hectares to settlers, but more than three times that amount was illegally cleared by migrants. The FAO estimates that over 36,000 hectares of Terai forests are cleared annually through squatting, and, at the present rate of cutting, all arable land will be occupied in little more than a decade. While the Terai has helped alleviate the population pressure in the hills temporarily, the end is in sight and officials wonder what migrating families will do in the future. Neighboring countries are experiencing a similar shortage of land, and soon there will be nowhere for transient families to go.

One grave indication of the trouble in the hills is the disappearance of many of the cottage industries. Most are dependant in some way on the forests or the fertility of the land for raw materials, and they cause, in themselves, a depletion of resources. Wood carving is disappearing as high-quality wood becomes scarce. Leather tanning requires the bark of certain trees that are also in short supply. Iron and copper mining, once a major activity of the Hedangna people in the Arun, is now virtually stopped due to a shortage of firewood for processing the ore. Similarly, blacksmithing is becoming increasingly difficult as firewood must be reserved for cooking. Cotton was once grown in many regions, but now all land is required for the cultivation of edible crops. The weaving of wool declines as the shortage of raw wool grows and the firewood required for dyeing the wool is no longer available. These cottage industries once provided

The villagers are forced to clear new forests to find agricultural land, but such areas usually have poor soils

an invaluable source of additional income for the hill people, and their disappearance puts a further burden on the people.

An even more frightening indication of trouble in the hills is the effect on the lands downstream of the environmental destruction in the mountains. Historically, the rivers of the Ganges plain have a pattern of alternating floods and droughts caused by natural fluctuations of the weather. But recently, these fluctuations have become erratic, and the cycles are increasing in frequency and magnitude. There is strong evidence to suggest that these changes result directly from the ecological degradation of the hills.

The massive erosion in the Himalayas, together with the incredible scouring effects of its streams and rivers, produces sand and silt in huge quantities, which is transported to the Gangetic plains. The Karnali in west Nepal, for example, shifts some 75 million cubic meters of solid material each year; this is equivalent to a 1.7-millimeter layer for the entire catchment area. This sand and silt, when deposited by the mountain torrents along the rivers of the plains, increases the height of the riverbeds there; this leads to flooding as well as to quite considerable shifts in the course of the river. The Kosi, into which the Arun River flows, has shifted its course over 85 kilometers within recent times, leaving behind an extensive area of once-fertile flat land buried under a mass of sand and debris. In the process, India estimates that almost 6 million people have been displaced from their original homes.

The implications are clear. For Nepal: Her soil is being washed away at a deadly rate and along with it the basis for life of her agriculturally dependant people. For India: Her watershed in the Himalayas is being destroyed and she must suffer the abuse of increasingly temperamental rivers in a country already plagued with other problems. The Himalayas are the major determinant in the weather system of the subcontinent and the principal watershed for the northern half of India, Pakistan, and Bangladesh. To tamper with their ecology is to tamper with the well-being of not only the 10 to 20 million people who live in their rugged arms, but also the very survival of the several hundred million people who dwell at their base.

And what is the future outlook? Nepal's population is growing at the annual rate of 2.2 percent. In real terms, this means that each year another 250,000 people are added to the population —

approximately half the total number of people now dwelling in Kathmandu, Nepal's capital and largest population center. If this geometric progression is continued, and the obvious limits of food and space are ignored, the population of Nepal would reach a ridiculous figure of 27 million people by the year 2000, more than twice the present number.

Meanwhile, the average life expectancy is still only 26 years. With only 350 doctors in the entire nation, Nepal continues to suffer from one of the highest infant mortality rates in the world; one out of every three babies born in the mountains dies before its first birthday. Per capita income is the equivalent of less than $90 per year. While the population grows at over two percent, food production grows at only one percent. While the population grows at over two percent, the forests are disappearing at the official rate of over two percent. The unofficial, and probably more accurate, rate is over eight percent. Obviously, the nation, like its environment, is deteriorating.

Nepal's dream of becoming an electricity exporter to India is slowly fading as her watershed disintegrates. Erosion has grown to the point where, if the rivers were ever dammed to trap their hydroelectric power, sedimentation would rapidly destroy the usefulness of such dams.

Tourism, at present a major earner of foreign exchange, is in jeopardy. When Nepal first opened her doors to the outside world in 1950, the number of foreign visitors was limited to a small handful, but now this emerging industry annually handles over 100,000 visitors who come to enjoy the scenic beauty of the mountains. Industry officials, however, have already expressed concern that there will be few visitors in the future if the landscape turns to barren, eroded slopes.

Nepal's hope of becoming a developed country with the mixed blessings of affluence is all but erased as the country has been rocked by worldwide inflation, skyrocketing oil prices, and its own environmental problems. The political leaders of the country search desperately for solutions, but while elaborate plans are quickly made in Kathmandu, each plan seems to fail before it is even initiated.

Obviously a new agricultural technology would revolutionize the hills. But the introduction of new techniques, such as motorized equipment, fertilizers, insecticides, et cetera, are impossible to contemplate when every pound of fertilizer, every gallon of

Some women spend much of their time hauling fodder back to their village to feed the insatiable appetites of their domestic animals

A village woman planting crops in an area that has recently been cleared by the slash-and-burn technique

gasoline, would need to be carried into the hills on human backs. Other techniques, for example, better seeds or educational programs to teach farmers about arresting erosion, are worthwhile but beyond the present capacity of the government to organize and support. It takes more years and more money than the government has at its disposal to create the extensive field service or enlist the thousands of teachers that would be required.

In addition, many hill tribes practice their present land-use techniques as cultural customs, and to suggest a change is an affront to their tribal identity. Nepalese is a second language to many hill people, and most women and older men are not conversant in it. Indeed, the majority of the hill people in the Arun refer to Kathmandu as "Nepal" — as if it were a foreign country and had little to do with them. The broad cultural diversity of the various tribes is an exciting study for an anthropologist, but a depressing obstacle to the government as it attempts any national reorganization.

Typical of the difficulties is the failure of a reforestation scheme in west Nepal. A government agency planted young saplings across a denuded slope and, after a perfunctory explanation, asked the villagers to care for the trees as they matured. The trees were safe enough as long as they were only a few inches tall, but as soon as they offered any value as fodder or firewood, the villagers immediately cut them. No trees grew to be more than five feet tall before they were cut, and the agency naturally abandoned its program. The villagers probably understood and appreciated the need for reforestation, but the immediate demand for the trees was too great to wait. In addition, the theory of the commons was doubtlessly at work, and each villager cut as much as he could as fast as he could, fearful that his neighbor would beat him to his share.

Lacking sufficient financial and manpower resources itself, the government has welcomed the assistance of foreign countries; but again there have been difficulties. The greatest problem has been that most foreign assistance has been based on short-term planning. The foreign countries (and Nepal herself) usually required immediate returns for their work to justify their efforts and to act as a measure by which such programs could be continued or discontinued. Many such programs, while giving signs of substantial short-term rewards, have actually had significant long-term negative effects on the ecology.

A classic example was the introduction of an intensive carpet industry into the Solu Khumbu Valley. Handwoven carpets made by the local Sherpa and Tibetan refugees had great appeal in Kathmandu and abroad; a thriving industry was created within a matter of a few years, and the program was judged a success. But the dyeing process for the wool required inordinate amounts of firewood which led to excessive destruction of the forests near the settlements. By the time these dangerous side effects were noticed it was too late, and the carpet industry disappeared as fast as it had appeared.

A similar situation occurred with the plan to manufacture cheese in the hills just north of Kathmandu. It seemed a brilliant plan at first. The initial products from dairy farming, such as milk, yogurt, and butter, were difficult to transport because of their weight and the short time before they experienced spoilage. But by changing the milk into cheese, the villagers could take their products to distant markets at their convenience. Aided by massive foreign help, Nepal launched a large-scale program that seemed destined for success. A delicious product was developed, a growing market was created, and there was even talk of exporting cheese. However, when the area was surveyed as a potential site for a national park it was discovered that there was widespread overgrazing and deforestation to provide pasture and fodder. Irreparable damage had been done to the environment, and while the industry continues to produce cheese, it is obvious that its potential for growth is greatly limited and that even its present production is continued at the expense of the integrity of the land.

Almost every foreign country interested in Nepal has expressed a willingness to help with population control programs, but again with little real success. Western medicine, in the form of antibiotics, vaccinations, and so forth, has been readily accepted wherever it has been made available, and one might think that birth control would be as easily accepted. But unlike antibiotics, which are easily administered and eagerly sought during the crisis of illness, birth control requires conscientious forethought and month-by-month planning.

Village women do not understand birth control pills and often horde them for when they get pregnant, at which time they take a month's supply at once. The proper manner of taking pills requires education, a society that lives by a calendar, and a culture familiar with the modern science of medicine. Other techniques of birth control often are despised or violate religious taboos. And family planning goes against the ancient Asian tradition whereby the number of children in the labor-intensive society constitutes the size of one's pension during debilitating old age. To the villager's mind, the problem is not one of too many people but merely not enough food.

The recent experience with birth control in India is also having its effects in Kathmandu. The failure of conventional techniques in India prompted the government in power to attempt stronger measures; they advocated vasectomies and tried to initiate a law of mandatory sterilization that required civil servants, among others, to undergo operations or suffer a loss of pay and certain benefits. The program met with such popular disfavor that it was partly responsible for the recent change in government leadership. The leaders in Kathmandu are apprehensive that similar repercussions might occur in Nepal if they push birth control too far.

Indeed the leadership in Kathmandu is caught in a predicament as seemingly insolvable as the environmental crisis itself. On the one hand, they face the depressing record of foreign assistance, the lack of cooperation of the hill tribes, and the difficulties of transportation and communication inherent in the topography. On the other hand, they face the severe limitations of their own bureaucratic machinery.

I remember one visit in particular to a government office. I had gone to meet with a middle-level official about the endangered status of many birds in the Arun Valley. The office I was visiting was tucked away inside the monstrous cavern of the Singha Durba, which for years served as the principal office building of the government, the Central Secretariat, a super ganglion in the network of agencies and ministries linking the people of Nepal with the policies of His Majesty's Government.

The Singha had been inherited from one of the earlier Rana Prime Ministers who had built it as a personal monument. It was a colossal edifice comprising a labyrinth of corridors, winding stairs, countless rooms and private chambers, secret passageways and false partitions that were the only entrance — or exit — for entire wings of the building. At the time the Rana Prime Minister lived there with his family and several hundred friends and servants, it was the largest private residence in the world. Its opulence set among the impoverished streets of Kathmandu was a sad symbol of the corruption and depravity that dominated the Rana period of Nepalese history.

After a confusing journey through a maze of dim, dust-covered hallways, I found my official quietly sleeping in a roomy office without windows. The office reflected the typical Nepalese sense of interior decorating by being so dark one had trouble seeing the far walls, and the high ceiling was lost in blackness. The desk, outlined by light from a small lamp, had papers dropping off one side and trailing out across the floor. The bookcase was stuffed to overflowing with spiral binders showing the protruding edges of hastily packed papers. There was one lonely teacup, I recall, stained and chipped from repeated use, lying on its side on the floor in a corner.

I was sorry to disturb the official during his nap. After a few yawns and embarrassed smiles, we exchanged pleasantries and he refused my offer of a Nepalese cigarette in favor of his own brand of American tobacco. At his invitation I sat down opposite him and began discussing my mission, while he made nervous and pretentious movements with a stack of documents on his desk. There was a solemnity about the occasion which I naïvely assumed meant that my request was being duly considered.

I explained my concern about several species of bird in the Arun. According to zoogeographic data, I knew that they should be common in the area, and yet I was unable to find them anywhere despite special efforts to look for them; many other species of bird were present but were suffering a decline in their populations caused by the widespread habitat destruction. It was true, I pointed out, that these species were all small inconspicuous creatures of relatively minor importance either to tourism or to what could be construed as significant parts of Nepal's wildlife heritage. But their disappearance suggested the need for monitoring all wildlife resources of the Arun.

By this stage in the conversation, I had reached prime form and launched into the arguments with all the passion of a scientific polemic. Ecosystem, bioclimatic functions, census transect, avian biology — the jargon popped from my mouth with the ease of a gospel preacher revealing the light to his congregation. I failed to notice the increasingly anxious manner in which my polite host was listening to my lengthy statements. He hunched over his papers, lower and lower, as if hanging onto something

familiar in the insanity which was descending upon him. Then
with the suddenness of a cornered animal, he turned to me with
a sentence-stopping expression — that bland yet biting smile common to officials — and condescendingly explained, "You know,
of course, that in Nepal conservation has nothing to do with
birds. In Nepal, conservation has to do with tigers and rhinos.
We are not concerned with birds. Please, I am very busy."

It was a stunning blow, and I limply excused myself as my
mind raced with thoughts about the incompetence and stupidity
of Nepalese officials. Like the dingy corridors I had to retrace
on my way out, his mind was littered with the encumbrances of
an antiquated bureaucracy superimposed on primitive percep-
tions about the environment. I came away from this experience
with a very low regard for the government and adopted that
fashionable opinion about Third World countries like Nepal, that
the faults of the country result from the sins of the government.
But from another point of view, what must the Nepalese government official think about when visited by the Western scientist
expressing alarm about "new problems"?

His view is doubtless tempered by the administrative world
in which he lives. His first concern might be just for a decent
place to work. His incentive might be low because his salary is
low, often less than a quarter of the normal pay scale in private
industry. No one else shows much enthusiasm; by tradition normal office hours do not begin until 10 A.M., a lengthy lunch break
is common, and the day ends punctually at 4 P.M. Even the telephone is a chancy device, often out-of-order, and a new telephone
directory has not been issued for over ten years, making even a
functioning phone useless unless one happens to know the numbers. The electrical system supplying his lamp usually breaks
down once a week, if not once a day. He is surrounded by
ineptitude.

Administrative procedure in Kathmandu has a special set of
hidden laws. Initiative is frowned upon — a tradition that dates
back to the days of the Rana regimen, when a mistake by a government official often was punished not only by his being ex-
pelled from Kathmandu, but, according to the letter of the law,
by forfeiting the rights of his children unto the seventh generation. In making any decision an official exposes himself to the
possibility of blame, in effect jeopardizing his own and his family's future.

Thus, when a proposal reaches him requiring a decision, his first reaction might well be to find some reason why it belongs in another's jurisdiction. If that fails, he will attempt to find a reason to reject a recommendation within it which will help him avoid a decision. He might seek to arrange a committee decision so that he can avoid personal responsibility, or possibly discover some aspect that requires him to send it to a higher authority for consultation. Should all these expedients fail, he should try to hold on to the file as long as possible in the hope that it will be forgotten. Decisions involving responsibility are to be avoided at all costs.

Within the bureaucratic world of Kathmandu, politics play the dominant role; caste and geography determine the political positions. In the past, promotion was dependant on family or personal connections, and although this has in a sense been replaced by a system of seniority, personal diplomacy is still far more important than specific achievements. Kathmandu is an extremely small world where only a few thousand people make all the important decisions. Everybody knows everybody else, and it is impossible to hide one's mistakes or to avoid one's enemies. Ideas of one's own are dangerous to the individual and to those associated with him. Ability, with the exception of specific skills such as engineering or medicine, seldom matters in either the effectiveness of one's department or the tides of one's personal fortunes.

Higher education is rarely an advantage. Administrative superiors do not take kindly to being upstaged, especially if a new official has been educated abroad and flaunts his more advanced knowledge. There is a lengthy delay in making new appointments so that, for example, a young statistician educated in Europe where his classmates will be making the equivalent of $1000 or more per month, can return to Nepal where he will linger for months or years before being given a position and then he will probably receive a salary of less than $75 per month. Conversely, it is almost impossible for the head of a department or ministry to get a job abolished, even if the need for it has long ago vanished. During the days of the Ranas "old age pension" meant never being fired. The halls of the Singha were always lined with idle workers with no real task at hand. Many officials never even bothered to come to the office.

The Kathmandu official must also recognize the limited resources that he has to accomplish any specific task. The Department of Wildlife Conservation, for example, has only recently been created within the Ministry of Forests. Less than a dozen men have been invested with the responsibility of regulating the entire country; not only must they direct the design and gazetting of new national parks and preserves, but also handle the regulation of hunting laws, research on endangered animals, development of new legislation for wildlife preservation, enforcement of existing laws, and so on. Many older officials have been drafted from odd jobs in other departments and have little understanding of their new task; there is constant friction between them and younger officials who have greater insight, but less seniority.

Jealousy between departments is the rule rather than the exception. Throughout the government, personality conflicts and family feuds determine policy decisions more often than the merit of any other consideration. Such conflicts are particularly intense when the decisions deal with issues that receive great public attention. The Wildlife Department mentioned above is not a fully autonomous organization but must seek approval for any action from the Ministry of Forests. This greatly hinders its ability to respond to sudden problems or carry out progressive programs, but the ministry insists on sharing the limelight created by international interest in wildlife.

There is also an appalling lack of communication between departments. In the past, most departments had well-defined areas of responsibility and there was little need for an exchange of information. But now the problems facing the country are of a nature that require coordinated efforts on the part of different departments. Soil erosion, for instance, really requires the combined assistance of the Department of Soil and Water Conservation, the Ministry of Forests, the Department of Hydrology, the Department of Education, and others. But the channels for exchanging information have never been established, and many programs started by individual departments are redundant. As a result, the programs are inefficient, often ineffectual, and sap what few resources the country has.

Ideally, all departments conduct their duties impartially for the well-being of the nation, but many departments still harbor vested interests from the days when the government was a commercial enterprise run by the Ranas. The Timber Corporation of

As incredible as it might seem, the Himalayas appear to be changing toward a semidesert ecology

Nepal is supposedly a government agency that is entrusted with regulating large forest tracts for the public. In fact, it is still directed by members of the old ruling class, who manipulate the corporation to their own benefit. The tradition of autocratic rule in Nepal leaves its imprint on the country in another damaging way; perhaps the power of the ruling class is largely diminished, but government workers continue to feel inadequate to act on their own. They look to the old ruling class for leadership and refuse to trust their own ability to operate independently.

I have come to sympathize with the plight of the government and now feel different toward the official I met with that day in the Singha Durba. Indeed, my overriding impression of the country is one of its helplessness. The degradation of the natural environment has reached a point where there is no instant cure. It is beyond the capacity of the hill people suddenly to change their ways. It is beyond the capacity of the government to mobilize some great plan to assist the hills. The spiral of tragedy has taken its own route. There is suffering in the hills now, and there will be considerably more suffering in the future. The Himalayas might well change completely to a semi-desert ecology. They might not. But things will get worse before they get better.

History provides a lesson for Nepal. Her problems are not new ones. The circle of human and environmental interactions that threaten her with ecological collapse are analogous, if not identical, to the experiences of certain earlier civilizations. The widespread environmental destruction that foreshadowed the downfall of the Roman Empire, the millions of square miles of barren desert throughout the Middle East, the disappearance of the ancient empires that once occupied North Africa, Mesopotomia, and Western Pakistan — all demonstrate the effects of an overburdening population using primitive agricultural and pastoral techniques on any environment.

Nepal still maintains its place in the Western mind as a land of great natural beauty, but that image of the Himalayas is going to change. The pervasive response to difficulties in Nepal is a shoulder-shrugging phrase, *"Ke garne!"* ("What to do?"). The people have little opportunity to affect the course of events. They are swept along in the tide of fate and doggedly get ready for the worst.

Appendix
Bibliography
Index

Appendix: Species List

There is great confusion with the common English names used for various Asian birds, mammals, and plants. Different authors use different names, depending on their country of origin or their background; there are some species of bird, for example, which have over five regularly used English names. Thus, it seems wise to include a list of scientific names for those species mentioned in the text by an English name so that readers anywhere can quickly and positively identify any particular species. Traditionally, species lists follow a phylogenetic order but I have arranged the entries in alphabetical order so that the uninitiated can more readily use the list.

MAMMALS

Bear, Brown · *Ursus arctos*
Bear, Himalayan Black · *Selenarctos thibetanus*
Buffalo, Wild Water · *Bubalus bubalis*
Cat, Fishing · *Felis viverrina*
Cat, Jungle · *Felis chaus*
Civet, Himalayan Palm · *Paguma larvata*
Deer, Chital · *Axis axis*
Deer, Hog · *Axis porcinus*
Bat, Fulvous Fruit · *Rousettus leschenaulti*
Ghoral · *Nemorhaedus goral*
Hare, Indian · *Lepus nigricollis*
Jackals · *Canis aureus*
Langur Monkeys · *Presbytis entellus*
Leopard, Snow · *Panthera unica*
Macaque, Rhesus · *Macaca mulatta*
Marten, Yellow-throated · *Martes flavigula*

Panda, Red · *Ailurus fulgens*
Pangolin, Chinese · *Manis pentadactyla*
Porcupine, Indian · *Hystrix indica*
Rat, Bay Bamboo · *Cannomys badius*
Serow · *Capricornis sumatraensis*
Squirrel, Giant Flying · *Petaurista petaurista*
Tahr, Himalayan · *Hemitragus jemlahicus*
Takin · *Budorcas taxicolor*
Tiger · *Panthera tigris*
Weasel, Himalayan · *Mustela sibirica*
Wolf · *Canis lupus*

BIRDS

Babbler, Chestnut-headed Tit · *Alcippe castaneceps*
Babbler, Dusky-green Tit · *Alcippe cinerea*
Babbler, Red-capped · *Timalia pileata*
Babbler, Rufous-necked Scimitar · *Pomatorhinus ruficollis*
Babbler, Scimitar · *Pomatorhinus* spp.
Babbler, Spiny · *Turdoides nipalensis*
Babbler, Spotted Wren · *Spelaeornis formosus*
Babbler, White-browed Tit · *Alcippe vinipectus*
Babbler, Wren · *Pnoepyga* spp.
Barbet, Crimson-breasted · *Megalaima haemacephala*
Barwings · *Actinodura* spp.
Bee-eaters · *Merops* spp.
Blackbird, White-collared · *Turdus albocinctus*
Bulbul, Black-headed Yellow · *Pycnonotus melanicterus*
Bulbul, Rufous-bellied · *Hypsipetes virescens*
Bulbul, White-cheeked · *Pycnonotus leucogenys*
Chough, Red-billed · *Pyrrhocorax pyrrhocorax*
Cochoa, Green · *Cochoa viridis*
Cormorant, Large · *Phalacrocorax carbo*
Cuckoo, Eurasian · *Cuculus canorus*
Cuckoo, Small · *Cuculus poliocephalus*
Cuckoo-Shrike, Large · *Coracina novaehollandiae*
Curlew · *Numenius arquata*
Dippers · *Cinclus* spp.
Dove, Spotted · *Streptopelia chinensis*
Drongo, Black · *Dicrurus adsimilis*
Drongo, Hair-crested · *Dicrurus hottentottus*
Drongo, Large Racquet-tailed · *Dicrurus paradiseus*
Eagle, Black · *Ictinaetus malayensis*
Forktail, Spotted · *Enicurus maculatus*
Flowerpeckers · *Dicaeum* spp.

Flycatcher, Brook's · *Muscicapa poliogenys*
Flycatcher, Gray-headed · *Culicicapa ceylonensis*
Flycatcher, Pale Blue · *Muscicapa unicolor*
Flycatcher, Verditer · *Muscicapa thalassina*
Flycatcher, Yellow-bellied Fantail · *Rhipidura hypoxantha*
Godwit, Black-tailed · *Limosa limosa*
Goldcrest · *Regulus regulus*
Goose, Bar-headed · *Anser indicus*
Grosbeaks · *Mycerobas* spp.
Honeyguide, Orange-rumped · *Indicator xanthonotus*
Honeyguide, Variegated · *Indicator variegatus*
Iora, Common · *Aegithina tiphia*
Jungle Fowl · *Gallus gallus*
Kingfisher, Eurasian · *Alcedo atthis*
Kingfisher, Large Pied · *Ceryle lugubris*
Kingfisher, Stork-billed · *Pelargopsis capensis*
Kingfisher, White-breasted · *Halcyon smyrnensis*
Lapwing, Gray-headed · *Vanellus cinereus*
Lapwing, Red-wattled · *Vanellus indicus*
Laughing-Thrush, Black-faced · *Garrulax affinis*
Laughing-Thrush, Large Necklaced · *Garrulax pectoralis*
Laughing-Thrush, White-crested · *Garrulax leucolophus*
Laughing-Thrush, White-spotted · *Garrulax ocellatus*
Leafbird, Golden-fronted · *Chloropsis aurifrons*
Leaf Warblers · *Phylloscopus* spp.
Leiothrix, Red-billed · *Leiothrix lutea*
Magpie, Red-billed Blue · *Cissa erythrorhyncha*
Malkoha, Large Green-billed · *Rhopodytes tristis*
Merganser · *Mergus merganser*
Mesia, Silver-eared · *Leiothrix argentauris*
Minivet, Yellow-throated · *Pericrocotus solaris*
Myna · *Acridotheres* spp.
Myzornis, Fire-tailed · *Myzornis pyrrhoura*
Niltava, Beautiful · *Muscicapa sundara*
Niltava, Large · *Muscicapa grandis*
Nutcracker · *Nucifraga caryocatactes*
Nuthatch, Chestnut-bellied · *Sitta castanea*
Owl, Scops · *Otus* spp.
Owl, Tawny Wood · *Strix aluco*
Parrotbill · *Paradoxornis* spp.
Partridge, Snow · *Lerwa lerwa*
Pheasant, Blood · *Ithaginis cruentus*
Pheasant, Crimson Horned · *Tragopan satyra*
Pheasant, Impeyan · *Lophophorus impejanus*
Pheasant, Kalij · *Lophura leucomelana*

Pigeon, Snow · *Columba leuconota*
Redstart, Blue-fronted · *Phonenicurus frontalis*
Redstart, White-capped · *Chaimarrornis leucocephalus*
Rosefinches · *Carpodacus* spp.
Sapsucker, Rufous-bellied · *Hypopicus hyperythrus*
Shortwing, Gould's · *Brachypteryx stellata*
Shrike Babbler, Red-winged · *Pteruthius flaviscapis*
Sibia, Black-capped · *Heterophasia capistrata*
Snipe, Painted · *Rostratula benghalensis*
Snipe, Pintail · *Capella stenura*
Snipe, Wood · *Capella nemoricola*
Snowcock, Himalayan · *Tetragallus himalayensis*
Sparrow, House · *Passer domesticus*
Stare, Spot-winged · *Saroglossa spiloptera*
Sunbirds · *Aethopyga* spp.
Tailor Bird · *Orthotomus sutorius*
Thrush, Blue Whistling · *Myiophoneus caeruleus*
Tit, Black-crested Coal · *Parus ater*
Tit, Green-backed · *Parus monticolus*
Tree Creeper, Northern · *Certhia familiaris*
Tree Pie, Himalayan · *Dendrocitta formosae*
Trogon, Red-headed · *Harpactes erythrocephalus*
Vulture, Beared · *Gypaetus barbatus*
Woodpecker, Large Golden-backed · *Chrysocolaptes lucidus*
Wren, Winter · *Troglodytes troglodytes*
Yuhina, White-bellied · *Yuhina zantholeuca*
Yuhina, Yellow-naped · *Yuhina flavicollis*

Bibliography

Acharya, B. N. 1976. "Interdependence of Cottage Industry and the Ecological Situation." In, *Mountain Environment and Development.* SATA, Univ. Press, Tribhuvan Univ., Kathmandu.

Ali, Salim, and S. Dillon Ripley. 1968–1974. *Handbook of the Birds of India and Pakistan.* 10 Vols. Oxford Univ. Press, Bombay.

Amma, S., and C. Akiba. 1967. "Geology of Arun River and Dudhkosi." *Jour. Geol. Soc. Japan,* 73: 8.

Bannerji, M. L. 1963. "Outline of Nepal Phyto-geography." *Vegetatio,* 11 (5, 6): 288–296.

———. 1965. "Contribution to the Flora of East Nepal." *Rec. Bot. Surv. India.* 19 (2): 88–90.

Bernstein, Jeremy. 1970. *The Wildest Dreams of Kew: A Profile of Nepal.* Simon and Schuster, New York.

Bhatt, D. D. 1973. "Nature Conservation in Nepal." *Swatantra Viswa,* No. 10.

———. 1976. *Proceedings of the Natural History Seminar.* Institute of Science, Tribhuvan Univ., Kathmandu.

Biswas, B. 1960–63, 1967. "The Birds of Nepal." *Jour. Bombay Nat. Hist. Soc.,* 12 parts, Vols. 57–60, 63.

Cronin, E. W., and Paul Sherman. 1976. "A Resource-based Mating System: The Orange-rumped Honeyguide." *The Living Bird.* Cornell Univ., Ithaca.

Dyhrenfurth, N. G. 1959. "Slick-Johnson Nepal Snowman Expedition." *American Alpine Jour.,* New York.

Eckholm, Erik. 1975. "Losing Ground in Shangri-La." *Sat. Review of Lit.,* Oct. 4.

Enders, Gordon, and Edward Anthony. 1935. *Nowhere Else in the World.* Farrar & Rinehart, New York.

Fleming, R. L., Jr. 1971. "Snakes of Nepal." *Swatantra Viswa.* Vol. 1, No. 2: 42–46.

Fleming, R. L., Sr., and R. L. Fleming, Jr., Lain Singh Bangdel. 1976. *Birds of Nepal*. Arun K. Mehta at Vakil and Sons, Bombay.

Friedmann, Herbert. 1955. *The Honeyguides*. U.S. Nat. Mus. Bulletin 208, Smithsonian Institution, Washington.

Furer-Hamendorf, Christoph. 1975. *Himalayan Traders*. John Murray, London.

Gansser, Augusto. 1964. *Geology of the Himalayas*. Interscience Publishers, London.

Haffner, W. 1968. "The Three-Dimensional Pattern of Climate, Vegetation and Land Use in the Himalayas." In, *Regional Seminar on the Ecology of Tropical Highlands*, Kathmandu.

Hagen, Toni. 1961. *Nepal and the Kingdom in the Himalayas*. Bern, Kummerly and Frey, London.

Hara, Hiroshi. 1966. "The Flora of Eastern Himalaya." First Report. *Univ. Mus. Tokyo*. Bull. 1: 744.

―――. 1971. "The Flora of Eastern Himalaya." Second Report. *Univ. Mus. Tokyo*. Bull. 2: 393.

Heuvelmans, Bernard. 1959. *On the Track of Unknown Animals*. Rupert, Hart, Davis, London.

Hooker, J. 1854. *Himalayan Journals*. London.

―――. 1875–1879. *The Flora of British India*. 7 Vols. London.

Houston, R. C., and L. William. 1955. "The Californian Himalayan Expedition to Makalu." *Sierra Club Bulletin*. Vol. 40: 1–17.

Howard-Bury, C. K. 1922. *Mount Everest, The Reconnaissance*. London.

Izzard, Ralph. 1955. *The Abominable Snowman Adventure*. Hodder and Stoughton, London.

Kanai, H. 1966. "Phyto-geography of Eastern Himalayas with Special Reference to the Relationship between Himalaya and Japan." In, *Flora of Eastern Himalaya*, Hara (ed.). Univ. Tokyo.

Kihara, H. (ed.). 1955. *Fauna and Flora of Nepal Himalaya*. Vol. 1. Tokyo.

Kinnear, N. B. 1922. "On the Birds Collected during the First Mt. Everest Expedition." *Jour. Bombay. Nat. Hist. Soc.* Vol. 1, iv: 495.

Koenigswold, G. H. R. von. 1939. "The Relationship of Fossil Mammalian Faunas." *Peking Nat. Hist. Bull.*, Vol. 13, Peking.

Kortlandt, Adriaan. 1962. "Chimpanzees in the Wild." *Scientific American*, Vol. 206 (5): 128–138.

Leviton, A., E. Meyers, and L. Swan. 1956. "Zoological Results of the California Expedition to Makalu, Eastern Nepal." *Papers of Nat. Hist. Mus., Stanford Univ.* No. 1. Palo Alto.

Lowdermilk, W. C. 1953. "Conquest of the Land Through 7000 Years." *U.S. Dept. Agri. Information Bull. No. 99*. Washington.

Mani, M. S. 1973. *Fundamentals of High Altitude Biology*. Oxford & IBH, New Delhi.

Mauch, S. P. 1976. "The Energy Situation in the Hills: Imperative for Development Strategies?" In, *Mountain Environment and Development*. SATA, Univ. Press, Tribhuvan Univ., Kathmandu.

Molnar, Peter, and Paul Tapponnier. 1977. "The Collision Between India and Eurasia." *Scientific American*, Vol. 236: 30–42.

Nicolson, Nigel. 1975. *The Himalayas*. Time-Life International, Amsterdam.

Ohsawa, M., P. R. Shakya, and M. Numata. 1973. "Occurrence of Deciduous Broad-Leaved Forests in the Cool-Temperate Zone of Humid Himalayas in Eastern Nepal." *Japanese Jour. Ecology*, Vol. 23 (5): 218–228.

Osmond, Edward. 1967. *Animals of Central Asia*. Abelard-Schuman, London.

Panday, K. K. 1976. "The Livestock, Fodder Situation, and the Potential of Additional Fodder Resource." In, *Mountain Environment and Development*. SATA, Univ. Press, Tribhuvan Univ., Kathmandu.

Prater, S. H. 1965. *The Book of Indian Animals*. Bombay Nat. Hist. Soc., Bombay.

Reynolds, Vernon. 1967. *The Apes*. E. P. Dutton, New York.

Rieger, H. C. 1976. "Floods and Droughts, The Himalaya and the Ganges Plain as an Ecological System." In, *Mountain Environment and Development*. SATA, Univ. Press, Tribhuvan Univ., Kathmandu.

Sanderson, Ivan. 1961. *Abominable Snowman: Legend Come to Life*. Philadelphia. Chilton, Radnor, Pa.

Schaller, George. 1964. *The Year of the Gorilla*. Univ. of Chicago Press, Chicago.

Shipton, Eric. 1952. *The Mount Everest Reconnaissance Expedition*. Hodder and Stoughton, London.

Simons, E. L., and P. E. Ettell. 1970. "Gigantopithecus." *Scientific American*, 222: 76–85.

Stainton, J. D. A. 1972. *Forests of Nepal*. John Murray, London.

Sterling, Claire. 1976. "Nepal." In, *The Atlantic Monthly*, October.

Stonor, Charles. 1955. *The Sherpa and the Snowman*. Hollis and Carter, London.

Swan, Lawrence. 1961. "Ecology of the High Himalayas." *Scientific American*, Vol. 205: 68–78.

———. 1967. "Alpine and Aeolian Regions of the World." In, *Arctic and Alpine Environments*, Weight and Osburn (eds.), Indiana Univ. Press. 29–54.

Szoke, P. 1962. "Zur Entstchung und Entwicklungsgeschichte der Musik." *Studia Musicologica*, 2: 33–85.

Tchernine, O. 1970. *The Yeti*. Neville Spearman, London.

Thorpe, W. H. 1961. *Bird Song: The Biology of Vocal Communication and Expression in Birds*. Cambridge.

Tschernesky, W. 1960. "A Reconstruction of the Foot of the Abominable Snowman." *Nature*, 186, May 7.

Ward, J. P. 1970. "The Iswa Khola Himalayan Expedition, 1969." *The Himalayan Journal*, Oxford Univ. Press, London.

Wharton, Charles. 1968. "Man, Fire, and Wild Cattle in Southeast Asia." *Proc. Annual Tall Timbers, Fire Ecology Conference.*

Yoda, Kyoji. 1967. "A Preliminary Survey of the Forest Vegetation of Eastern Nepal." *Jour. of College of Arts and Sciences*, Chiba Univ. Vol. 5 (1): 99–140.

Index